An Invitation to Social Construction

Kenneth J. Gergen

SAGE Publications
London · Thousand Oaks · New Delhi

First published 1999

Reprinted 2000, 2001

 SAGE Publications Ltd
6 Bonhill Street
London EC2A 4PU

SAGE Publications Inc
2455 Teller Road
Thousand Oaks, California 91320

SAGE Publications India Pvt Ltd
32, M-Block Market
Greater Kailash - I
New Delhi 110 048

British Library Cataloguing in Publication data

A catalogue record for this book is available
from the British Library

ISBN 0 8039 8376 X
ISBN 0 8039 8377 8 (pbk)

Library of Congress catalog card number 99-72824

Typeset by Type Study, Scarborough, North Yorkshire
Printed in Great Britain by The Cromwell Press Ltd,
Trowbridge, Wiltshire

An Invitation to Social Construction

CONTENTS

PROLOGUE:
HOW ARE WE TO GO ON?

My aspirations for this book are not meager. In fact my dearest hope is that these pages can provide the reader with insight into a range of exciting dialogues taking place across the academic disciplines, within sectors of the culture at large, and around the globe. For many participants these discussions are momentous in implication. They seem equivalent to the radical changes in thinking and societal practices taking place in sixteenth and seventeenth century European culture, when we moved from the "Dark Ages" into the "Enlightenment." As I see the present dialogues, they not only unsettle the grounds for all that we know to be real and good; they also offer unparalleled opportunities for creative deliberation and action. They invite us into new spaces of understanding from which a more promising world can emerge. They have changed my life; they have so for many of my acquaintance. In contrast, others view these discussions with alarm. The ideas and practices seem to destroy the foundations of knowledge and morality, to plunge us into an imperiling chaos where there is nothing to believe and nothing to do. Controversy abounds. If this book is successful, however, you should be able to join these discussions, appreciate their significance, sample their potentials, worry about their shortcomings – and most hopefully, take away something of value. This book is not intended as "the last word," but as a beginning.

Yet, how are we – author and reader – to go on together? We both bring important limitations to these pages now uniting us. I am limited by the fact that I have lived the better part of my life as a scholar. My habits of expression are acceptable enough in professional circles, but outside these circles they may seem exotic or obscure. For non-scholars the tendency toward abstract analysis may seem irrelevant to the practical challenges of daily life. My task is all the more difficult because I deeply hope to communicate with many different kinds of readers, including university students, practitioners, graduate students, scholars desiring a first hand account, and many for whom English is a second language. I suspect that I shall not always be clear. And too, some will find I have treated important issues too lightly; they will wish for more detailed accounts. To help in such matters I have included at the end of each chapter a range of more detailed writings.

Yet, my limitations as author exceed those of literary style. My life experiences are also bounded. It is not only that my words will inevitably carry the traces of nationality, gender, age and sexual preference, but my life experiences are also limiting. I have lived a life of some privilege: I have had a steady job, never fought on a field of battle, and never lived in poverty. Yes, I have had my share of suffering, but I cannot write out of the depth of fear and pain that has affected many families during my lifetime. I can only hope that there is sufficient communality remaining that all may locate themselves somewhere in these pages.

As I write I try to imagine you as the reader sitting and talking with me as an interested friend. Yet, these words will be more or less significant to you depending on how you imagine me. In these pages you will get to know me through the rhythms and melodies of relationship I have shared with others across time and circumstance. However, you can do as you wish with these words – work, play, invent, fantasize, devour, spit. Perhaps we shall best make meaning together if you can imagine me as someone who can be educated by your reactions to the text. It is not my aim here to persuade, to win, or to educate you in "the right way." It is you who must breathe life into these words. And if we are successful in this author–reader relationship, perhaps new paths will open. As we relate together so do we construct our future.

In appreciation to all those dialogic companions
whose voices are echoed here
and to
Jenna and John
who will inherit the realities we thus create

1

TRADITIONS IN TROUBLE

> The major advances in civilization are processes that all but wreck the societies in which they occur.
>
> Alfred North Whitehead

I grew up with fountain pens. As a child they were as "natural" to me as my family. My father's pen seemed to produce an endless stream of mathematical scribbles that somehow transformed themselves into papers in journals. Meanwhile my mother's musings gave way to bursts of inspirational writing – short stories, travelogues, and the best letters a boy away from home could ever receive. The pen was destined to become my life. And so it did, as I slowly worked my way toward a professorship in psychology. I loved to ponder and to write; the sound of the pen on paper, the flowing of the ink, the mounting columns of "my thoughts" – all produced a special thrill. And wonder of wonders, I could be paid for it! But now the pen is gone. Some years ago I was informed there would be no more secretaries to transform my handiwork into solid print. I was to write by computer. I loathed the idea. Writing was a craft, not a technology; I needed to touch the paper physically; feel the words flowing from fingers to shaft and shaft to "my being made visible." The act of writing was very close to physical contact with the reader. In contrast, the computer was a wedge between us – a piece of brutish machinery separating our humanity. I refused to purchase a computer. Finally, in frustration, the college administration delivered one as a gift. A goose quill now sits nearby on the desk to remind me of my roots. I use my pen only for signing letters.

This machine has virtually transformed my life. It's not simply the ease of writing; there are the possibilities for endless experimenting, storing of random ideas, and the like. It also delivers electronic mail and opens the vast horizons of the World Wide Web. Everywhere relationships are "going electronic" and they are going rapidly in all directions to all points. Dozens of times daily I receive messages, not only from colleagues down the hall, or across town, but from around the world: Oslo, Istanbul, Vienna, Buenos Aires, Adelaide, Kyoto, Hong Kong, Delhi. My interlocutors aren't "somewhere else;" their expressions are here, right in front of me. I log on to the Web and find myself careening around the mountainous roads of information, insight, polemics, humor, sexy conversation and more. My computer screen moves like a magic carpet around the globe, into people's offices, their private spaces, their very private fantasies.

I write of these matters because we find here a living illustration of a condition we all now confront: rapid and sweeping global change – in politics, economics, in the movement of peoples around the globe, the worldwide circulation of lifestyles, and more. Although global in sweep, these changes insinuate themselves into the interstices of our life. With these changes we confront profound questions of value: what is worth valuing, holding on to, and defending in our lives, and what can we abandon in favor of the new and exotic? In Johnny Cash's words, how do we "know when to show, and know when to hold 'em?" Or more extremely, how are we to go on when alien – even hostile – ways of life begin to replace those we hold dear? Such questions become more acute when I consider the multiple voices that increasingly vie for a place on the world platform. It once seemed easy enough to distinguish between truth and falsity, objectivity and subjectivity, good reasons and bad, and even morality and immorality. Yet, those days have largely vanished, as television, radio, books, newspapers, e-mail and passing acquaintances inundate us with differences in perspective, values, and understanding. In what particular words can we place our trust when confronted with infinite variations in the real and the good? Who "has it right," and by what right? Or is trust possible at all?

It is in precisely this context that the present volume takes shape. To focus more sharply, consider Don DeLillo's account of a father driving his 14-year-old son, Heinrich, to school.[1] Heinrich begins the conversation:

> "It's going to rain tonight."
> "It's raining now," I said.
> "The radio said tonight." . . .
> "Look at the windshield," I said. "Is that rain or isn't it?"
> "I'm only telling you what they said."
> "Just because it's on the radio doesn't mean we have to suspend belief in the evidence of our senses."
> "Our senses? Our senses are wrong a lot more often than they're right. This has been proved in the laboratory. Don't you know about all those theorems that say nothing is what it seems? There's no past, present or future outside our own mind . . . Even sound can trick the mind. Just because you don't hear a sound doesn't mean it's not out there. Dogs can hear it. Other animals. And I'm sure there are sounds even dogs can't hear. . . ."
> "Is it raining," I said, "or isn't it?"
> "I wouldn't want to have to say."
> "What if someone held a gun to your head?"
> "Who, you?"
> "Someone. A man in a trenchcoat and smoky glasses. He holds a gun to your head and he says, 'Is it raining or isn't it? All you have to do is tell the truth and I'll put away my gun and take the next flight out of here.'"
> "What truth does he want? Does he want the truth of someone traveling at

almost the speed of light in another galaxy? Does he want the truth of someone in orbit around a neutron star? . . ."

"He's holding the gun to your head. He wants *your* truth."

"What good is my truth? My truth means nothing. What if this guy with the gun comes from a planet in a whole different solar system? What we call rain he calls soap. What we call apples he calls rain. So what am I supposed to tell him?"

"His name is Frank J. Smalley and he comes from St Louis."

"He wants to know if it's raining *now*, at this very minute?"

"Here and now. That's right."

"Is there such a thing as now? 'Now' comes and goes as soon as you say it. How can I say it's raining now if your so-called 'now' becomes 'then' as soon as I say it?"

". . . Just give me an answer, okay, Heinrich?"

"The best I could do is make a guess."

"Either it's raining or it isn't," I said.

"Exactly. That's my whole point. You'd be guessing. Six of one, half dozen of the other."

"But you *see* it's raining."

"You see the sun moving across the sky. But is the sun moving across the sky or is the earth turning? . . . What *is* rain anyway?"

"It's the stuff that falls from the sky and gets you what is called wet."

"I'm not wet. Are you wet?"

"All right," I said. "Very good."

"No, seriously, are you wet?"

"First-rate," I told him. "A victory for uncertainty, randomness and chaos. Science's finest hour."[2]

On one level this is a hilarious interchange – the powerful father exasperated by the unrelenting sophistry of the son. Yet, there is also a moment of painful self-consciousness. Aren't there ways in which both father and son speak for us, both expressing views that we hold dear? Don't we resonate with the father's faith in no-nonsense facts, the importance of reason, and the truth of science? Doesn't Heinrich seem like a bratty kid, a smart aleck nerd? Yet, don't we simultaneously appreciate Heinrich's awareness of multiple perspectives, the limits of common reason, and the shortsightedness of the taken-for-granted? Here the father seems parochial and old-fashioned. In effect, DeLillo's fictitious dialogue is giving voice to a broadly shared tension in contemporary society.

Is this an important conflict? For students entering the academic world the future may hang on it; jobs are gained or lost depending on whether one sounds more like the father or Heinrich. Universities are steeped in these conflicts. The conflicts are labeled in various ways in differing sectors and with differing emphases: foundationalism vs. post-foundationalism, structuralism vs. post-structuralism, empiricism vs. post-empiricism, colonial vs. post-colonial, and most popularly, modern vs. postmodern. In my own department of psychology, the majority of the faculty are traditionalists; roughly a third dwell in the land of the "posts."

It is difficult to communicate across the divide. In the departments of literature and languages, almost the entire faculty has shifted in the "post" direction. In many universities, departments have split up and entire new programs have sprung to life. The critical heat is also directed toward the long-secure natural sciences. The intensity of the debate has yielded the phrase, "the science wars." One can scarcely be neutral.

Are we speaking here only of an intellectual in-fight? Not according to many cultural commentators. As many see it, we are perhaps witnessing a shift in cultural beliefs that is equal in significance to movement from the Dark Ages of Western history to the Enlightenment. For many the present transformation is catastrophic. It represents the erosion of beliefs central to our ways of life, including our sense of truth and morality, the value of the individual self, and promise of a better future. Traditions of democracy, religion, education, and nationhood are all placed under threat. Yet, for many others this same shift is pregnant with potential. As many feel, the traditional Western beliefs – for example, in truth, rationality, and the self – are severely delimited. In the globalized world of today, they seem increasingly parochial, and possibly deadly in implication. Further, the grand institutions of science, religion, government, education – designed for the benefit of all – have not only fallen dramatically short of their aims, but often seem to generate oppression, environmental degrading, and armed warfare. As Jean-Francois Lyotard, doyen of postmodernism, has put it, "The nineteenth and twentieth centuries have given us as much terror as we can take. We have paid a high enough price for the nostalgia of the whole and the one experience."[3] The search, then, is for fresh ideas and practices for a more promising millennium. To what, then, do we hold fast; what do we abandon; what is worth doing?

The Present Volume

It is this context of conflict and change that gives rise to the present book. For over twenty years I have been deeply involved with these conflicts in my relations with academic colleagues and students, mental health professionals, organizational managers, friends, and family. Early in my career I sounded very much like Heinrich's father; slowly, however, I turned skeptical – and then pointedly critical. I was scarcely alone in this shift; it was everywhere in evidence. In recent years, however, I have become far more optimistic. I have come to see that we can move beyond both traditionalism and skepticism, foundationalism and nihilism. These new potentials are most fully realized in the writings and practices of social constructionism, the topic of this book. As I hope to demonstrate in the pages that follow, constructionism welcomes both the voices of tradition and critique into dialogue, while granting neither an ultimate privilege. Commitments do not require rigidity, nor critique eradication of the past. More importantly, the constructionist dialogues contain enormous potential; they open new spans of possibility for creating the future. This is so in the intellectual/scientific world, in the world of professional practice, and in our daily lives.

About the organization of the book: this initial chapter will explore the dark side. We shall put into sharper focus the traditions in peril, and try to understand why their condition is so precarious. We enter, then, into the corridors of critique. In Chapter 2 we shall begin digging from the rubble. We shall see that if we examine the shards of the critique, we begin to locate alternative visions of knowledge, truth, and the self. The dialogues surrounding these alternatives are essentially those of social construction. After exploring some of the basic ideas of social construction, we turn, in Chapter 3, to a major form of inquiry invited by constructionism, namely reflection on our existing beliefs about reality, the self, and the good. Here we find that deliberating on our common discourses – in science and everyday life – can have liberating consequences. Critique gives way to emancipation and creative construction of alternatives. In Chapter 4 we consider ways of exploring social life specifically invited by social constructionism. We do not lose the old traditions of study, but rather, through constructionism we add significantly to the potentials of human science inquiry. As I suggested, social constructionism invites the creation of new, more inhabitable ways of going on together. Chapter 5 will illustrate these potentials by exploring an alternative to the long-standing view of the individual self. The attempt is to place the view of individual self with relational being.

As the arguments of the book take shape we shall find theory and practice converging: constructionist scholarship and societal practice become one. Concern with the conditions of society and the possibility for alternative futures occupies the next three chapters. In the first of these (Chapter 6) we move from a theoretical concern with human understanding, to forms of dialogue holding promise for reducing conflict and hostility. Of special concern will be components of transformative dialogue, promising alternatives to social alienation. Chapter 7 explores the burgeoning of new practices favored by social constructionism. Attention will be directed specifically to psychotherapy, organizational management, education, and forms of scholarly communication. In each case we locate new possibilities for coordinating relations to build new futures. Then, in Chapter 8, we shall move to ways in which constructionist inquiry is directed toward the conditions of society itself. Of interest here will be ways in which communication technology and the swirl of information, images, opinions, advertisements and so on increasingly dominate our daily lives.

Throughout these discussions you will certainly experience reservations – possibly even strong criticisms. You could scarcely grow up in modern society without some doubts about what will unfold here. From time to time I will try to take account of some of these misgivings. However, in the final chapter, Chapter 9, I shall consider head-on some of the major criticisms of social constructionism. Issues of truth, objectivity, science, moral relativism, political activism, and the like will all be treated. You are invited, of course, to peek into this chapter at any point in your reading.

Let us begin, then, with a set of assumptions, comfortable and comforting. Specifically, let's consider our sense of self as rational agents, who make choices and direct our own actions. We don't easily want to part with such a belief, let's say trading it for a view of ourselves as so many robots, or the victims of our genes. This sense of ourselves as directing our own actions is central to who we are. As we shall find, such beliefs in self are also closely allied to assumptions about science and truth. In turn, our commitment to individual selves and scientific knowledge are closely tied to major institutions in society, including our systems of morality, education, and democracy. All these beliefs are interlocking; each relies on the other to survive. In the present context, however, we begin to confront the voices of doubt. Even we who live in these traditions do not always find them so nurturing. And our path toward the future should be informed about the downside of our commitments.

This reflexive treatment of the self and its close companions will prepare us for the uprooting critiques of recent years. So powerful are these newly emerging arguments that many believe they threaten the annihilation of these traditions. All that seemed essential becomes groundless. How much do we wish to hold on to, what are we willing to abandon?

The Shaky Scaffold of the Self

> The whole dear notion of one's own Self – marvelous old free-willed, free-enterprising, autonomous, independent, isolated island of the Self – is a myth.
>
> Lewis Thomas, *The Lives of a Cell*

If you were in an auto crash and it was necessary to sacrifice some bodily organ to stay alive, what would you least wish to lose? Chances are you will pick the brain, and specifically those brain processes that permit conscious thought. For most of us losing the capacity for conscious thought and choice would be to lose the self, that which makes us distinctive and significant as human beings. In street talk, the loss would make us vegetables. The prime importance we place on the self can be traced to an extended cultural history. We inherit today over two thousand years of deliberation on and celebration of the subjective self, our sense of being reasoning and choice-making individuals. From Plato's discussion of "pure ideas," the Christian celebration of the human soul, through contemporary cognitive psychology, we have held the individual self in highest regard.[4]

This is no place for a full review of this history. However, most would credit the Enlightenment as the birthplace of our contemporary – or modernist – beliefs about the self.[5] For centuries, the people of Europe had labored under autocratic rule – the crown and the cross often working in oppressive tandem. Common people had little control over their fates, and life or death could often be determined by whim from on high. How were these shackles to be removed? At least one means was by developing a rationale that would honor the individual, that would grant to each individual those capacities and dignities that would challenge the right of any authority to rule without consent. The Judeao-Christian tradition had already endowed individuals with souls, a connection to a spiritual father. Enlightenment thinkers of the sixteenth and seventeenth centuries – philosophers, statesmen, scientists among them – added important elements to this conception of the individual. Most particularly they gave intelligibility to the idea that each individual is capable of observing the world for what it is, and deliberating about the best course of action – that is, the capacities to *observe* for oneself, to *think*, *evaluate*, and then to *choose* one's actions. Neither royalty nor clergy could declare themselves superior in these universal capacities.

Thus the socio-political importance of René Descartes' disquisition on doubt. As he reasoned in *Discourse on Method* (1637), he could doubt all authority and public opinion, and even the senses; but in the end he could not doubt the process of doubting itself. Thought is at the center of what it is to be human. *Cogito ergo sum.* Likewise, when John Locke's *Essay Concerning Human Understanding* (1690) laid out the foundations of human knowledge, his central concern was with the way in which observations of the world were recorded within the mind. Knowledge was thus defined as private and personal, and not dictated by decree from on high. And as Thomas Hobbes proposed in the *Leviathan* (1651), the state gains its rights to create laws and maintain order from the consent – manifest within a *social contract* – of those individuals who make it up. There is no authority that is not reduced to the minds of individual citizens. It is this legacy that stoked the fires of the French Revolution, and formed the basis of what has come to be called cultural Modernism.

Today the echoes of the Enlightenment conception of the self are everywhere in evidence. The very idea of democracy – each individual endowed with the right to vote – derives from Enlightenment presumptions. Public education also owes its existence to the same investments. As individuals grow in knowledge, so does the state gain in efficacy. Within this same vein, we praise the non-conformist and delight in signs of independent thought – in children, in college students, and in organizations. We marvel at the heroic stories of those sacrificing themselves for their beliefs, and who are ultimately proved right. We condemn obedience, and praise autonomy; we bridle at those who would try to gain control over us; we wish to be free. Free and equal.

In many ways this is a glorious history. We prize our capacities for conscious thought, self-determination, the freedom to determine our own futures. Yet there is an irony here. How did we come by these prized possessions? Were not centuries of skilled writing, political struggle, warfare and more required to secure our modernist sensibility? Without our religious and philosophic heritage, would we still set such importance on the conscious choice of the single individual? Many other cultures do not. In effect, the treasure of individual autonomy is a gift from others. We didn't choose it; it was chosen for us. This irony opens the way for further reflection. The same history that we celebrate for its modernist legacy, has also left a repository of doubt. Let us allow this doubt some room for expansion. Specifically we turn to three conceptual problems at the heart of the presumption of individual minds: the problem of two worlds, of individual knowledge of the world, and of self-knowledge. These problems are central to the modernist tradition of the self; without adequate answers we begin to realize the fragility of the tradition.

The Two World Problem: "Out There" vs. "In Here"

To value the self is to value a private, interior consciousness ("me," "here") in contrast to an exterior world ("out there.") In effect, we presume the existence of a psychological world of the self (which perceives, deliberates, decides), and at the same time a material world (that which exists outside of our thoughts). This arrangement seems self-evident enough . . . but only so long as it remains unexamined. In philosophical terms, we find ourselves comfortably committed to a *dualist ontology* – the reality of mind and of world. Yet, as a long history of philosophical writing has taught us, dualist beliefs create problems as profound as they are insoluble. Among the most thorny challenges is comprehending how a mental and a physical world can be causally related. That "the spirit is made flesh" is an old religious idea; but it is a mystery left for God to answer. In present day terms we might ask, how does "a thought" ("I should call her") make its way into action ("picking up the phone"); how does a wish or an intention produce actual muscle movements? You may say to yourself, "I intend to move," but this intention does not activate neurons in the spinal cord. We have little difficulty in comprehending causality *within* the physical word (e.g. "how smoking can cause lung cancer") or *within* the mental world (e.g. "how our thoughts can influence our emotions.") But can a "thought" or an "emotion" cause cancer; and if so, how does the psychological impact on the physical? Descartes believed that this mysterious transformation took place in the pineal gland, a view long abandoned by brain scientists. The question of how "mind stuff" produces changes in material, or vice-versa, remains unanswered to this day.

Finding ontological dualism unsatisfactory, philosophers have sought replacement in various forms of *monism*, that is, the presumption of only one world. Most prominently in the nineteenth century philosophers believed there is only one world and it is in the mind; this thesis is called *philosophical idealism*. The assertion is that all that we can be sure of is our own experience (Descartes again); the presumption that there is a material world is something we generate within our minds. Although idealist views remain alive in certain quarters, they are generally rejected. Few wish to accept the *solipsism* invited by this view, that is, the assumption that we each live in totally private worlds, and that even the belief that other persons exist is nothing more than a private fantasy. One can neither prove nor disprove solipsism, so why, philosophers ask, accept such a grim conclusion?

Perhaps owing to the dramatic developments in twentieth century technology – from telephones and radio to the atom bomb – idealism has largely been replaced by a second form of monism, namely *materialism*: there is only one world, and it is material. From this standpoint, whatever "the mind" is, it must be an expression of material (brain) processes. There is no mental process that is independent of cortical functioning. Or to put it another way, whatever we call psychology is only neurology at another level of description. Yet, on closer inspection the materialist position proves no more compelling than the idealist. On the one hand, how do we know that there is material? Presumably, it is through our experience. But on what basis can we conclude from our experience that the world is material? This is not simply obvious; we would have to "imagine" or "infer" it; in effect, the world is material only because we *think* it is. Enter the mind once again.

Further, the reduction of the mind to material ultimately destroys the tradition of the autonomous self. We generally understand the material world as a world of cause and effect, of antecedents and consequences linked in predictable ways. There is no room in this conception of the material world for "freely selected decisions," decisions that would interrupt "the laws of nature." One cannot simply decide to jump ten meters in the air, or choose against growing old. Thus, to embrace the material view of persons ultimately turns the idea of free and conscious deliberation into cultural mythology. If we are only machines then whatever we think is already determined in advance. There is little to distinguish the human machine from a robot. And, we might conclude, there is little reason we should place greater value on a human life than that of a machine.

The Problem of Knowledge: Mind as Mirror

The presumption of an "in here" world of subjectivity and "out there" world of objects, creates further riddles of great magnitude. Among the most profound, how do we as subjects acquire knowledge of the objective world? In philosophy this is the problem of *epistemology*. The central epistemological challenge is to understand how individual consciousness comes to have knowledge of the external world. Perhaps you can already sense the emerging predicament. If we can't understand how it is that the objective and the subjective world are causally related, as just discussed, how will we ever determine how the objective world is accurately registered in (or has effects on) the mind? For over 2000 years philosophers have deliberated on this problem; for over a century psychologists have sought answers with the most rigorous laboratory methods. The ideal for most has been to demonstrate that – metaphorically speaking – the mind functions as a *mirror to nature*. Only if we can assume that the mind reflects the world as it is – that we don't experience a rabbit when there is a duck or see a bouquet of flowers when in reality it is a gun – that we can speak of having objective knowledge of the world. If the mind doesn't function like a mirror, and we are simply "making it up," then the very idea of individual knowledge begins to crumble.

Within the tradition of philosophical writing, attempts to justify the view of mind as mirror are typically identified as *empiricist* – the source of all knowledge deriving from experience. Although empiricist views can be traced to Aristotle, within Enlightenment writing John Locke's seventeenth century *Essay Concerning Human Understanding* formed a landmark. As Locke proposed, the mind of the individual is at birth a blank slate, or *tabula rasa*, and it is experience of the world that fills the slate. All abstract ideas and complex thoughts owe their origins to our basic experience of the world. In concert with Locke, the philosopher and statesman Francis Bacon proposed that knowledge of the world must be built up through rigorous *rules of induction* – moving from the particulars of observation to empirically based generalities. Be careful, he warned in *The New Organon* (1620), to avoid the "influences of the marketplace," that is, the common ways people have of talking, as "words" improperly bias the "mind." Later philosophers – including Bishop Berkeley, David Hume, John Stuart Mill – are all identified with the empiricist view.

However, in their strong form empiricist views of knowledge have never been wholly convincing. First, the "world as it is" doesn't seem to demand any particular form of categorization or thought; if a botanist were to look out my window he/she would make one description, a landscaper another, and still other itemizations would be offered by an artist, a real estate agent, or a thief. How then can we conclude that the world shapes our knowledge? Nor can any convincing account be given of how "abstract ideas" are built up from "raw sensations" – how we could derive, for example, concepts of "justice," "democracy," or "God" from the information delivered to the brain by the sensory nerves. What, then, is the origin of our ideas? Finally, it is asked, how can the empiricist stand outside his or her experience to know whether there is actually a world that is being mirrored correctly. If all we have is the reflection in our minds, how can we be certain what is "out there" producing this image?

Such doubts are among those giving rise to a competing school of epistemology, commonly called *rationalism*. For rationalists – from Platonic philosophy to contemporary cognitive psychology – mental processes inherent within the individual play the critical role in fashioning our knowledge. Rationalists seldom make claims that we can know the world directly. Plato used the metaphor of the cave to illustrate our relationship to material reality: as described in *The Republic*, we might see ourselves as born into a cave, capable of observing only the shadows of objects cast upon the wall. It is through our reason that we must come into knowledge about what the shadows mean. In this vein many scholars have been swayed by Immanual Kant's argument (*Critique of Pure Reason*, 1781) that in order to understand the world we must come prepared with certain innate ideas. We could not derive from observation the concepts of number, causality, or time, for example; and so central are these concepts to our understanding of the world that they must be innate. Much the same argument undergirds the view of contemporary cognitive psychologists. In order to draw information from the world, it is proposed, we must approach it with concepts already in mind. The world does not produce our concepts; rather our concepts help us organize the world in various ways. The botanist, landscaper, and real estate agent see my yard differently because they each approach the scene with different mental categories.

Yet, as the debate has continued over the centuries, rationalism fares no better than empiricism in solving the riddle of mental knowledge. For one, it is asked, how did the botanist, landscaper and so on ever acquire their concepts? If you answer "they are learned," then you again enter the empiricist camp: the concepts are built up through observation. Yet we couldn't make sense of this view. You might, as Kant, then argue that they are innate. Many psychologists are drawn to such nativist explanations. However, in this case it is difficult to understand how new concepts are always emerging in culture. From whence our concepts of "black holes" and "postmodernism?" Further, to argue that concepts or ideas are innate again begs the question of mind–body relationships. How is it that chromosomal composition produces abstract concepts? To answer this we should have to solve the thorny problem of how material events cause mental events.

In short, after 2000 years of study, the problem of knowledge remains unsolved. In his important work, *Philosophy and the Mirror of Nature*, Richard Rorty argues for abandoning the entire tradition. "To think of knowledge which presents a 'problem,' and about which we ought to have a 'theory,'" he writes, "is a product of viewing knowledge as an assemblage of representations." That is, we inherit the epistemological riddle because of the metaphor of mind as mirror. This "view of knowledge . . . is a product of the seventeenth century. The moral to be drawn is that if this way of thinking of knowledge is optional, then so is epistemology . . ."[6] In effect, the insoluble problem of knowledge is only insoluble because of the dualist metaphor used to define the problem. We could abandon dualism and the problem would go away – or at least be revised in a more treatable form.

Self-knowledge: the Problem of the Inner Eye

Someone asks you what you think about abortion rights, another asks you about your feelings toward your father, and a third asks what you want to do this weekend. Chances are you will respond easily to each. But, how exactly is it that you know what you think, feel, or want? "You just do," you might say, but how? What follows if we cannot answer this question? We should have to admit not only that we don't know our "real thoughts, feelings, or desires," but that in truth, we can't even be certain that we have such mental events. And we couldn't honestly say "I love you," or "I didn't mean to," for we couldn't know whether we possess love or intention. This is the *problem of self-knowledge* and it poses difficulties no less profound and intractable as those of dualism and individual knowledge. To appreciate the complexities, let's break the problem of self-knowledge down into several components. In each case we find ourselves in a cul de sac.

- What are the characteristics of mental states by which we can identify them? By what criteria do we distinguish among, let's say, states of thought, desire, or intention? What is the color of a thought, the shape of a desire, or the weight of an intention? Why do none of these attributes seem quite applicable to mental states? Is it because our observations of the states demonstrate to us that they are not?
- If we try to observe our mental states, what part of the mind is doing the observing and what part is functioning as the observed? Following our earlier discussion, if we conceive of the mind as some form of mirror, how can the mirror turn on itself to record its own reflections? If we see the world with our eyes, what serves as the "eye of the inner world," and what is its object?
- Could we identify our mental states through their physiological manifestations – blood pressure, heart rate, and so on? Could we find out whether we truly loved someone by looking at our GSR or MRI readings? And if we did have highly sensitive readings of our physiology, how would we know to which states these readings applied? Does an increased pulse rate indicate anger more than love, hope more than despair? Without knowing what states exist, how could we link physiological conditions with the mental world?
- How can we be certain when we identify such states correctly? What if certain mental processes (for example, repression or cognitive biases) prevent accurate self-appraisal? How would we know that they did not? And if you could be certain you were unbiased, how would you know when you were correct, when you had seen your mind "for what it is?" What would be your criterion of "correct?" What is your criterion for knowing, for example, that you are "depressed," as opposed to "sad," "blue," "uninspired," "preoccupied," or just a little tired?
- Although we may all agree on our use of mental terms (for example, that we experience happiness, sadness or anger on particular occasions), how do we know that what we experience privately is the same for others? I can never see into your mind, so how can I be certain that what you are calling "fear" is not what I call "anger," and that my word "happiness" refers to the state you call "anxiety?" You might

reply that you learned to recognize your feelings and other major states during early socialization. You came to know you possessed a specific state of "sadness," when your mother, for example, said something like, "Oh Sara, you seem so sad . . ." But how did your mother know you were sad in this case, as opposed to depressed, uninspired or angry? Your experiences were not on the table for her to examine; no one has access to your "inner life," nor vice versa. Perhaps your mother had it wrong all the time, and perhaps you do now as well.

Again, 2000 years of deliberation – in philosophy, psychology, and biology – have failed to yield answers to such questions. In the meantime many begin to wonder whether we haven't been victims of a *fallacy of misplaced concreteness*. We have words such as "thinking," "feeling," "wanting," "intending," and so on; these seem concrete enough. But we mistakenly attribute the concreteness to an imaginary object – "the thought in the head," "the feeling in my heart," and so on. Even though it seems self-evident that we can think, observe, desire, and so on, perhaps it is only self-evident because we don't question the supposition. In Friedrich Nietzsche's terms, perhaps "It is an illusion" that "after long use seems firm, canonical, and obligatory to a people," and thus an "illusion of which one has forgotten that it is an illusion."[7]

The Gathering Storm: Truth, Rationality, and Morality

> Things fall apart; the centre cannot hold;
> Mere anarchy is loosed upon the world.
>
> W.B. Yeats, "The Second Coming"

Problems of the self are challenging and important. However, far more hangs on these questions than justifying the self alone. Beliefs in the individual mind also form the cornerstone of much else that is central to the Western tradition – in everyday life and most of our major institutions. To raise serious questions about the self is to send shock waves into every corner of cultural life. Before traveling further into the dangerous waters of critique, let us pause to consider several significant repercussions.

Objectivity, Truth, and the Science Question

If the idea of individual minds with knowledge of the external world is suspect, then what are we to make of those who claim the privilege of knowledge? More specifically, what does it mean to claim *objective* knowledge – knowledge based on experience of the world as opposed to subjective imagination? With all the problems of subject–object dualism, what privilege are we to give to those whose claims to knowledge are based on "experience of the world?" Such questions are closely related to the concept of truth. True statements about the world, we hold, reflect the world as it is, and not as we might wish it to be. We gain candidacy as "truth tellers" when we (1) accurately observe a phenomenon, and (2) accurately report on our observations. If all those who are exposed to the phenomenon reach the same conclusion, then we hold the conclusion to be true beyond anyone's private view – beyond history and culture. Yet, if the idea of the mind as a "mirror of nature" is suspect – as reasoned above – then so is the concept of accurate observation. And if we cannot make sense of how the mind could know its own contents (self-knowledge), we begin to threaten the idea of accurately reporting on private observations. If the concepts of truth and objectivity depend on states of knowing mind, they are unsteady indeed.

Let us be more concrete: we generally prize the natural sciences – physics, chemistry, biology, astronomy, and the like – for their advances in knowledge. They tell us about the world as it is. Truth claims within these disciplines are also lodged in the concept of the individual knower – the individual scientist who observes carefully, thinks rigorously, and tests his/her conclusions against the world. Knowledge begins, it is said, with careful observation. Yet consider this configuration that I call "my desk." In my world the desk is solid, mahogany colored, weighs some 80 lb, and is odorless. Yet, the atomic physicist approaches this configuration and tells me that it is not solid after all (it is primarily constituted by empty space); the psychologist informs me that it has no color (as the experience of color is produced by light waves reflected on the retina); the rocket scientist announces that it only appears to weigh 80 lb (as weight depends on the surrounding gravitational field), and the biologist proposes that my sense of smell is inferior to that of my dog for whom the desk is rich in olfactory information. As carefully as I might observe, I would never reach any of these conclusions.

Consider further: each of these professionals employs a different vocabulary for understanding what I call my desk. Physicists speak of it in terms of atoms, biologists of cellulose, engineers of static properties, art historians in terms of Victorian style, and economists in terms of its market value. None of these vocabularies is simply derived from individual observation. I could not read them from nature. Rather, the vocabularies seem to spring from the professional disciplines; they are the forms of description and explanation particular to these traditions of practice. A physicist as such will never "observe" cellulose, nor a biologist a static property, and so on. If this seems reasonable, then scientific truths might be viewed as outgrowths of communities and not observing minds. Likewise, to extend the logic, objectivity and truth would not be byproducts of individual minds but of community traditions. And too, science could not make claims to universal truth, as all truth claims would be specific to particular traditions – lodged in culture and history. We shall return to these possibilities in the next chapter.

Rationality and the Role of Education

If we thrust the concept of knowing minds into question so do we place in jeopardy the assumption of human reason – thinking, planning, rational choice. If the idea of *interior* knowledge of an *exterior* world is abandoned, what would the mind "think about?" What would be its "objects?" Philosophers have conjectured about the possibility of "pure thought" but they have never been able to clarify how the thinker could look inside to know his/her own thoughts. And, if individual knowledge and private reason are suspect, we rapidly bring into question the rationale behind our educational systems. Schools are traditionally dedicated to improving the quality of *individual* minds – increasing knowledge and reasoning skills. It is the individual student who must master the subject matter, write term papers, take exams, and be penalized or rewarded accordingly. Groups of students are seldom graded as groups; a student's family is never evaluated for their contribution (or lack of it); nor is the relationship between teacher and student ("are we together being productive?") subjected to test.

If education is doubtfully about truth, objectivity, knowledge, and rationality, then how are we to understand the process? Again, we begin to make headway when we consider the idea of professional vocabularies. If I as teacher ask you about your reasoning on a given problem, chances are you will respond with an array of words. Whether these words are a reflection of your thoughts I will never know, but when it comes to evaluating your reasons and giving you a grade, it is the words that I will examine. And if the class is in biology I will expect your words to reflect this tradition; in psychology I will anticipate a different set of words; in mathematics I may not want words from the dictionary at all but an array of symbols. Is it possible that what we mean by reasoning, then, is not a private ability but a public action? Is education primarily about socialization into different traditions, different vocabularies, and different practices? Again, we shall return to these possibilities in later pages.

Morality and Responsibility

Beliefs in individual knowledge and reason are closely related to yet another cultural talisman: moral principles. In a sense, most of our actions are congenial with a *moral order* – standards of what is appropriate or acceptable. And it is because we endow individuals with the capacity for knowledge and conscious reasoning that we hold them responsible for deviations from this order. Consider the classroom: there are severe limits placed on what you can say, how long you can talk, how loudly you can speak, to whom you can speak, your tone of voice, your facial expressions, your clothing, and more. The range of acceptability is narrow indeed. At the same time, you may find yourself reasonably comfortable with the situation; the moral order is your order. However, if you deviate you will be punished for violations – by your teacher, classmates, parents and so on. On a larger scale, the dictates of the moral order become realized in our legal codes. We hold individuals responsible for murder, rape, robbery, drug dealing, child molesting, and the like, and wish to see them penalized and corrected. They have chosen on their own to violate the moral codes of the culture.

This is all familiar enough. However, when you consider the problems encountered earlier with the idea of rational self-direction, you can begin to sense the shakiness of this tradition. Why should we presume that moral order is achieved through individual moral thought? More directly to the point, we may ask how an individual can ever make a *free* choice, reflecting his/her own moral beliefs. Can I *alone* choose? For example, how can a person independently deliberate the pros and cons of racing through a traffic signal? Can I even begin to consider the issue without society's influence? I could scarcely think about "the law," because the concept of law is supplied by the culture; to think in these terms would be to "think in a cultural way," not as a private individual. Similarly, concepts like "insurance," "imprisonment," and "bravery" would have to be eliminated from my deliberation. In fact, the very concept of "immorality" itself – the idea of evil as opposed to good – would be unavailable without a culture to supply the terms. Morality – like knowledge and reason – seems to be defined within specific cultures. To hold the individual – and the individual alone – morally responsible, may obscure our own complicity. In important degree, perhaps evil actions speak for us all.

As we find, when we question the common belief in private, knowing selves, so too are assumptions about science, truth, objectivity, rationality, education, and moral choice thrown into doubt. Nor do the reverberations stop here. For example, nothing is more central to the concept of democracy than the belief in independent thought and judgment, "One man, one vote." Our system of economy is also heavily dependent on the presumption of individual minds. Within a capitalist economy we presume the existence of individual decision makers, each motivated to increase his or her own profits. Most of our organizations – businesses, government, the military, and so on – are also lodged in the view of individual competence; it is the individual who is hired, evaluated, paid and/or fired. All these institutions are placed in question. Meddle with the self and all the bones of tradition begin to rattle.

Pulsing Toward the Postmodern

Thus far we have done little more than survey the weak foundations of an otherwise robust tradition. But why bother with the weaknesses – whistle a happy tune and get on with life. These are simply "our beliefs" and they support "our ways of life." They need no more in the way of rational basis than the fact that we generally prefer to eat three as opposed to five meals a day. This is just the way we do it; full stop.

Yet, we must pause at this point to ask who is the "we" who rests satisfied with these traditions? First, it is clear that the family of suppositions and practices in question are all byproducts of Western culture, and chiefly byproducts of recent centuries. If we simply take them for granted, we stop asking questions. In particular, we fail to ask about the downside – what are the negative repercussions for society. Further, we fail to address whether these beliefs and practices can successfully function within the new century. For example, with the development of globe-spanning technologies of communication and transportation – from telephone, radio, television and jet transportation to computers, satellite transmission, the internet, and World Wide Web – the world's peoples increasingly confront each other. And rather than the *global village* for which many hoped,[8] we confront increasing numbers of contentious factions, expansionist movements, exploitative practices, animosities and resistances. Under these conditions we must ask whether any culture – and particularly a powerful one – can afford commitment without question? Consider some of the implications of our traditional commitments to self, truth, reason and moral principles:

Cultural imperialism: As elsewhere, we in the West typically presume the universality of our truths, reasons, and morals. Our scientific truths are not "ours" in particular, we hold, but candidates for universal truth. That the world is made up of atoms and individuals who possess emotions is not for us a matter of cultural belief. Any reasonable person would reach the same conclusion. Yet, as we presume the reality and truth of our own beliefs, so do we trample on the realities of others. We unwittingly become cultural imperialists, suppressing and antagonizing. For example, while a visiting professor in Japan, a senior professor confided in me his sense of loneliness and isolation. Bitterly he recounted the years after the Second World War, when the Americans re-organized the university. Before the Americans, he recounted, all the professors shared the same large office. "We talked, shared, and laughed. The Americans thought this 'backward,' and re-organized the university so that each professor was confined to a separate office. Now we don't talk, share or laugh very much." Individualism at work. The reaction can be far more bitter. Consider the sentiments of a Maori from New Zealand:

> Psychology . . . has created the mass abnormalization of Maori people by virtue of the fact that Maori people have been . . . recipients of [English] defined labels and treatments . . . Clinical psychology is a form of social control . . . and offers no more "truth" about the realities of Maori people's lives than a regular reading of the horoscope page in the local newspaper.[9]

Knowledge and the new totalitarianism: Enlightenment ideas were highly successful in undermining the totalitarian rule of royalty and religion. We hold that each individual is endowed with powers of observation and reason, and thus an inalienable right to participate in the process of governance. While we continue to cherish this right, we have also seen this valorization of individual knowledge as instrumental to the rise of science, objectivity and truth. As scientific communities have grown strong, so have they developed specialized vocabularies, methodologies, modes of analysis and practices of reason. Thus, we confront the emergence of a new "knowledge class," groups who claim superiority of voice over all others. Further, without initiation into the class (typically through an advanced degree) one cannot challenge these claims. Opinions based on anything other than the standards of the knowledge class – for example, on personal values, spiritual insights, commitments to another tradition – are largely discounted. In effect, where the Enlightenment initially functioned to democratize the society, it has now succeeded in generating a new form of totalitarianism.[10] As many now feel, "when the trumpets of truth begin to sound, run for cover!"

Communal erosion: If we hold the individual to be the fundamental atom of society, so do we emphasize separation as opposed to community. We evaluate, judge, measure, heal, and incarcerate separate individuals. As a result we give little attention to relations – to the coordinated efforts required, for example, to generate knowledge, reason and morality. We judge the individual student, while failing to appreciate how it is that cooperation is required among students and teachers to achieve a process of education. We emphasize individual rights while paying little attention to the duties required to sustain our communities. Our conception of individual selves is also duplicated at the international level: we place a premium on strengthening the individual nation, with secondary concern for relations with others. Yet, as is becoming increasingly clear on the international level, the economic and political fate of any nation is tied to its alliances – NATO, EC, UN, NAFTA and so on. Attention to individual units leads to blindness of relationship.

Instrumental relations: If the individual is prized, then all that is "not the self" is "other." Cast in the position of other, the fundamental question one asks is "whether you will help me or hurt me." My powers of reason are thus enlisted to ensure my well-being, and all must be evaluated in terms of outcomes. As commonly put, I am invited into an *instrumental* posture toward others: they are primarily means to the ends of my fulfillment. They possess no intrinsic worth. This attitude enters into relations with family, friends, and colleagues – generating distance and distrust. One has value only so long as he "profits" the other. Why remain friends if the other doesn't "do anything for me." Why remain married if "my needs are being stifled?" The same individualist view has now become virtually synonymous with business life. In the service of expanding profits anyone can be sacrificed at any time – from single individuals ("downsized") to communities ("the business went south"), to nations ("they can make it cheaper in China"). When the world turns instrumental no one can be trusted.

Exploitation of nature: The posture of instrumentality also enters into our orientation to nature. If self is first, then nature is evaluated in terms of its benefits (or threats) "to me." It is this mentality – extended to organizations such as business and government – that many view as catastrophic. Natural resources (coal, iron, oil) are pillaged, forests turned to stubble, water resources fouled and depleted, and vast ranges of animal species eradicated – all for purposes of increasing individual gain. As many argue, unless we shift from a posture of instrumental expansion (more growth, gain, profit, well-being) to one of *sustainability*, the planet will be laid waste.[11]

These are only a few of the critiques of the Western tradition of individual selves and its allied beliefs in truth, reason and moral principles. We shall encounter others as the book unfolds (see especially Chapter 5). This is not to argue for abandoning these traditions. Rather it is to open the commonplace to critical inspection and to explore the possibility of fresh and more viable alternatives.

Agitation in the Academy: Beware the Word

> . . . We multiply distinctions, then
> Deem that our puny boundaries are things
> That we perceive, and not that which we have made.
>
> William Wordsworth, "The Prelude", Book III

In this context of broad misgiving, three new developments have taken root in the intellectual sphere. Their primary thrust has been critical. Many believe these developments – working separately and together – function like death warrants for the traditions in question. While creating enormous controversy and resistance, these developments also form the beginning of a brave new dialogue, dangerous yes, but one both exciting and profound in consequence. The dialogue is variously called post-foundational, post-Enlightenment, post-empiricist, post-structural, and *postmodern*. You will understand this family of concepts ("the posts") more fully as the story moves on. For now, let us concentrate on the chief elements of the dialogue. They are essential background for appreciating the emergence of social construction.

Words as Pictures: the Crisis of Representation

The major lines of postmodern critique can be traced to a single, but long-ignored weakness in the traditional accounts of self, truth, science, and their relatives. The weakness is in the taken-for-granted character of language. As suggested, most of the problems inherent in the idea of individual knowing minds have to do with the relation of self and world (problems of "in here" vs. "out there.") That people use language to share the contents of their minds has been relatively uncontested. Naturally, we have presumed, we use words to describe what we experience, and to

share our thoughts and observations with others. In the case of observations, we presume something like a *picture theory of language*. That is, our
words can function as pictures. If you have never been to Marrakech, I
could return from a visit and my descriptions would give you a picture of
what I saw. More formally, this view is treated in the philosophy of science
as *the correspondence theory of language*. How is it, philosophers ask, that
words can correspond to the world as it is? Much hangs on the answer. It
is through words that we communicate what we take to be true – whether
in daily life, courts of law, or science. If words do not correspond to the
events or objects in the world – if they cannot picture the world as it is –
then how can we communicate the truth? If a psychologist tells us that
"persons with angry dispositions have shorter life spans than those who
are more content" we presume the statement corresponds to an observed
reality. Other scientists can determine the accuracy of such a statement,
and if it is corroborated we might wish to change our ways. However, if
words do not correspond with what there is, then we learn nothing. The
statement is little more than a fairy story.

Interestingly, philosophers of science have never been able to supply an
account of how words can correspond to experienced realities. You may
begin to appreciate their problems by returning momentarily to the
assumption of the interior self. How can we accurately convey our private
experience to others – report accurately on what we feel or see? Consider
the case of emotional feelings. How can you reduce the complex, ever
changing flow of consciousness to a single word like "sadness" or "love?"
And what is the object of the word in any case; what precise bit of experience is captured by the word? Further, you didn't choose the vocabulary
with which to convey your internal states; all you have is the hand-me-
down vocabulary available within the culture. Are these words adequate
to picture your states; and indeed, for what states are they pictures? How
is it, then, that words correspond to – or "tell the truth" about – our experiences?

At this point you might reply that truth in language may be difficult to
justify in the case of psychological states like experience, but this is not so
in the case of scientific truth. In the case of science we are speaking of publicly observable phenomena; here words and objects can correspond. Consider, however, the classic critique of the philosopher W.V.O. Quine. In his
volume *Word and Object*[12] he asks how it is that words and objects match,
so that we can all know we mean the same thing. He considers the hypo-
thetical case of a linguist who visits an exotic tribe and tries to translate
their language. He notices that the people use the term *gavagai* when a
rabbit scurries by. However, the same term is used for what he calls a
running rabbit, a dead rabbit, pieces of rabbit cooking in a pot, and the
ears of a rabbit seen through the brush. The specific objects bear little
resemblance to each other. To what specific observable, then, does the
word *gavagai* apply? And, even if we had the animal standing before us,
would the natives mean the same thing by *gavagai* that we do by rabbit?

Perhaps the native is referring to the collection of independent rabbit parts, while some of us would mean the animal as a single whole.

As Quine concluded, we confront a profound *indeterminacy of reference*, that is, an enormous vagueness concerning the referents of our words. And when you stop to consider, to what specific object, in what specific state, does your personal name correspond? You are in a state of continuous flux, moving in this way and that, growing and changing, expressing one thing and then another. Yet, you use the same word for all configurations, and you cannot know whether other people are using your name for the same configurations. We shall return to the problem of truth in language in the following chapter. For now, however, it is useful to see the critique of correspondence as setting the stage for two more lethal lines of analysis.

Ideological Critique: the Crisis of Value Neutrality

> We do not address inquiries to nature and she does not answer us. We put questions to ourselves and we organize observation and experiment in such a way as to obtain an answer.
>
> Mikhail Bakhtin, *The Problem of the Text*

Each year I receive numerous requests from my students for recommendations. These students usually have good reason to expect my letters to be positive. But what does "positive" mean in this case? Without any sense of misrepresentation I could describe the same student as "a good worker," "an able performer," "intelligent," or "intellectually a delight." Each of these descriptions is positive; more important, I cannot select one over the other on the basis of objective accuracy. So how do I select? As you quickly realize, what is distinctive about these differing descriptors is what they suggest about my disposition toward the student. If I really care about the student's success, I will not describe him or her as "a good worker" or an "able performer." The words are positive, but simply convey no enthusiasm. Even "intelligent" does not carry the intensity of "intellectually a delight." Depending on my investment in the student, then, I can – without being objectively unfair – tip the balance in one direction or another.

This possibility that my *interests* bias my descriptions of the world may seem trivial. However, if you play out the implications they are devastating in consequence. To the extent that my interests determine how it is I describe the world, then my descriptions lose the capacity to objectively describe. To the extent that you believe I am personally invested, you will cease to listen to me as an objective observer and hear what I say as an expression of personal interests. My authority on the subject of my student's abilities (in this case) is suspect if not demolished. More broadly, if you can detect my personal interests you throw my authority into disrepute. The significance of this argument was made particularly apparent by early Marxist writings. As Marx and his allies proposed, capitalist economic theory offers itself as an accurate reading of the world of economics. However, because the theory favors a system in which its proponents are benefited, it is suspicious. The theory rationalizes a condition in which the "haves" continue to profit through exploited labor of the "have nots." Or in Marxist terms, the theory *mystifies* the public, leading them to believe a falsehood that keeps them enslaved. Marx mounted the same argument against religious authority. Religious teachings, on this account, do not illuminate the world of spirit; rather religion serves as an "opiate of the masses," diminishing consciousness of suppression and exploitation.

Yet, this line of critique is scarcely the preserve of Marxist theorists. As social theorist Jürgen Habermas demonstrated in his influential volume *Knowledge and Human Interests*,[13] all knowledge-seeking privileges certain interests over others, favors a certain political and economic configuration to the detriment of alternatives. As we thus find, virtually any authority – whether a scientist, scholar, supreme court judge, or religious leader – could be subjected to *ideological critique*, that is, critique aimed at revealing the interests, values, doctrines, or myths that underlie seemingly neutral claims to truth. As ideological critique suggests, their words are not pictures of the world; rather, their interests lead them to select certain accounts and not others. What has been left out, what descriptions are they suppressing? Further, given the distinct possibility of self-interest, we are encouraged to ask how the authorities gain by way of their particular accounts? Who is being silenced, exploited, or erased?

Of course, such critiques may seem applicable enough in the case of politics, religion, and the social sciences – where the terms are often ambiguous and the facts are scarce. However, aren't the natural sciences immune from such critiques? Scientists don't seem to be ideologically invested; and their findings are open to public scrutiny. Yet, for the astute ideological critic, it is this seeming neutrality of science that is most misleading, most mystifying. Critical scrutiny is essential. In this light, consider Emily Martin's analysis of the ways in which biological science characterizes the woman's body. Martin's particular concern is in the way biological texts, in both the classroom and laboratory, represent or describe the female body. She concludes from her analysis that the woman's body is largely portrayed as a "factory" whose primary purpose is to reproduce the species. It follows that the processes of menstruation and menopause are characterized as wasteful if not dysfunctional, for they are periods of "nonproduction." To illustrate, note the negative terms in which standard biology texts describe menstruation (italics mine): "the fall in blood progesterone and estrogen *deprives* the highly developed endometrial lining of its hormonal support"; "*constriction*" of blood vessels leads to a "*diminished* supply of oxygen and nutrients"; and when "*disintegration* starts, the entire lining begins to *slough*, and the menstrual flow begins." "The loss of hormonal stimulation causes *decrosis*" (death of tissue). Another text says that menstruation is like "the uterus crying for lack of a baby."[14]

Martin makes two essential points. First, these scientific descriptions are anything but neutral. In subtle ways they inform the reader that menstruation and menopause are forms of breakdown or failure. These negative implications have broad social consequences. For the woman, to accept such accounts is to alienate herself from her body. Such descriptions furnish grounds for judging herself negatively – both on a monthly basis during most of her adult years and then permanently after the years of fertility have passed. Women who are childless are condemned, by implication, for their *unproductivity*. Of equal importance, these characterizations could be otherwise. Such negative descriptions are not required by "the way things are," but reflect masculine interests, an ideology that reduces the woman to "baby maker."

To secure the case, Martin points out that there are other bodily processes – some even exclusive to men – that could be described in the same manner but are not. The lining of the stomach is shed and replaced regularly, and seminal fluid picks up cells that have been shed as it flows through the male ducts. However, biological texts characterize the change in the stomach walls as a "renewal" and make no mention of males "losing" or "wasting" in describing ejaculation. In effect, many different descriptions are possible, and the dominant choice in the biological sciences reflects male interests to the detriment of women.

Martin's analysis is but one illustration of ideological critique at work. It is also but a single manifestation of an enormous body of feminist critique – sophisticated and sharply pointed scholarship that spans the humanities, social sciences, and natural sciences. Nor are Marxists and feminists the only groups to make use of ideological critique. Currently such critique is used by virtually all groups that find themselves marginalized, oppressed, misrepresented, or "unheard" by society at large – by African American, feminists, Native American, gay and lesbian, Chicano, Asian, and Arab activists, to name but a few. In all cases, the critique calls into question the taken-for-granted logics or realities of the dominant culture, shows how these logics both support the self-interest of the dominant groups and perpetuate injustice, and casts suspicion on the motives of the prominently placed.

Nor is it an easy matter for the targets of such criticism to defend themselves. Any defense of what appears to be a self-serving statement will itself give rise to the same suspicion. The target can make no further recourse to "the facts" that will not seem to issue from the same self-serving investments. And, because ideological critique is typically directed against those in power – who have wealth, position, privileges, security, and the like – their defenses seem especially flimsy. Would "the haves" say anything that wasn't designed, in the end, to protect their own interests? Some see ideological critique as a great new defender of democracy; others see it as democracy's end. We shall explore these issues as the volume unfolds. Let us now turn to a second major threat to the prevailing traditions.

From Semiotics to Deconstruction: the End of Reason

> There is nothing outside of text.
>
> Jacques Derrida, *Positions*

A second slide into skepticism began quietly in a small corner of the scholarly world; its once elfin voice now bellows. To appreciate what is at stake we again visit the word, but this time the early study of language. One of the most important approaches to understanding language was initially formalized in the work of the Swiss linguist Ferdinand de Saussure (1857–1913).[15] In his influential volume *A Course in General Linguistics*, Saussure laid out the rationale for what became the discipline of *semiotics*. The field of semiotics (or semiology) was conceived as a *science of signs*, that is, a science focussed on the systems by which we communicate. Two of Saussure's ideas are particularly important to our discussion: first, a distinction is made between the *signifier* and the *signified*, with the signifier referring to a word (or some other signal), and the signified to that which we believe is signaled by the word (that for which it stands.) As Saussure proposed, *the relationship between signifiers and signifieds is ultimately arbitrary*. In the simplest case, each of us was assigned a first name at birth (a signifier), but our parents were free to choose almost any name they wished. Saussure's second significant proposal was that *sign systems are governed by their own internal logics*. Put simply, our language (as a sign system) can be described in terms of various rules, such as rules of grammar or syntax. When we speak or write we must approximate these rules (or internal logics); otherwise we fail to make sense.

All this seems simple enough, and has lead to a long line of traditional research on grammar, phonemes, syntax, the history of language, and the like. However, the plot begins to thicken when you return to the correspondence theory of language discussed above. Recall here that the concepts of accuracy, objectivity and truth all depend on the assumption that certain words correspond to what is the case. On this view, certain words "tell it like it is," while others are biased, exaggerated, or simply untrue representations. If, however, the relationship between signifier and signified is ultimately arbitrary, then in principle any word can stand for any signified – any object, person, or events. What then privileges any particular arrangement of words as being "true to fact?" Is it not simply social convention that cements word to world, that "makes it true" that I am Kenneth and not Samuel or Susan? It is not because the word is a map or picture of me, but because of local conventions.

A lovely illustration of the extent to which "truth in language" depends on convention is given in Raymond Queneau's beguiling little volume *Exercises in Style*.[16] In this work Queneau generates 195 different descriptions of a single occasion. Variously he relies on metaphor, verse, scientific notation, and other genres of writing to give the reader a heady sense of the many ways we *could* describe a given situation. Consider first one of the more colorful descriptions:

> In the centre of the day, tossed among the shoals of traveling sardines in a coleopter with a big white carapace, a chicken with a long, featureless neck suddenly harangued one, a peace-abiding one, of their number, and its parlance, moist with protest, was unfolded upon the airs. Then, attracted by a void, the fledgling precipitated itself thereunto.
>
> In a bleak, urban desert, I saw it again the self-same day, drinking the cup of humiliation offered by a lowly button.

For most of us, this account doesn't seem to be objective – true to the facts. It seems whimsical and poetic, a play with words. Let's turn to a second account:

> In the S bus, in the rush hour, a chap of about 26, felt hat with a cord instead of a ribbon, neck too long, as if someone's been having a tug-of-war with it. People getting off. The chap in question gets annoyed with one of the men standing next to him. He accuses him of jostling him every time anyone goes past. A sniveling tone which is meant to be aggressive. When he sees a vacant seat he throws himself on to it.
>
> Two hours later, I meet him in the Cour de Rome, in front of the gare Saint-Lazare. He's with a friend who's saying: "You ought to get an extra button put on your overcoat." He shows him where (at the lapels) and why.

Here we breathe a sigh of relief. Now we have a glimpse of what's *really* going on. But why do we draw such a conclusion? Is it because the language is more precise? Consider, then, good scientifically acceptable prose:

> In a bus of the S-line, 10 meters long, 3 wide, 6 high, at 3 km. 600 m. from its starting point, loaded with 48 people, at 12.17 p.m., a person of the masculine sex aged 27 years, 3 months and 8 days, 1 m. 72 cm. tall and weighing 65 kg. and wearing a hat 3.5 cm. in height around the crown of which was a ribbon 60 cm. long, interpellated a man aged 48 years 4 months and 3 days, 1 m. 68 cm. tall and weighing 77 kg., by means of 14 words whose enunciation lasted 5 seconds and which alluded to some involuntary displacements of from 15 to 20 mm. Then he went and sat down about 1m. 10 cm. away.
>
> 57 minutes later he was 10 meters away from the suburban entrance to the gare Saint-Lazare and was walking up and down over a distance of 30 m. with a friend aged 28, 1 m. 70 cm. tall and weighing 71 kg. who advised him in 15 words to move by 5 cm. in the direction of the zenith a button which was 3 cm. in diameter.

Now we have precise details, without color or passion, but again we aren't certain about "what truly happened." What is it, then, that makes one language "objectively accurate" and another "aesthetic" or "obscuring?" It does not appear to be the correspondence of the words to the world; nowhere in these accounts have we confronted "the world" to which they refer. Rather we have confronted only variations in styles of writing. Is truth, then, simply "being in style"?

Although such a conclusion may seem extreme, this focus on language does invite a robust skepticism. When claims are made to "truth," "objectivity" or "accuracy in reporting," we should be aware that we are only being exposed to "one way of putting things." These are "truths by convention," which is to say, privileged by certain groups of people. But, we must ask, who are these people, what is not being said, whose voices are absent? These are all questions that will concern us as the book develops. We must continue at this point to examine more sweeping repercussions of the linguistic arguments.

The preceding treats only the arbitrary relationship between the signifier and the signified. Recall, however, the second aspect of semiotic study: that language can be studied as a system unto itself. Although this assumption seems tame enough – similar to saying that we can study music or plant life independent of everything else – its implications are profound. What is most interesting is that if language use is determined by an inner logic, then what we call "meaning" may be independent of the world outside language. Or to put in another way, words and phrases may gain their meaning from their relationship to other words and phrases, and without regard to "the way the world really is." This possibility seems clear enough in the case of definitions. Every entry in the dictionary is defined in terms of other words; you don't have to exit the dictionary to find meaning. However, if meaning is generated out of words alone is it possible that our understandings of the world and ourselves are primarily driven by the relationship among words? We treat propositions about the world and the self as reflections of what is the case. As we now find, such propositions depend for their intelligibility on their place in a history of language use.

It is this possibility that has sparked major interest in literary theory, and particularly the works of French theorist Jacques Derrida.[17] Although highly ambiguous in themselves, scholars have extended the implications of Derrida's writings on linguistic *deconstruction* in many significant directions. Two of these implications are especially relevant to us: first, deconstruction theory suggests that all our attempts to make sense – to make rational decisions, to provide good answers to life's major challenges – first depend on a *massive suppression of meaning*. In an important sense, all rationality is myopic. Second, we find, under close scrutiny that the coherence of our most rational accounts will collapse. Rationality, then, is not a foundation for anything – for our institutions of government and science, for example, or a way of deciding on what is moral or worthwhile. Rather, Derrida suggests, our "good reasons" are in the end both suppressive and empty. These are strong – even outrageous – conclusions. How can Derrida and those following the deconstructive path support them?

First, how can deconstruction theorists conclude that rationality requires suppression or a degradation of sense? Drawing from early semiotic theory, Derrida views language first as a system of *differences*. Language is not like a flowing stream, but is divided into discrete units (or words). Each word is distinct from all others. Another way of talking about these differences is in terms of *binaries* (the division into two). That is, the distinctiveness of words depends on a simple split between "the word" and "not the word." The meaning of "white," then, depends on differentiating it from what is "non-white" (or "black" for instance). Word meaning depends, then, on differentiating between a *presence* and an *absence*, that which is designated by the word against what is not designated. To make sense in language is to speak in terms of presences, what is designated, against a backdrop of absences. As you can see, the presences are privileged; they are brought into focus by the words themselves; the absences may only be there by implication; or we may simply forget them altogether. But take careful note: these presences would not make sense without the absences. Without the binary distinction there is no meaning.

Let us put this argument into action: consider the widely accepted view of science, that the cosmos is made up of material. We as humans, then, are essentially material beings – whether we speak of this material in terms of neurons, chemical elements, or atoms. Take away the material and there is nothing left over to call a person. Humanists and spiritualists are deeply troubled by this view; it seems to repudiate everything we hold valuable about people. We want to believe there is something that gives human life more value than an automobile or a new television. Yet, materialism as a world-view seems so obviously true! But now consider the deconstructionist's arguments: the word "material" gains its meaning only by virtue of a binary, that is, in contrast to "non-material." Consider this binary in terms of material/spirit. To say that "the cosmos is material" makes no sense unless you can distinguish it from what is spirit. Something identifiable as spirit must exist then, in order to say what material is. Yet, if spirit must exist in order to give material any meaning, then the cosmos cannot be altogether material. To put it another way, in the world-view of materialism, the spiritual world is *marginalized* (thrust into the unnoticed margins of the page.) The spirit is an unspoken absence. However, without the presence of this absence, the very sense of "the cosmos is material" is destroyed. As we might say, the entire world-view of the materialist rests on a suppression of the spirit.

As Derrida also proposes, in the Western tradition there are many binaries for which there is a strong tendency to privilege or value one side over the other. In Western culture we generally prize the rational over the emotional, mind over body, order over disorder, and leaders over followers. As many social critics have pointed out, there is also a tendency for the dominant groups in society to lay claim to the privileged pole, while viewing "others" as the opposite. Consider, for example, the ways in which masculinity is commonly associated with rationality, mental control, order, and leadership, while women are typically said to be emotional, bodily oriented, disorganized followers. Because of the oppressive implications of our common distinctions, deconstructionist critics are drawn to upsetting the binaries or blurring the boundaries. These issues will occupy us later in the book.

The assault on rationality does not terminate with its suppressive character. Rather, from a deconstructionist perspective we find that under close scrutiny the coherence of our most rational accounts will collapse. Rationality, then, is not a foundation for anything – for our institutions of government and science, for example, or a way of deciding on what is moral or worthwhile. Everywhere we are exposed to experts, confident and knowledgeable authorities with strong contentions. Yet, from Derrida's perspective, there are no grounds for such confidence. When closely examined, reason lies empty. How is this so? Return again to the idea of language as a self-contained system, where the meaning of each term depends on its relationship to other terms. As Derrida proposes, we might see this dependency as made up of two components, *difference* and *deferral*. Each word first gains its meaning by virtue of differing from other words. The word "bat" has no meaning in itself, but begins to acquire meaning when it is contrasted with other terms – such as "hat" or "mat." This difference, however, is insufficient to give "bat" its meaning. Rather, in order to understand the term we must defer to other terms that will tell us what "bat" means. Realize at this juncture that we have more than one choice in this process of deferring. We can, for example, say that a "bat is a flying mammal," or alternatively that a "bat" is a "wooden club used in the game of baseball." More formally, we may say that the term *bears traces* of meaning from various linguistic or textual histories, here from biology and athletics. Realize as well that once you have entered the process of *différance* (Derrida's binary-breaking elision of "differing" and "deferring"), there is no principled exit. That is, the meaning of "flying mammal" or "wooden club" is not given in these terms themselves. To understand them we must again defer to still other terms. We search for traces, and we find only further traces. "Nothing . . . is anywhere simply present or absent. There are only, everywhere, differences and traces of traces."[18]

To give these arguments a critical edge consider a term such as democracy. We speak about democracy as an existing form of government, a form to be cherished, studied, theorized, and protected if necessary with human life. Yet, the meaning of the term "democracy" is not derived from our simply observing people moving about. The word is not a picture of people's actions. Rather, to use the term meaningfully depends on a literary distinction between "democracy" and, for example, contrasting terms such as "totalitarianism" and "monarchy." Yet, the difference alone is insufficient to understand the term. What is democracy other than "not being a monarchy?" To gain clarity we find ourselves deferring to other words, words such as "freedom" and "equality." Yet what do these latter terms mean? What exactly is "freedom" and "equality"? For clarity we again resort to the process of *différance*. "Equality," we might say, is the opposite of "inequality"; it is reflected in societies that are "fair" and "just." But what precisely is "inequality," and what is it to be "fair" or "just?" The search continues, and there is no means of exiting the self-referring texts of democracy to encounter "the real thing." The meaning of democracy is fundamentally *undecidable*.

From this standpoint, whatever is argued clearly and confidently masks a profound fragility – the fact that all the terms making up the argument are deeply ambiguous. Clarity and confidence can be maintained only so long as one does not ask too many questions, such as "what exactly is democracy . . . justice . . . warfare . . . love . . . depression?" and so on. When examined closely, all authoritative arguments – indeed all meaning – begins to vanish.

The Valley of Despair

We began this chapter by considering a number of closely related beliefs: the sense of ourselves as knowing, rational, and autonomous, and the correlative assumptions of objective knowledge, reason, and moral foundations. Such beliefs are all central to what is often called cultural modernism. Although fortifying many cultural traditions (democracy, education, organizational structures, the economy), we also found that the grounds for such beliefs were fragile; long-standing questions of fundamental importance could not be answered. Of course, beliefs or traditions don't necessarily erode because they are flawed; life is never perfect. However, as we confronted the major changes occurring in the global context, we also began to see the potential dangers of the modernist commitments and to raise questions about their future viability. This growing consciousness of the historical and cultural limitations of these beliefs set the stage for considering major lines of critique emerging in the scholarly world. Because these latter forms of critique place modernist assumptions in severe jeopardy, they are typically identified as postmodern. In their questioning the relationship between word and world, all claims to truth – as represented or conveyed in language – were brought into question. Within the domain of ideological critique we found all authoritative statements – on self and world – open to suspicion. Semiotic and deconstructionist critique pointed the way to unraveling all propositions, descriptions, and rational arguments. We were left, then, without any significant grounds for the configuration of modernist beliefs. We confront, then, what is said to be a *legitimation crisis*: all claims to knowledge of self and world lose their authority.[19] This crisis now leaps the boundaries of the books and becomes fuel for action. Terms such as "identity politics," the "science wars," the "culture wars," and "political correctness" are only a few of the indicators of ferment. Everywhere there is questioning, challenging, mistrust, and resistance.

But one final turn must be made in this story. For many it is a downward turn that leaves a deposit of despair. As the arguments unfold not only do the traditions seem groundless, so many balloons afloat on hot air, but so do the critiques. The critiques initially seem to offer moments of insight, new ways of understanding, possibly some positive alternatives. And yet, if this is the termination of the dialogue we end in a sorry state. The chief problem is that the critiques are so powerful that they also destroy themselves – in effect, undermining their capacity to do more than form a chorus of corrosive nattering. Consider, for example, the ideological critic who finds every rational defense of tradition shot through with self-interest. For example, feminists argue that research on women's depression paints a picture of women as weak and dependent – thus sustaining the patriarchal order. What then of the critic's observations; are they not also dipped in the same ink – colored in this case by feminist biases? As many traditionalists have now learned, the best defense against ideological critique is to locate the self-interested and oppressive character of the criticism. Herein lies the basis for the counter-charge of *political correctness*. Aren't the ideological critics themselves suppressing those they criticize, with the banner of "liberation" serving as a mystifying device? The result is a standoff between critics and targets, with no obvious means of resolution.

And what is the self-defeating consequence of deconstructionist critique? Such critique demonstrates the meaningless character of rational argumentation, but rests its case on exactly such argumentation. As Derrida was fully aware, his own arguments should also be placed "under erasure" (as he called it); they cannot sustain themselves. Descartes was moved to doubt his senses, all authority, all common opinion, but in the end could not doubt the fact of doubt. This left him with a center, a place to stand and to build. In the current debates we find that even the doubt must be doubted. There is no center that can hold.

It is in this soil of critique and dead-end despair that social constructionism takes root. For many constructionists the hope has been to build from the existing rubble in new and more promising directions. The postmodern arguments are indeed significant, but serve not as an end but a beginning. Further, it we are careful and caring in the elaboration of the constructionist alternative, we shall also find ways of reconstituting the modernist tradition so as to retain some of its virtues while removing its threatening potentials. In the next chapter I will develop some of the rudiments of constructionism. Several paths will be opened by the constructionist clearing. As further chapters unfold we shall find some of these paths will be scholarly, others political, some personal, and others very practical in implication. We move then from a prevailing despair to more positive possibilities – from deconstruction to reconstruction.

Reflection

I have used this chapter to create a sense of historical movement – history as an unfolding story in which we now find ourselves burdened by a problematic tradition and in which we must act to create our future. But it must be realized that the "sense of history" created here is not a true reflection of the past – a picture revealing life as lived, the world as it has come to be – but is itself the result of a particular configuration of words on paper. I could have written all this otherwise ... in many different ways, and with far different implications. This does not make the account inaccurate or wrong. After all, how can any words accurately picture the world? The very idea of words as pictures is misleading. So, let's treat this introduction in another way – not my "telling the truth," but as a form of invitation. Consider it as something like an invitation to dance, to play, and to deliberate about our lives, our relationships, our societies and our future. If you find it an attractive invitation, and I surely hope you do, then you will enjoy reading on. The story becomes increasingly fascinating and the implications profound.

Notes

1 DeLillo, D. (1985) *White Noise*. New York: Penguin.
2 Ibid., from pp. 22–4.
3 Lyotard, J. (1984) *The Postmodern Condition: A Report on Knowledge*. Minneapolis, MN: University of Minnesota Press.
4 For a detailed discussion of early conceptions of mind and self, see Onians, R.B. (1951) *The Origins of European Thought about the Body, the Mind, the Soul, the World, Time and Fate*. Cambridge: Cambridge University Press.
5 For more extended discussion see Lyons, J.O. (1978) *The Invention of the Self: The Hinge of Consciousness in the Eighteenth Century*. Carbondale, IL: Southern Illinois University Press.
6 Rorty, R. (1979) *Philosophy and the Mirror of Nature*. Princeton, NJ: Princeton University Press. p. 136.
7 Nietzsche, F. (1979) On truth and falsity in their ultramoral sense. In O. Levy (Ed.) *The Complete Works of Friedrich Nietzsche*. New York: Russell & Russell. (Originally published in 1873.) p. 174.
8 McLuhan, M. and Powers, B.R. (1989) *The Global Village: Transformation in World Life and Media in the 21st Century*. New York: Oxford University Press.
9 Lawson-Te Aho (1993) The socially constructed nature of psychology and the abnormalisation of Maori. *New Zealand Psychological Society Bulletin*, 76, 25–30.
10 See for example Willard, C.A. (1998) *Expert Knowledge: Liberalism and the Problem of Knowledge*. Chicago: University of Chicago Press.
11 For further discussion see Meadows, D.H., Meadows, D.L., and Raners, J. (1992) *Beyond the Limits: Confronting Global Collapse, Envisioning a Sustainable Future*. Post Mills, VT: Chelsea Green.
12 Quine, W.V.O. (1960) *Word and Object*. Cambridge, MA: MIT Press.
13 Habermas, J. (1971) *Knowledge and Human Interests*. Boston: Beacon Press.

14   From E. Martin (1987) *The Woman in the Body: A Cultural Analysis of Reproduction*. Boston, MA: Beacon.
15   Saussure, F. de (1974) *Course in General Linguistics*. London: Fontana.
16   Queneau, R. (1981) *Exercises in Style*. New York: New Directions.
17   See especially Derrida, J. *Of Grammatology*. Baltimore, MD: Johns Hopkins University Press.
18   Derrida, J. (1981) *Positions*. Chicago: University of Chicago Press. p. 38.
19   Habermas, J. (1975) *Legitimation Crisis*. Boston, MA: Beacon Press. See also Lyotard, J.F. (1984) *The Post-modern Condition: A Report on Knowledge*. Minneapolis, MN: University of Minnesota Press.

Further Resources

The Self in Question

Austin, J.L. (1962) *Sense and Sensibilia*. London: Oxford University Press.
Bonjour, L. (1998) *In Defense of Pure Reason: A Rationalist Account of A Priori Justification*. New York: Cambridge University Press.
Goldman, A.H. (1988) *Empirical Knowledge*. Berkeley, CA: University of California Press.
Levine, G. (Ed.) (1992) *Constructions of the Self*. New Brunswick, NJ: Rutgers University Press.
Malcolm, N. (1971) *Problems of Mind, Descartes to Wittgenstein*. New York: Harper & Row.
Rorty, R. (1979) *Philosophy and the Mirror of Nature*. Princeton, NJ: Princeton University Press.
Ryle, G. (1949) *The Concept of Mind*. London: Hutchinson.
Smith, P. (1988) *Discerning the Subject*. Minneapolis, MN: University of Minnesota Press.
Vesey, G.N.A. (1991) *Inner and Outer: Essays on a Philosophical Myth*. New York: St Martin's Press.

Postmodern Critique

Anderson, W.T. (Ed.) (1995) *The Truth about the Truth*. New York: Putnam.
Culler, J. (1982) *On Deconstruction, Theory and Criticism after Structuralism*. Ithaca, NY: Cornell University Press.
Fox, D. and Prilleltensky, I. (Eds.) (1997) *Critical Psychology, An Introduction*. Thousand Oaks, CA: Sage.
Harvey, D. (1989) *The Condition of Postmodernity*. Oxford: Blackwell.
Lyotard, J.F. (1984) *The Post-modern Condition: A Report on Knowledge*. Minneapolis, MN: University of Minnesota Press.
Nencel, L. and Pels, P. (Eds.) (1991) *Constructing Knowledge: Authority and Critique in Social Science*. London: Sage.

2

THE COMMUNAL CONSTRUCTION OF
THE REAL AND THE GOOD

If I ask about the world, you can offer to tell me how it is under one or more frames of reference; but if I insist that you tell me how it is apart from all frames, what can you say?

Nelson Goodman, *Ways of Worldmaking*

Several years ago two students enrolled in my honors seminar recoiled at the constructionist readings I had assigned. "Without any truth, how can we ever make sound decisions?" they asked; "without a sound sense of personal identity, how are decisions even possible; and without a firm view of moral good, what is worth doing?" Everything they believed worthwhile seemed destroyed by the seminar. So moved were they that they took their complaints to the provost: the seminar was both immoral and nihilistic in their view and should be stricken from the curriculum. Fortunately the tradition of academic freedom saved the seminar. And while I can fully understand the depth of their concerns, in my view this dark night of doubt is but a transitional phase, perhaps necessary for appreciating the enormous potentials of social constructionist inquiry. It is not that social constructionist ideas annihilate self, truth, objectivity, science, and morality. Rather, it is the way in which we have understood and practiced them that is thrown into question. In the end, social constructionism allows us to reconstitute the past in far more promising ways.

We begin this chapter by returning to the key question of language. In developing an alternative to the traditional view of language, we can locate answers to the pivotal critiques of the preceding chapter. When seen in light of the new view of language, the sense of hopelessness that accompanied these critiques is replaced by more positive possibilities. It is within the elaboration of these possibilities that we enter most directly the realm of social construction. After detailing major working assumptions within social constructionism, we shall turn our attention more specifically to the social origins of scientific knowledge.

Language: From the Picture to the Game

> Doesn't the fact that sentences have the same sense
> consist in their having the same *use*?
>
> Ludwig Wittgenstein, *Philosophical Investigations*

First recall the problems we faced in the traditional view of language as a reflection of the world – a picture or map of events and objects. This view is wedded to the assumption that truth can be carried by language, and that some languages (and chiefly those which are scientific) are closer to the truth than others. As we found, however, there is no privileged relationship between world and word. For any situation multiple descriptions are usually possible, and in principle there is no upper limit on our forms of description. Nor did we find any ultimate means of ruling among competing descriptions, of declaring one as corresponding more "truly" to the nature of reality than another. However, these puzzlements left us in a poor position, essentially without answers to some very important questions. If language does not describe or explain the world as it is, then what is the status of travel guides, weather reports or scientific findings? If words don't correspond or picture the world, then how can we meaningfully warn each other that drinking and driving are a dangerous combination, or that there is an acute danger of forest fires? If we become ill, surely we would prefer the account of the trained physician to that of a child or a witch doctor. All descriptions are not equal; some give us useful information while others are fanciful or absurd. The critique of the picture metaphor of language is not very useful without an alternative.

A vision of this alternative is furnished in arguably the most important work of philosophy of the twentieth century, Ludwig Wittgenstein's *Philosophical Investigations*.[1] We shall revisit this work several times in this book, but for now let us consider only his account of language. Essentially Wittgenstein replaces the *picture metaphor* of language with that of *the game*. "What is a word really?" asks Wittgenstein. It is equivalent to asking "What is a piece in chess?"[2] How are we to make sense of this metaphor? Consider first the game of chess, in which the two opponents take turns in moving pieces of various sizes and shapes across a checkered board. There are explicit rules about when and how each piece can be played, along with implicit rules of proper social conduct (for example, you may not curse or spit at your opponent). Here it is possible to say that each piece in the chess set acquires its meaning from the game as a whole. The small wooden chess pieces would mean nothing outside the game; however, once in the game, even the tiniest of pieces can topple "kings" and "queens."

Words acquire their meaning in the same way, proposes Wittgenstein. To say "good morning" gains its meaning from a game-like relationship called a greeting. There are implicit rules for carrying out greetings: each participant takes a turn, typically there is an exchange of mutual glances, and there are only a limited number of moves that one can legitimately make after the other has said "good morning." You may respond identically, or ask "how are you," for example, but you would be considered "out of the game," if you responded by screaming or cuffing the other in the head. Further, the words "good morning" are generally meaningless outside the game of greeting. If we are in the midst of a heated argument on unemployment, and I suddenly say, "good morning," you would be puzzled. Have I lost my mind? Wittgenstein termed the "language and the actions into which it is woven, the 'language game.' "[3] Words, then, gain their meaning through their use within the game. Or, for Wittgenstein, "the meaning of a word is its use in the language."[4]

Forms of Life and the "Game of Truth"

If the meaning of our world is generated through the way we use words together, what is this to say about the nature of truth? Is the idea of "truth" totally misleading? How can this possibly be so? To answer these questions it is useful to return to the game of chess and consider the specific words shared by the players. For example, there are words for the various pieces (for example, "rook," "knight," "king,"), and various moves (for example, "checkmate"). Yet consider, these words gain their meaning not only from our patterns of talking – that is, the language game – but from the entire game. In order to make sense of "checkmate," we need the chess board, pieces laid out in a certain configuration, at least two players, and so on. As Wittgenstein put it, language games are embedded in broader patterns of actions and objects, which he called *forms of life*. Without the form of life we call the game of chess, the words "rook" and "checkmate" have little meaning; without the words there is no form of life called the game of chess. Language, in this sense, is not a mirror of life, it is the doing of life itself.

It is not, then, that language pictures the world, but rather, as Wittgenstein's protégé, J.L. Austin put it, we "do things with words;"[5] as we describe, so are we engaging in a performance of some kind – doing something with our interlocutor. In Austin's terms, we must attend to the *performative* character of our language, how it functions within a relationship. We see this most clearly in utterances such as "I now pronounce you man and wife," or "I christen you John Bennett Woods." Here the sentences perform the ceremony of marriage or christening. However, the same may be said of "Hi Sue," "Just a minute . . ." or "Piss Off!" which typically function as a greeting, a request, and a belligerent command. As later theorists put it, we may conceptualize all of our meaningful utterances as *speech acts*,[6] that is, actions which accomplish something within the interpersonal world.

But how does "doing things with words," help us to understand why some accounts of the world seem to give us important or "true" information while others are false or misleading? The answer is that telling the truth is much like playing a very specific game. Although the rules are not formalized, we may speak of *the game of truth*. This is to say that when we engage in actions such as "describing," "explaining" or "theorizing" we are also performing a kind of cultural ritual. After I announce, "Let me tell you what happened this morning," I cannot say just anything, shout, or jump up and down. There are implicit rules – just as in games – for what counts as a proper description. In contrast, if I tell you, "Let me show you how I *felt* about what happened to me this morning" I enter another kind of game; in this case shouting and jumping might be perfectly acceptable. So, while the presumption of transcendental truth – beyond culture, history, and circumstance – seems ill-conceived, we may say, "there is truth," but always within the rules of a specific or circumscribed game.

Let's press further: these language games of truth are typically embedded within broader forms of life. Far more than words and actions are required in order to play the game. We typically require objects of various kinds within particular settings. Let me illustrate the social process of "achieving truth" with an example from my adolescence. I was serving as a summer assistant to an ill-tempered, foul-mouthed wall plasterer named Marvin. Despite his personal shortcomings, Marvin was very good at his job. And when he climbed to the top of a ladder, his arms working the plaster to perfection on the ceiling overhead, it was crucial that I serve up mixtures of water and plastering compound exactly to his specification. At times the mixture had to be moist – so it could be subtly worked and reworked; at others it had to be dry, so that it could rapidly seal the contours. Thus, depending on his progress, he would bellow, "skosh" (for a wet mixture) and "dry-un" (for a drier compound). Of course these words meant nothing to me when I began my servitude, but within a few days I became proficient in producing the desired mixtures. In effect, "skosh" and "dry-un" became part of a form of life in which we were engaged.

Yet, consider what has been achieved as a byproduct of this primitive dance of words, actions, and objects. After two weeks of practice in this procedure, Marvin and I could have observed a series of plaster mixtures, and with very little error, we could have agreed on which were "skosh" and which "dry-uns." And, if I said "dry-un cumin' up" this would also inform Marvin of what he might predict on that occasion. This prediction could have been confirmed or disconfirmed by what I delivered. In effect, by virtue of their function within the relational game, such terms as "skosh" and "dry-un" began to function as descriptions that could tell the truth. No, the words themselves do not describe the world; but because of their successful functioning within the relational ritual, they became truth telling.

What is this to say of our newspapers, or of eye-witness testimony, or of science? Essentially, when we say that a certain description is "accurate" (as opposed to or "inaccurate") or "true" (as opposed to "false") we are not judging it according to how well it depicts the world. Rather, we are saying that the words have come to function as "truth telling" within the rules of a particular game – or more generally, according to certain conventions of certain groups. The proposition that "the world is round and not flat" is neither true nor false in terms of pictorial value, that is, correspondence with "what there is." However, by current standards, it is more acceptable to play the game of "round-world-truth" when flying from Kansas to Cologne; and more useful to "play it flat" when touring the state of Kansas itself. Nor is it true beyond any game that the world is composed of atoms; however, "atom talk" is extremely useful if you are "playing the game of physics" and carrying out experiments on fission. In the same way, we can properly say that people do indeed have souls, so long as we are participating in a form of life that we call religion. The existence of atoms is no more or less true than the existence of souls in any universal sense; each exists within a particular form of life.

As we find, in the game metaphor of language human relationships are of pivotal significance. We also find that on this view we can resuscitate the concept of truth. The term may be very useful within a community but the utterance, "it is true" loses its privilege to command assent (or silence) beyond a specific form of life. With this alternative view of language in place we may now return to the two forms of critique treated in the previous chapter. Recall the general state of intellectual despair resulting from the ideological and literary critiques of recent decades. A reconsideration is now in order. Specifically, by placing these critiques in the context of the alternative view of meaning, we can appreciate their force but simultaneously avoid the nihilistic conclusions they seemed to favor.

Ideology Critique Reconsidered

Recall first the charge that because personal or political motives may bias their accounts of the world, there is reason to be distrustful of all authorities. All declarations of fact, from this standpoint, could be clouded by personal motives. Yet, as we also found, the ideological critic has no means of separating the true account from the biased one. As soon as an authority declares "truth" on his/her side, the critic can demonstrate ideological bias. At the same time, the critic is also subject to the counter-charge of ideological contamination. We soon reach an impasse, with distrust and antagonism dominating the relationship. Yet, if we employ the metaphor of the language game, we can revise this analysis. We can also do so in ways that do not result in full-scale antagonism but simultaneously sustain the importance of critique.

To realize this possibility, we must first abandon the true/false binary in its traditional form. In light of all that has been said so far, we may readily abandon the assumption that some word patterns are true by virtue of correspondence with the world. However, from the view of language games, we can replace "Truth" with "truth," that is, now locating truth as a way of talking or writing that achieves its validity within a local form of life. On this view, the value of ideological critique remains paramount: to engage in critique is to defend a mode of life, a tradition, a network of human relationships. At the same time, the critic is not left in the arrogant and indefensible position of claiming the "truly true." Truth, as an ultimate rationale for eliminating the target is removed. Rather, the critic is enjoined to understand the target in terms of his or her immersion in a tradition.

The game metaphor of meaning leads to a second improvement on the ideological critique. Here we find that we can abandon concern with the hidden reservoirs of motivation or ideological bias said to be lurking behind people's words. We need not impute evil intent to the other. Nor must we locate the true motives *behind* the words – a challenge that can never be satisfactorily resolved. Rather, our attention moves to the forms of life that are favored (or destroyed) by various ways of putting things. If physicists define people as "nothing but atoms," for example, how does this characterization function within society; how do we come to treat people within this form of life; how will our actions differ if we characterize people as "possessing a soul?" What kinds of people, institutions, laws, and so on are favored when we speak in one set of terms as opposed to another; what traditions or ways of life are suppressed or destroyed? An illustration will be helpful.

Mental Disorder: Foucault and Further

> Madness cannot be found in a wild state. Madness exists only within a society, it does not exist outside the forms of sensibility which isolate it and the forms of repulsion which exclude it or capture it.
>
> Michel Foucault, *Madness and Civilization*

The profound significance of these arguments is realized in the works of one of the most catalytic social theorists of the century, Michel Foucault. Much more will be said about Foucault's work in Chapter 8, but illuminating in the present context is his concern with the way in which people quite willingly subjugate themselves to subtle forms of power.[7] We are not speaking here of the obvious forms of power – control by law and arms, but rather, the insinuation of power into the ordinary. In spite of our tremendous capacities for variation, for the most part we live very ordered lives; with few questions or qualms, we attend school, enter professions, pay for our purchases, go to doctors, and so on. For Foucault, in the very exercise of these taken-for-granted practices, we demonstrate our subjugation to power. For Foucault, "power is . . . an open, more or less coordinated . . . cluster of relations."[8]

Language is a critical feature of such power relations, and in particular the discourse of knowledge. Foucault was centrally concerned with *zoning of libels' control* (handwritten)

subjugation by various groups who claim "to know," or to be in possession of "the truth" – especially about who we are as human selves. Consider, for example, the disciplines of medicine, psychiatry, sociology, anthropology, education, and the like. These *disciplinary regimes*, as Foucault called them, generate languages of description and explanation – classifications of selves as healthy or unhealthy, normal or abnormal, upper or lower class, intelligent or unintelligent – along with explanations as to why they are so. The regimes also employ various research procedures, whereby we are scrutinized and classified in their terms. In effect, when we offer ourselves for examinations of various sorts – from medical examinations to college board assessments – we are giving ourselves over to the disciplinary regimes, to be labeled and explained in their terms. And when we carry these terminologies into our daily lives, speaking to others of our cholesterol level, our depression, or academic grades, we are engaging in power relations – essentially extending the control of the disciplinary regimes. As our disciplines of study begin to influence public policy and practices, we become further ordered in their terms. Ultimately we participate in our own subjugation.

To appreciate Foucault's argument let's begin with the ordinary: one day you are feeling down, a little blue, perhaps self-critical and a friend asks "what's wrong . . . ?" Chances are you might respond, "Oh, I'm just a little depressed." Although describing yourself as "depressed" is wholly unremarkable in today's culture, it was not always so. The first classification of mental disorders in the United States, occurring in 1840, contained only a handful of distinctions and was closely tied to organic dysfunction. In those days the term "depression" did not exist. It was only in the 1930s, with the emergence of psychiatry and psychology, that "mental disorders" began to mushroom. By 1938, some 40 disturbances were recognized (including moral deficiency, misanthropy, and masturbation!). Since that time the *Diagnostic and Statistical Manual of Mental Disorders*, the official handbook for diagnosis, has gone through four editions, and the number of deficit terms has now mounted to over 300 (which include such disorders as inhibition of orgasm, gambling, academic deficiency, bereavement, and negative attitudes toward medical treatment). Depression is not only a significant entry in the present manual, but there are several sub-types as well (for example, chronic, melancholic, bipolar). Mental health professionals now believe that more than 10% of the population suffers from depression. Anti-depressant drugs, virtually unknown a quarter of a century ago, are now a billion dollar industry. And if you continued to find yourself "feeling blue" this would probably be your future as well.

Interestingly, this dramatic expansion of identified disorders roughly parallels the growing numbers of mental health professionals. For example, at the turn of the century the American Psychiatric Association numbered less than 400; today there are approximately 40,000 members – a hundred-fold increase. The costs of mental health have increased in similar magnitude. By 1980 mental illness was the third most expensive category of health disorder in the United States. In effect, we find ourselves facing what appears to be a *cycle of progressive infirmity*: consider the phases: (1) as mental health professionals declare the truth of a discourse of dysfunction, and (2) as this truth is disseminated through education, public policy, and the media, so do we come (3) to understand ourselves in these terms. ("I'm just a little depressed.") With such understandings in place, we will (4) seek out mental health professionals for cure. As cure is sought, (5) so is the need for mental health professionals expanded. And (6) as the professional ranks expand, so does the vocabulary of mental disorder prosper. The cycle is continuous and ever-expanding in its effects.[9]

Is there a limit to the dysfunctional disciplining of the population? I recently received an announcement for a conference on the latest research and cure for addiction, called, "the number one health and social problem facing our country today." Among the addictions to be discussed were exercise, religion, eating, work, and sex. If all these activities, when pursued with intensity or gusto, can be defined as illnesses that require cure, there seems little in cultural life that can withstand subjugation to the professions. Unless we can mount a collective refusal.[10]

A critique such as this is designed to mobilize resistance. Indeed, Foucault's own writings were focally concerned with ways of combating the expanding domains of *power/knowledge*, as he termed the process of cultural disciplining. Foucault urged his readers to fight against these forces through resistance, subversion, and self-transformation. Yet, while rousing the spirit of revolution, we must also realize the limits to the rebellious response to power/knowledge invasion. An appreciation of these limits also demonstrates the advantages of the present form of critique over the ideological attacks of the preceding chapter. Consider, then, two substantial problems with the unrelenting posture of antagonism toward the dominant order.

First, there is the problem of freedom. To fight against the invasive influence of power, is to hold out a promise that we might one day become free – no one controlling or containing us with an alien knowledge. Yet, freedom from the ordering effects of language, from forms of life, from all traditions or conventions is not freedom: it is essentially a step into insignificance – a space where there is no freedom because there are no distinctions, and thus no choices. This is not at all to undermine the critical impulse; however, it is to place strong emphasis on visioning the alternative. We cannot step out of meaning or avoid ordering of any kind. If we wish to refuse one form of disciplining, what form of ordering do we suggest in its place? For example, there is good reason to put a lid on the expansion of psychiatric diagnosis. However, we do not therefore step into an arena of pure freedom. The invitation is to generate alternative understandings of greater promise.

Closely related is a second major problem with an unrelenting critical posture: it fails to take account of the positive effects of ordering. To reject all that Foucault might call "disciplining" or "ordering" would be to erase virtually all that we value. We cannot have another's love without participating in a social ordering of some kind; parents cannot give their children love without the regime we call "family;" we can scarcely achieve justice without an institution of law. Rather than wholesale rejection of all forms of ordering, we might adopt a posture of *differentiating appraisal*. Given a range of language games, forms of life, or disciplinary traditions, we may launch inquiry into consequences – both negative and positive. In what ways does a tradition sustain that which we hold to be good, in what ways does it fail? How could it be otherwise? The professional practices of classifying and curing mental disease, for example, have the negative effects of inviting us to see normal problems of daily life as "illnesses," diminishing our abilities to generate local solutions (believing these are problems for professionals), and providing us with multiple means of finding fault in others and ourselves (for example, "He is obese," "She is anorexic," "He is addicted to his work,"). Yet, the classifications of "mental illness" do give many people the sense that they are not personally responsible for their problems ("I can't help it, I'm ill"), and that there are professionals who can alleviate their suffering. They are not alone, nor are they hopeless. In this kind of differentiating appraisal, then, we may bring forth alternatives that retain some of the virtues of a problematic tradition while removing those we believe harmful.

From Text to Cultural Representation

> Like any common living thing, I fear and reprove classification and the death it entails, and I will not allow its clutches to lock down on me . . .
>
> Trin Minh-ha, *Woman Native Other*

The preceding account shows how a vision of language as social practice helps to restore a positive function to otherwise debilitating critique. Recall now the second of the doomsday critiques of the preceding chapter, that is, the reduction of all truth to text. As we saw, from the textual standpoint the meaning of our words depends not on the features of the world, but on their interdependency with other words. We can make sense of nothing "outside of text," it seemed, because it is only in text (or language) that sense is made. Yet, in spite of its compelling power, this critique also left us at an impasse. Not only did it reduce all traditions of science and scholarship to mere word-play, but the argument was essentially self-refuting (for example, the argument itself was a text and therefore only a play of signifiers). The use-dependent view of meaning with which we began this chapter helps us to re-vision the textual critique, and to do so in a way that the impasse is overcome.

Consider: if meaning is generated through human interchange, as in the Wittgensteinian sense, then the textual critique suppresses the more plausible source of meaning. That is, the critique treats the text (or words in themselves) as having meaning, while inert texts (as a collection of markings or syllables) can never themselves mean anything. We give to texts their meaning. Or, we may say, texts only come into meaning through their function within relationships. It is the community that is prior to textual meaning and we must see texts in terms of their function within human relationships.

By embedding the meaning of texts within human communities, we retain much of the power of the textual critique, but avoid the deadening consequences of reducing the word to pure words. We continue to appreciate the multiple constructions that are possible in any given situation, the incapacity of the referent to determine the choice of construction, the principled undecidability of meaning in any situation, and the power of linguistic conventions to compel our descriptions and understandings. We need not conclude that there is nothing outside of text. However, critical concern now moves from texts in themselves to the social pragmatics of textuality, that is, the ways in which texts are constructed by communities for certain purposes. Here we are more likely to ask, for example, about the social traditions or dynamics that give rise to certain literary forms, how various texts are used to unite a group in opposition to an enemy, or how various genres of writing sustain values, prejudices, or the economic structure. In a broader sense, we move from a concern with text in itself to text as rhetoric, that is, a language designed to do something within a community. To illustrate "text in action" consider:

The Case of Identity Politics

In our daily relations, we act but it is often the public interpretation of our acts that determines the outcome. In particular, much depends on the way we are represented in others' talk – their descriptions, explanations, criticisms, or congratulations. These representations constitute our social reputation. Yet, these are not the words we would necessarily choose; they are generated by others – our friends, family, neighbors, teachers and so on. It is our identity which is at stake, but we neither own nor control the way we are represented. Consider the problem on a societal level: all of us are identified with one or more social groups – woman, man, Christian, Jew, black, white, German, Irish, and so on. Such groups are often the subject of media interest – film, novels, news reports, advertising, etc. When our group is represented to millions of people we confront helplessness writ large. When women are depicted as helpless and emotional, Asians as obedient, Germans as menacing, Irish as aggressive and so on, we are implicated. It is not only a matter of public reputation, but as these reputations become shared so do they come to be the taken-for-granted realities. And it is these realities that inform public policies, educational practices, police actions, and so on. Further, these same public portrayals inform those depicted. Here one may learn what it is to be a woman, Asian, heterosexual, and so on. A mutually sustaining symmetry develops between self-knowledge and others' knowledge of you.

In terms of the present discussion we may say that our identities are importantly fashioned by the texts of media representation. Concern with such injurious effects is scarcely limited to the scholarly world. However, constructionist scholars have joined with sectors of the concerned public to create a consciousness of *identity politics* – that is, deliberation on the ways in which group identities figure within the sociopolitical landscape. Engagement in identity politics may take many forms. However, during the past several decades one can discern three overlapping waves – different emphases with different outcomes.

Reflecting long-standing irritation in various ethnic groups, the first wave is that of *resistance*. There were early critiques by Italian Americans for their media image as gangsters, by African Americans for their caricature as Uncle Toms and Aunt Jemimahs, and women for their one-dimensional depiction as sex objects. Now such resistance is multiplied manifold. Native Americans reject the ways in which they are represented in museums – as savage and primitive; gays and lesbians show how Hollywood films enkindle homophobia; numerous studies now explore the constructions of subaltern (or "subordinate") peoples within the common media of the day.[11] Further explorations delve into the early roots of contemporary constructions, showing how minority identities have been treated in earlier times, earlier texts, paintings, photographs, and the like.[12]

This derogatory creation of the other also carries into the scholarly arena. Much social science is, after all, about depiction. Social scientists typically attempt to describe and explain people's actions; sociologists often focus on marginal peoples, anthropologists on peoples of other cultures, historians on peoples of the past, and so on. These writings, too, enter the political arena, creating images of different classes, cultures, and traditions. Perhaps the classic writing of resistance is that of Edward Said, on the social construction of the Orient.[13] For centuries European depictions of "Oriental people" – the manners, customs, beliefs, and traditions of cultures from the East – have accumulated, generating in the present century the grounds for entire academic departments. Yet, as Said proposes, the Orient is essentially a "European invention" – a representation of the other that grows from the soil of European interests. These interests, Said points out, are not merely ones of curiosity and entertainment. Rather, he sees "Orientalism as a Western style for dominating, restructuring, and having authority over the Orient."[14] In the mode of describing and explaining "the Orientals" there was subtly created a sense of superiority and justification for political domination.

This problematic construction of the other has led to acute concern in the field of anthropology, as all too often ethnographic description seems to enhance colonialist attitudes and aspirations. Ethnographic study not only provides the colonial powers information to strengthen their control, but succeeds in characterizing the people in just those ways that would justify such rule.[15] As related by an African "native," Anthropology is "the diary of the white man on a mission; the white man commissioned by the historical sovereignty of European thinking and its peculiar vision of man."[16] Such critiques have had powerful effects on forms of social science research, a topic we shall take up in Chapter 4.

For many of those engaged in identity politics, these forms of resistance are only a beginning. More important is the challenge of gaining the capacity for self-representation. Thus a second wave of identity politics, oriented in this case toward *self-representation* has emerged. In the terms of social theorist Ernesto Lauclau, "The crucial question . . . is not who the social agents are, but the extent to which they manage to constitute themselves."[17] Or as black feminist Patricia Hill Collins has put the case, "The insistence on Black female self-definition reframes the entire dialogue from one of protesting the technical accuracy of an image – namely refuting the Black matriarchy thesis – to one of stressing the power dynamics underlying the very process of definition itself . . . the act of insisting on Black female self-definition validates Black women's power as human subjects."[18] Put in this light, one's ethnic, racial or religious identity is a site of struggle – often bitter. At a simple level it is a contest between your control vs. the control of others.

Growing awareness of this struggle has provoked broadscale action – to gain control over the representation of one's group identity and to use these representations as a means of sparking group consciousness and political activism. The most important work here does not take place in the scholarly world but in the sphere of public writing and performance. Thus we find television networks pressed to expand their fare to include and fairly present the experiences of the under-represented groups. Oprah Winfrey, for example, has been singled out for the way in which she has transformed the public image of both women and black culture.[19] We also find a proliferation of niche magazines by and about feminists, African Americans, the gay community, and so on; and a spate of films, plays and books revealing the lives of the downtrodden and voiceless.

Yet, the movement to take control of one's public identity is not without its problems. If you write or make a film about "your people," *you* are representing *them* – and effectively, they continue to be without control. Further, many within such groups object to the way they are depicted "by their kind." For example, if an author wishes to reveal the miseries resulting from an oppressive society – emphasizing for example, suffering, drugs and violence – the identified group often feels betrayed. They appear as abnormal, incapacitated victims. On the other hand, if the author wishes to stress the richness of a tradition, the joys, the communal bonds, and so on, antagonism again erupts. Here the work is faulted for the pretty picture it paints, a picture that provokes no political action but

suggests the status quo is just fine. Consider the reaction of black feminist bell hooks to the way black film-maker Spike Lee portrays blacks and
women:

> The portraits of black men conform to popular stereotypes in the white racist
> imagination. Rather than threaten white audiences, they assuage their fear. [The
> film] excludes black women and their role in liberation struggle . . . every black
> female in the film, whether she be mother, daughter, or sister, is constructed at
> some point as sex object.[20]

We must ask then, can anyone be trusted to represent any group? Must
the answer be "every person for him/herself?" Wouldn't this bring an end
to the political power of group unity?

Questions such as these have sparked a third significant wave of identity politics, *political reconstruction*. Central to this third wave is a growing
concern with the ways in which all representations of a people – regardless of the author or content — tend to *essentialize* their object. To essentialize in this case is to treat a social category (for example, women, gays,
Asians) as standing for an essence – a set of intrinsic qualities or characteristics residing within a people. We have long had this problem with the
concept of race, a category commonly used as if to mirror a specific set of
essences that distinguish one group from another. Yet, there is no essence
– no essential nature – lurking within people of which skin color, height,
facial hair, and so on are the "manifestations." As the cultural studies
scholar Stuart Hall, puts it, "What is at issue here is the recognition . . . that
'black' is essentially a politically and culturally constructed category,
which cannot be grounded in a set of fixed transcultural or transcendental racial categories and which therefore has no guarantees in nature."[21]
The problem, however, is not simply the essentializing carried by group
characterizations. There is further the tendency of such categories to
destroy differences, to suppress the enormous variations in values, sexual
preferences, tastes, and ways of life among those classified within a group.
So great are the variations that not all those who can be identified with a
group wish to espouse its positions. There are many Asians who are committed Christians, Pakistanis who are gay activists, African Americans
engaged in Muslim causes. Labels are too often suppressive. Finally, there
are ways in which group divisions foster *antagonism* – avoidance, distrust,
and hatred. For insiders it suggests that "we are different, and you can
neither understand nor authentically participate in our community." For
the outsider, every group thus becomes the Other – alien, self-seeking and
ultimately antagonistic. So many and so politically active are the divisions
within American society, that political theorist James Davison Hunter
coins the phrase *culture wars* to characterize the condition.[22]

Given these problems how is political reconstruction to proceed? There
is no single answer here; the dialogues are in motion. There are first those
who feel betrayed by these critiques of essentialism. As they argue, just

when women and minorities are beginning to gain a sense of autonomy and self-direction – taking charge of their own identities – the critics begin to fault their essentialism. To do this removes the grounds for social critique, and the rationale for changing society. If there are no "women" (the category of "woman" is only a label), for example, how can we fight for equal rights for women? For feminist Naomi Weisstein those who see gender and other categories as socially constructed represent "a high cult of critique," and she laments, "Sometimes I think that, when the fashion passes, we will find many bodies, drowned in their own wordy words, like the Druids in the bogs."[23]

There are more promising possibilities. For example, African American scholar Cornell West emphasizes the importance of developing a *love ethic*, within the black community in this case, which can enable people to work together in a context of heightened self-esteem.[24] Such an ethic might eventually enable better relations within the society more generally. Sociologist Tod Gitlin looks to popular movements and organizations that can cross the "identity trenches" to link otherwise disparate groups of minorities. Labor unions once served this purpose; new groups are now needed.[25] Others believe we must radically expand the democratic process, so that people in all sectors of society can participate in dialogue. Agreeing with this recreation of a *public commons* (or meeting place) others make strong arguments for civilizing our forms of public debate, finding less hostile ways of speaking together.[26] More radical are those who propose to reconstruct our very conceptions of what it is to be a person, to possess an identity. As African American bell hooks puts it, "We have too long had imposed on us from both the outside and the inside a narrow, constricting notion of blackness . . . Critiques of essentialism . . . can open up new possibilities for the construction of the self . . ."[27] In this context, feminist theorist Judith Butler urges a wholesale challenging of the familiar binaries, men/women, heterosexual/homosexual and the like.[28] Because being female, for example, is not a "natural fact" but a form of "cultural performance," we are free to perform in new ways. In revolutionary fashion, she opts for performances that blur the common distinctions; "gender bending" and "bisexuality" are illustrative. Others argue for a more fluid or nomadic conception of self, one that is not fixed in any category but which moves with time and circumstance – taking political stands but not permanently so.[29] Clearly the reconstructive wave is in a fledgling state; more will be said on these issues in Chapter 6.

Social Construction: the Emerging Contours

> Rationality is one tradition among many rather than a standard to which traditions must conform.
>
> Paul Feyerabend, *Science in a Free Society*

The moment is at hand for taking stock. In the preceding chapter we took a look at several significant but troubled assumptions in the Western tradition – assumptions of self, truth, rationality, and moral principle. We also examined two forms of recent critique – ideological and literary – that seem to obliterate the grounds for any justifiable belief. In the present chapter we have attempted to take more positive steps. Specifically I introduced a communal view of language and with this view reformulated the two lines of critique in more promising ways. Yet, as these arguments have unfolded, another goal has been accomplished. Built into the present arguments are a set of assumptions that, when stated more directly, form the basis for the subject of this book: social constructionism. It is now time to bring these assumptions into clear focus, for they form the essential backbone for the remainder of the book. It is important to realize that not all those who participate in social constructionist dialogues necessarily agree with all the assumptions; these should be considered working assumptions rather than confident conclusions.[30] Further, realize that these assumptions are not candidates for truth, but entries into conversations, insinuations into relationships. As we animate these assumptions in our work and our lives more generally, they may have significant if not dramatic potential; to ask whether they are true or false misses the point of constructionism. Consider then the following four working assumptions.

1 THE TERMS BY WHICH WE UNDERSTAND OUR WORLD AND OUR SELF ARE NEITHER REQUIRED NOR DEMANDED BY "WHAT THERE IS"   This assumption gives voice to all that we have said about the failure of language to map or picture an independent world. Given whatever is the case, there is no arrangement of syllables, words or phrases that necessarily follows. It should also be realized that the assumption applies not only to spoken and written words, but to any other form of representation, including, for example, photographs, maps, microscopes, and MRI scans. Another way of stating this assumption is that for any state of affairs a potentially unlimited number of descriptions and explanations is possible. In principle (though not in practice) not one of these descriptions or explanations can be ruled superior in terms of its capacity to map, picture, or capture the features of the "situation in question."

Although this assumption may seem reasonable enough at this point, do not underestimate its implications. First, we must suppose that everything we have learned about our world and ourselves – that gravity holds us to the earth, people cannot fly like birds, cancer kills, or that punishment deters bad behavior – could be otherwise. There is nothing about "what there is" that demands these particular accounts; we could use our language to construct alternative worlds in which there is no gravity or cancer, or in which persons and birds are equivalent, and punishment adored. For many people this supposition is deeply threatening, for it suggests there is nothing we can hold onto, nothing solid on which we can rest our beliefs, nothing secure. Yet, for others this dark night of insecurity gives way to an enormous sense of liberation. In daily life, so many of our categories of understanding – of gender, age, race, intelligence, emotion, reason, and the like – seem to create untold suffering. And in the world more generally, so many common understandings – of religion, nationality, ethnicity, economics and the like – seem to generate conflict, alienation, injustice, and even genocide. From the constructionist standpoint we are not locked within any convention of understanding.

2 OUR MODES OF DESCRIPTION, EXPLANATION AND/OR REPRESENTATION ARE DERIVED FROM RELATIONSHIP   This assumption follows largely from the use-view of language with which we began the chapter. On this account, language and all other forms of representation gain their meaning from the ways in which they are used within relationships. What we take to be true about the world or self, is not thus a product of the individual mind. The individual mind (thought, experience) does not thus originate meaning, create language, or discover the nature of the world. Meanings are born of co-ordinations among persons – agreements, negotiations, affirmations. From this standpoint, relationships stand prior to all that is intelligible. Nothing exists for us – as an intelligible world of objects and persons – until there are relationships. This suggests that any words, phrases or sentences that are perfectly sensible to us now could, under certain conditions of relationship, be reduced to nonsense. Or conversely, even the most brutish grunt can be endowed with deepest significance. If we do quest for certainty, something to count on, a sense of grounded reality, it can only be achieved through relationship.

One caveat is required: although there is a strong tendency in this book to treat relationships as human endeavors – as in the *social* construction of reality – this emphasis is ultimately misleading. Relations among people are ultimately inseparable from the relations of people to what we call their natural environment. Our communication cannot exist without all that sustains us – oxygen, plant life, the sun, and so on. In a broad sense, we are not independent of our surrounds; our surrounds inhabit us and vice versa. Nor can we determine, as human beings, the nature of these surrounds and our relation with them beyond the languages we develop together. In effect, all understandings of relationship are themselves limited by culture and history. In the end we are left with a profound sense of relatedness – of all with all – that we cannot adequately comprehend.

3 AS WE DESCRIBE, EXPLAIN OR OTHERWISE REPRESENT, SO DO WE FASHION OUR FUTURE   As our practices of language are bound within relationships, so are relationships bound within broader patterns of practice – rituals, traditions, "forms of life." For example, words like "crime," "plaintiff," "witness," and "law" are essential to carrying out the practice of law; our world of higher education depends on a discourse of "students," "professors," "curricula," and "learning." Without these shared languages of description and explanation these institutions would fail to exist in their present

form. More informally, it would be difficult to carry out a recognizable love affair without such words as "love," "desire," "care," and "hope." In a broad sense, language is a major ingredient of our worlds of action; it constitutes social life itself.

Consider the implications: if we agree that there is nothing about the world that demands any particular form of language or representation, then all our institutions – our long-standing traditions of cultural life – could be dissolved. If we obliterate our languages of the real and the good, so do we destroy forms of life. From this standpoint, to sustain our traditions – including those of self, truth, morality, education, and so on – depends on a continuous process of generating meaning together. In this sense, history is not destiny – either in terms of one's personal past determining one's future, or with respect to the culture's history proscribing its potential. The past guarantees nothing. If we wish to maintain our traditions in a world of rapid global change, we confront the everyday task of sustaining intelligibility. That is, we must carry out the forms of relationship, and the generation of rationality within these relationships, that will enable these traditions to remain sensible. It has been continuously necessary, for example, to rewrite or reconstruct Christianity in order to give it vitality in today's world. The same is true of our intimate connections in daily life, in our families, and circles of friendship; we must continuously reconstruct their nature (for example, "who we are to each other") in order to keep them alive.

At the same time, constructionism offers a bold invitation to transform social life, to build new futures. Transforming ourselves, our relationships, or our culture need not await the intervention of some expert, a set of laws, public policies or the like. As we speak and write at this moment we participate in creating the future – for good or ill. If we long for change, we must also confront the challenge of generating new meanings, of becoming *poetic activists*. New patterns of social life are not secured simply by refusing or rejecting the meanings as given – for example, avoiding sexist or racist language. Rather, the strong invitation is for the emergence of new forms of language, ways of interpreting the world, patterns of representation. Invited are *generative discourses*, that is, ways of talking and writing (and otherwise representing) that simultaneously challenge existing traditions of understanding, and offer new possibilities for action. We shall take up the challenge of generative discourse again in Chapter 5.

4 REFLECTION ON OUR FORMS OF UNDERSTANDING IS VITAL TO OUR FUTURE WELL-BEING   The challenge of sustaining valued traditions on the one side, and creating new futures on the other, is no small matter. Every tradition closes the doors to the new; every bold creation undermines a tradition. What shall we save; what shall we resist and destroy; what worlds should we create? These are not only complex questions, but in a world of multiple and competing constructions of the good we see that there can be no universal answers. Whatever there is places no demands on our modes of understanding. There is

a strong tendency under these conditions to resort to "good reasons, good evidence, and good values." That is, if we simply think about a given tradition, evaluate the evidence, consider its moral and political implications, we can arrive at an acceptable conclusion. However, from a constructionist standpoint, there is reason for critical pause. The generation of good reasons, good evidence and good values is always *from within a tradition*; already accepted are certain constructions of the real and the good, and implicit rejections of alternatives. Whether we should ban smoking from public buildings, allow child pornography, oppose land mines, or support feminist liberation in Arab countries are questions that can only be treated from within some tradition of discourse. Thus, our "considered judgments" are typically blind to alternatives lying outside our tradition.

For constructionists such considerations lead to a celebration of *reflexivity*, that is, the attempt to place one's premises into question, to suspend the "obvious," to listen to alternative framings of reality, and to grapple with the comparative outcomes of multiple standpoints. For the constructionist this means an unrelenting concern with the blinding potential of the "taken-for-granted." If we are to build together toward a more viable future then we must be prepared to doubt everything we have accepted as real, true, right, necessary or essential. This kind of critical reflection is not necessarily a prelude to rejecting our major traditions. It is simply to recognize them as traditions – historically and culturally situated; it is to recognize the legitimacy of other traditions within their own terms. And it is to invite the kind of dialogue that might lead to common ground.

This set of working assumptions is simple enough; yet the implications are profound. Already you can begin to appreciate the generative implications of constructionist dialogues themselves, the way they begin to unsettle long-standing distinctions between the knowers and the ignorant, the teacher and the student, the highbrow and the lowbrow. And you can appreciate the invitation to the scholar to recognize his or her lodgment in traditions of value, and the vital connections between scholarly work and societal futures. Much more will be said about these matters in later chapters. However, in preparation for these explorations, and by way of demonstrating the significance of constructionist ideas, let us close this chapter by considering the challenging case of scientific knowledge.

The Social Construction of Scientific Knowledge

> It is hard to popularize science because it is designed to force out most people in the first place.
>
> Bruno Latour, *Science in Action*

Many people consider science to be the crowning jewel of Western civilization. Where others have mere *opinions*, scientists have the hard *facts*;

where others have armchair ideas, scientists produce real-world effects: cures, rockets, and atomic power. In part, our respect for science is born of our cultural traditions. We glimpsed in the preceding chapter the ways in which scientific thinking grew from the soil of Enlightenment resistance to church and crown, and beliefs in scientific knowledge now inhabit our practices, education, national policy making, news reporting, criminal investigation, military planning, and more. Of special importance, however, is the link between science and social equality.

Recall that Enlightenment thinking was vastly important in terms of its granting to each and every individual the right to a voice. The privilege of royalty and religion to speak for all, to rule on the nature of the real and the good, was removed. Over time science became the model for equal rights to reason. In the scientific world, everyone has the privilege of independent observation, reason, and reporting. If one follows rigorous methods of investigation he or she can demand an audience. But now consider, what do you as reader have to say about the "PE surface for polyatomic molecules," "the indeterminacy of cyclopentane-1,3-diyl," or "*Hox* genes"? Chances are you have no opinion; you know little about such matters. Moreover you may scarcely understand the phrases. So you are forced to accept these realities; and why not? Don't scientists simply "tell it like it is?" Ironically, then, this bastion of equality now functions to remove equality: all voices save its own are moved to silence. Are we witnessing here the emergence of a new breed of high priests, a subtle dictatorship for which we are merely docile bodies?

It is this possibility, this closing of the common dialogue, that gives us reason to lay open scientific knowledge to social constructionist analysis. The point of this discussion is not to undermine scientific efforts, but to remove their authority and to place them into the orbit of everyday scrutiny. The focus, then, is on scientific interpretations of the world – the choice of certain languages of description and explanation as opposed to others. Recall, no particular language is privileged in terms of its picturing the world for what it is; innumerable accounts are possible. Most importantly, because scientists do make claims to the truth, their accounts have a way of creeping out into society, of forming society's conceptions of what is the case. In response to headlines about the origins of the universe, genetic coding, and the greenhouse effect, we are not likely to say "well, that's one way of putting it." Rather, the news media report these as universal facts, and we are inclined to accept them as such – until they are corrected by other scientists. As scientific accounts enter society as "truth beyond tradition, beyond value, beyond question" so do they affect our ways of life – undermining, disrupting, and refashioning. And there is little critical questioning of these effects, not only because the common person is mystified by scientific language, but as well because scientists have traditionally been unable to escape their premises to ask reflexive questions from alternative standpoints.

Are such effects significant? We have already touched on the adverse effects on society of mental illness terminology. But consider as well the way in which spiritual issues have been systematically replaced by science within academic curricula – both in secondary education and universities. It would now be almost laughable for a student to ask whether a creationist account of human existence could be superior to a Darwinian explanation. Yet there are the more subtle effects of a curriculum that defines human beings merely as material – just another mass open to scientific inspection and manipulation – and which defines values as forms of bias or contamination. It is science that has reduced the enormities in human variation to a handful of racial categories, informed society that there are hereditary differences in intelligence and certain races are more intelligent than others; and has supported the idea that one's fundamental motivation in life is to sustain his/her genes. By interpreting nature in just these ways, society is ill served.

Removing the mantle of scientific authority and fostering democratic participation has been a chief aim of constructionist inquiry. However, this form of argument has not always been the same. The history of the social construction of science bears brief recounting. Essentially we may distinguish between two historical periods, an early emphasis on the *social determination* of scientific fact, and a more recent turn to the *relational emergence* of scientific knowledge.

The Social Determination of Fact

> Man has created death.
>
> William Butler Yeats, *Death*

Karl Mannheim's 1929 volume, translated from the German as *Ideology and Utopia*, was perhaps the groundbreaking work on the social construction of scientific knowledge.[31] As Mannheim proposed, (1) the scientist's theoretical commitments may usefully be traced to social (as opposed to empirical) origins; (2) scientific groups are often organized around certain theories; (3) theoretical disagreements are therefore issues of group conflict; and (4) what we assume to be scientific knowledge is therefore a byproduct of a social process. These suppositions reverberated widely. In Poland and Germany, Ludwig Fleck's 1935 work *Genesis and Development of a Scientific Fact*[32] proposed that in the scientific laboratory, "one must know before one can see" and traced such knowing to the scientist's social lodgment. In England, Peter Winch's influential volume *The Idea of a Social Science* (1946)[33] demonstrated ways in which theoretical propositions are "constitutive of the phenomena" of the social science. For the French, George Gurvitch's *The Social Frameworks of Knowledge* (1966)[34] traced scientific knowledge to particular frameworks of understandings, themselves the outgrowth of particular communities. And in the United States, Peter Berger and Thomas Luckmann's *The Social Construction of Reality* (1966)[35] developed one of the most challenging themes implicit in much of the earlier work: the social constitution of subjectivity. Here the scientist's private experience of the world – what is seen, heard, or distinguished by touch – is traced to the social sphere.

To elaborate this point, Berger and Luckmann propose that we are socialized into *plausibility structures*, that is, conceptual understandings of the world and rational supports for these understandings. As we come to rely on these plausibility structures, so do we develop a *natural attitude*, that is, a sense of a natural, taken-for-granted reality. "I apprehend the reality of everyday life as an ordered reality," they write. "Its phenomena are prearranged in patterns that seem to be independent of my apprehension of them . . . The language used in everyday life continuously provides me with the necessary objectification and posits the order within which these make sense and within which everyday life has meaning for me . . . In this manner language marks the co-ordinates of my life in society and fills that life with meaningful objects."[36] To illustrate, consider the way in which we seem to experience time, and the way in which the clock (an eighteenth century invention) now orders our life. As Berger and Luckmann write, "All my existence in this world is continuously ordered by [clock time] . . . I have only a certain amount of time available for the realization of my projects, and the knowledge of this affects my attitude to these projects. Also, since I do not want to die, this knowledge injects an underlying anxiety into my projects. Thus I cannot endlessly repeat my participating in sports events. I know that I am getting older. It may be that this is the last occasion on which I have the chance to participate . . ."[37] Perhaps you can appreciate their point.

A similar view of socially constituted subjectivity lies at the heart of the single most influential constructionist volume of the century, Thomas Kuhn's *The Structure of Scientific Revolutions* (1962).[38] Partly catching the wave of interest generated by its predecessors, partly appealing to the revolutionary movements of the 1960s, Kuhn's work became at one time the most widely cited work in the English language – including the Bible. Most importantly, this work represented a frontal challenge to the long-standing presumption that scientific knowledge is progressive, that with continued research – testing hypotheses against reality – we come ever closer to the truth. Few can doubt, for example, that the shift from a Ptolemaic view of the earth as the center of the universe to the Copernican account of the earth's revolutions around the sun is not progress; or that the shift from Newtonian mechanics to relativity theory in physics is not a gain in understanding. Kuhn did, and his reasoning sent shock waves across the intellectual world. As Kuhn proposed, our propositions about the world are embedded within *paradigms*, roughly a network of interrelated commitments – to a particular theory, conception of a subject matter, and methodological practices (or "form of life" in a Wittgensteinian sense). Thus, even our most exacting measurements are only sensible from within the paradigm. A look into a microscope tells you nothing unless you are already informed about the nature of the instrument and what you are supposed to be looking at. Here Kuhn is at one with his predecessors.

What we call progress in science, for Kuhn, is not then movement from a less to a more objectively accurate paradigm. Objective accuracy is only achieved from within the terms of the paradigm. Findings within an alternative paradigm are *incommensurable*, that is, beyond measurement from another perspective (for example, a neurologist cannot measure the depth of a soul because the soul is not a fact within neurology). Rather, new paradigms are generated by *anomalies*, data that fall outside the range of problems capable of solution within a given paradigm. As new problems are explored, so do they give rise to alternative paradigms – new conceptions, apparatus, and objects of study. Scientific revolution is essentially the shift from one paradigm to another. For Kuhn, "the scientist with a new paradigm sees differently from the way he had seen before."[39] In the end, Kuhn opined, we may "have to relinquish the notion, explicit or implicit, that changes of paradigm carry scientists and those who learn from them closer and closer to the truth."[40] While Kuhn subsequently came to regret the radical implications of his arguments, others extended them with even greater force.[41] No longer was it possible to justify science as a quest for *the* truth.

This initial wave of writing on the social determination of scientific knowledge has been enormously influential – both in transforming the common understanding of science and putting teeth into the mouth of social constructionism. However, it is not a line of argument without flaws. First, some critics find it lacking because it conceptualizes the scientist as a simple pawn to social forces. It suggests that the scientist is nothing but a byproduct of his/her sub-culture, little more than a robot or puppet. Further, if everyone is simply a byproduct of group belief, then how did the group come by its particular conceptualizations? Wouldn't the group simply be a collection of robots? How would ideas originate; why would they change? Second, many of these accounts are built on the assumption of a subjective mind (the mind of the scientist), biased by conceptions absorbed from the social world. Such a formulation borrows most of the problems of dualism discussed in the preceding chapter. Especially plaguing is the difficulty of explaining how the individual mind can absorb the ideas of others. If understanding others requires concepts, how would the unsocialized infant – born into the world without concepts – ever come to understand what others were saying?

A third problem inheres in the lack of self-reflexivity displayed by many social determinists. They argue against the possibility of objective knowledge in science, and yet, seem to treat these arguments as factually based, objective, and true. The inconsistency is left unresolved. Finally, the social determination view seems to emphasize only the constructions we make of the world, while blind to non-social or material aspects of knowledge making. Is scientific knowledge simply word play? As argued earlier, language games also take place within a context that includes material objects. Where is the material world in these analyses? This latter critique sets the stage for the second important movement in the social account of science.

Scientific Fact as Emerging from Relationship

> The reeds give
> way to the
> wind and give
> the wind away.
>
> A.R. Ammons, "Small Song"

The social determination arguments are very important in underscoring the significance of interpretive communities in shaping the taken-for-granted realities of science. However, because of the problems inherent in their extreme form (for example, "Scientific knowledge is nothing but social convention"), more recent work has shifted the emphasis in important ways. In particular, scholars increasingly seek ways of understanding scientific knowledge as the result of relational processes – emerging from the interchange of persons, objects, physical surrounds, and so on. Individual scientists, in this case, are not so much pawns to social forces, but full participants in a range of complex relationships out of which common understandings emerge. Perhaps the best example of this approach is the work of Bruno Latour and his colleagues.[42] Latour is particularly concerned with how a proposition acquires the status of a scientific *fact*. We say that it is simply a fact that smoking causes cancer and the world is round. But given the possibility of multiple interpretations – that truth cannot be read from nature – how did these particular statements acquire such broad acceptance while others are considered only hypotheses, conjectures, or mere nonsense? Latour proposes that the world of science is no less messy than that of daily life, and that producing a sense of order out of this chaotic condition is a difficult social and material achievement.

So how are facts brought forth from chaos? Primarily, through an elaborate process of *conscription* (literally, "writing with"). That is, the scientist may propose a candidate for truth, but the naked statement is scarcely convincing. There are innumerable ways of faulting anything that is said, noting its ambiguities, disagreeing over premises, attacking underlying motives, and so on. There are also myriad ways of supporting, praising, or prizing the statement. The problem for the scientist, then, is to generate supporters while reducing detractors. In effect, the scientist must conscript those sources that will celebrate the proposal and protect it from doubters. As Latour proposes, there are many targets of conscription. Consider, for example, *the fact* that smoking causes cancer. In order to make this a fact (from the daily clutter of papers, specimens, laboratory apparatus, subjects, numbers, etc.) scientists had to conscript from at least four domains:

Allies: To "make a fact" it is essential to enroll others who support your interpretations or give you the benefit of the doubt. To say to a colleague, "Frank, I think we are really on to something, and it could save millions of lives" is designed to conscript in a way that saying, "We are puttering along here, but I like the work" is not. Making friends is no less important in science than politics.

Former texts: Published papers in science represent "what is known" or established. The acceptability of a new proposal benefits, then, from resting its arguments on the former texts of the field. To say that, "Jones discovered that . . .; Smith corroborated the fact; and the present study vindicates the conclusion that . . ." is not only a means of adding a chorus of approval to one's report. It suggests as well that the conclusions are equivalent to "what is established." Seldom, however, will the scientist return to the earlier work to examine its ambiguities and shortcomings; to question the work would raise doubts about one's own.

Rhetorical devices: In scientific writing there are particular literary forms or devices that are accorded high status in terms of "truth-telling capacity." For example, the use of numbers suggests precision, astute attention to detail, and clear differences upon which to base one's count. The use of figures or graphs not only embodies numbers, but gives the reader the sense of "seeing the phenomenon." By using figures and graphs the scientist implicitly says, "You don't have to take my word for it, look for yourself." Of course, one is not actually viewing the phenomenon in itself, but rather taking the scientist's "word for it," now in graphic form. Although the abstract, technical, and complex character of much scientific writing is esteemed within the scientific culture, Latour tells us to be on the alert. Wherever the scientist moves into murky formulations, you as reader are being pushed away. You are not being allowed to understand, to know too much about what is presumed or has taken place.

Inscription devices: Latour proposes that if you doubt the scientific report and actually visit the scientific laboratory for proof, you will seldom confront the "phenomenon in itself." For example, you will see neither smoke nor cancer. Rather, in modern science you will typically be shown a machine or instrument that produces non-linguistic representations – for example, X-ray machines, MRI scanners, GSR recorders, and the like. These *inscription devices*, as Latour calls them, effectively "write the world" for us. So long as we accept the scientist's view of how such devices operate (how they "measure" or translate "the world as it is"), their results come to stand in for "the phenomenon."

As we extend this view, we find what we call "scientific facts" to emerge from an array of interacting influences – scholarly organizations, journals, apparatus, the public and so on. Recent theory casts these multiple influences in terms of *actor networks*.[43] Here theorists dispense with the traditional distinctions between the social and the natural world, or between humans and technology. Rather, any participant in the total system of relationships is termed an *actant*. To illustrate, if time plays an important role in organizing our lives, we may be informed of the hour by the voice of a radio announcer, the position of the sun, or the ringing of an alarm. The human voice, the sun, and the technological device all play the same powerful role. In principle, each could be substituted for the other. The process by which actants come into an interdependent relationship is called *enrolling*. If I am a psychologist and I use a tachistoscope in my studies of perception, I am enrolling the apparatus for purposes of producing an outcome. If, however, my colleagues convince me that a dichotic listening device would better serve my purposes, my colleagues and the new apparatus enroll me within another network. From this perspective, what we call "scientific knowledge" can be viewed as a by product of a cluster of inter-related and mutually supportive actants.

Finally, to return to the issue of science vs. society, if scientists are becoming a new breed of high priests – beyond question from the unannointed – the present analysis tells us why. It is essentially because we have no means of direct confrontation with its truths. At every point we try to dig in, we find our questions deflected. If we try to question a scientist's findings on cancer, we will be directed to allies who support the findings, a previous literature on the subject, tables and graphs, and to machinery. Each of these sources, says Latour, is like a *black box*. If you try to open it, you find yourself directed to another black box, and so on . . . In the end you realize that to question a scientific fact is to question an enormous interlocking arrangement of assumptions, equipments, writings, and so on – in effect, an entire tradition or form of life.

All this is not to say that a proposition such as "smoking causes cancer" is untrue, or that all the evidence is not yet in. Recall that we have now left the "game of truth" at the door. Rather, it is to remove the armanent from scientific annunciations, the justificatory grounds by which scientists can claim truth beyond interpretation, values, and cultural ways of life. It is to reveal the confusions, competitions, strategies, and negotiations underlying what is passed on to a public as immutable fact. In this unmasking science loses its status as *above* culture, and is brought closer to the common dialogues.

At the same time, the analysis does not argue that we should pay no attention to such propositions as smoking causes cancer. Rather, given the common constructions of the culture, and the value placed on what we call "life," this proposition has important functional value. We can use it to adjust our actions to relatively reliable patterns of events. In the same way we say that "the sun will rise at 6:40am," and adjust our lives accordingly – even if scientists tell us that the sun does not rise, but the world turns. In the case of cancer, the scientific view has largely become the cultural reality; to the chagrin of millions of smokers, the scientific and cultural values are increasingly at one.

Reflection

My early training was in scientific psychology, that is, a psychology based on the promise that through the application of empirical methods, sound measures, and statistical analysis we would begin to approach the truth of mental functioning. Most of my graduate training was thus occupied by seminars and research practice devoted to "establishing knowledge." I learned my lessons well, how to produce from the messy confines of laboratory life the kinds of clear and compelling "facts" acceptable to the professional journals. A few tricks of the trade: pre-test the experimental manipulations so to ensure that the desired effects are obtained; use multiple measures so to ensure that at least one will demonstrate the effects; if the first statistical test doesn't yield a reliable difference, try others that will; if there are subjects who dramatically contradict the desired effect, try to find a bias that will disqualify their data; if you run enough subjects even the smallest effect can reach significance; be sure to cite early research to express historical depth; cite recent research to demonstrate "up-to-date" knowledge; do not cite Freud, Jung or any other "pre-scientific" psychologist; cite the research of scientists who are supported by the findings as they are likely to be asked for evaluations by the journal. Nor was it simply that mastering the craft of research management allowed me to "generate facts" in the scientific journals; success also meant research grants, reputation, and higher status jobs.

I no longer do this kind of work. Yet, in spite of my consciousness of the constructed character of the "truth," I would scarcely be pleased at the withering of all such research. I would like to see the pretensions of truth and objectivity abandoned, and a greater emphasis placed on dialogue as opposed to the traditional attempt by scholars to secure "the last and only word." Most important, I would like to see more discussion on the values and potentials of such research on grounds other than "establishing the truth." We must ask questions of the kind inspired by Foucault's work: what happens when the scientific ways of interpreting the world are set loose in the society? Who gains, who loses, and how do we wish to build our future together?

Notes

1 Wittgenstein, L. (1978) *Philosophical Investigations*. Oxford: Blackwell.
2 Ibid., section 108.
3 Ibid., section 7.
4 Ibid., section 20e.
5 Austin, J.L. (1962) *How to Do Things With Words*. New York: Oxford University Press.
6 See for example Searle, J.R. (1970) *Speech Acts*. London: Cambridge University Press.

7   See especially Foucault, M. (1979) *Discipline and Punish*. New York: Vintage; and (1978) *The History of Sexuality*, vol. 1. New York: Pantheon.

8   In Gordon, C. (Ed.) (1980) *Power/Knowledge: Selected Interviews and Other Writings by Michel Foucault, 1972–1977*. New York: Pantheon. p. 199.

9   For further elaboration see Gergen, K.J. (1994) *Realities and Relationships*. Cambridge, MA: Harvard University Press.

10   For further steps toward refusal see http://www.swarthmore.edu/SocSci/Kgergen1/Psychodiagnostics/index.html

11   See for example Naylor, G. (1982) *The Women of Brewster Place*. New York: Viking; Bad Object-Choices (Ed.) (1991) *How Do I Look? Queer Film and Video*. Seattle: Bay Press.

12   See for example Riley, D. (1988) *Am I That Name? Feminism and the Category of 'Woman' in History*. Minneapolis: University of Minnesota Press; Sharpe, J. (1993) *Allegories of Empire: The Figure of Woman in the Colonial Text*. Minneapolis, MN: University of Minnesota Press.

13   Said, E. (1979) *Orientalism*. New York: Random House.

14   Ibid., p. 3.

15   Representative writings are included in Further Resources at the chapter's end.

16   Trin Minh-ha (1989) *Woman Native Other*. Bloomington, IN: Indiana University Press. p. 48.

17   Lauclau, E. (1990) *New Reflections on the Revolution of Our Time*. London: Verso. p. 36.

18   Hill Collins, P. (1990) *Black Feminist Thought*. New York: Routledge. pp. 106, 107.

19   See for example Squire, C. (1994) Empowering women? The Oprah Winfrey Show. In K. Bhavnani and A. Phoenix (Eds.) *Shifting Identities, Shifting Racisms*. London: Sage.

20   hooks, b. (1990) *Yearning, Race, Gender, and Cultural Politics*. Boston, MA: South End Press. pp. 179–182.

21   Hall, S. (1996) New ethnicities. In D. Morley and K. Chen (Eds.) *Stuart Hall: Critical Dialogues in Cultural Studies*. London: Routledge. p. 443.

22   Hunter, J.D. (1991) *Culture Wars: The Struggle to Define America*. New York: Basic Books.

23   Weisstein, N. (1993) Power, resistance and science: a call for a revitalized feminist psychology. *Feminism and Psychology*, 3, 239–245; at p. 244.

24   West, C. (1993) *Race Matters*. New York: Random House.

25   Gitlin, T. (1995) *The Twilight of Common Dreams*. New York: Henry Holt.

26   See for example Kingwell, M. (1995) *A Civil Tongue: Justice, Dialogue, and the Politics of Pluralism*. University Park: Pennsylvania State University Press; Hunter, J.D. (1994) *Before the Shooting Begins*. New York: Free Press.

27   hooks, *Yearning*, p. 25.

28   Butler, J. (1990) *Gender Trouble: Feminism and the Subversion of Identity*. New York: Routledge.

29   See for example Flax, J. (1993) *Multiples*. New York: Routledge; Deleuze, G. and Guattari, F. (1986) *A Thousand Plateaus*. Minneapolis, MN: University of Minnesota Press.

30   Deliberations on reality construction have taken many forms over the centuries, and contemporary dialogues are replete with differences in emphasis and outlook. For those searching this broader literature it is useful to distinguish between:

Radical constructivism: a perspective with deep roots in rationalist philosophy, that emphasizes the way in which the individual mind constructs what it takes to be reality. Scholars such as Claude Levi Strauss and Ernst von Glazersfeld are often identified with this view.

Constructivism: a more moderate view in which the mind constructs reality but within a systematic relationship to the external world. The names of Jean Piaget and George Kelly are often associated with this position.

Social constructivism: here it is argued that while the mind constructs reality in its relationship to the world, this mental process is significantly informed by influences from social relationships. Works of Lev Vygotsky and Jerome Bruner exemplify this approach. The work of Serge Moscovici and his colleagues on *social representation* often takes this view, but places special emphasis on the broad societal conventions in which the individual participates.

Social constructionism: here the primary emphasis is on discourse as the vehicle through which self and world are articulated, and the way in which such discourse functions within social relationships. This is the pervasive – though not exclusive – theme of the present volume.

Sociological constructionism: here the emphasis is on the way understandings of self and world are influenced by the power that social structures (such as schools, science, and government) exert over people. Works of Henri Giroux and Nikolas Rose are illustrative.

31 Mannheim, K. (1951) *Ideology and Utopia*. New York: Harcourt Brace.
32 Fleck, L. (1979) *Genesis and Development of a Scientific Fact*. Chicago: University of Chicago Press.
33 Winch, P. (1946) *The Idea of a Social Science*. London: Routledge & Kegan Paul.
34 Gurvitch, G. (1971) *The Social Frameworks of Knowledge*. New York: Harper & Row.
35 Berger, P. and Luckmann, T. (1966) *The Social Construction of Reality*. New York: Doubleday.
36 Ibid., p. 21.
37 Ibid., p. 26.
38 Kuhn, T.S. (1962) *The Structure of Scientific Revolutions*. Chicago: University of Chicago Press.
39 Ibid., (1970 edn) p. 115.
40 Ibid., (1970 edn) p. 169.
41 For Kuhn's regrets, see Kuhn, T.S. (1977) *The Essential Tension*. Chicago: University of Chicago Press. For a more extreme view of the social determination of science, see Barnes, B. (1974) *Scientific Knowledge and Sociological Theory*. London: Routledge & Kegan Paul; and Bloor, D. (1976) *Knowledge and Social Imagery*. London: Routledge & Kegan Paul.
42 See especially Latour, B. and Woolgar, S. (1979) *Laboratory Life: The Social Construction of Scientific Facts*. Beverly Hills, CA: Sage; and Latour, B. (1987) *Science in Action*. Cambridge, MA: Harvard University Press.
43 For a review of this literature, see Michael, M. (1996) *Constructing Identities*. London: Sage. Law, J. and Hassard, J. (Eds.) (1999) *Actor Network Theory and After*. Oxford: Blackwell.

Further Resources

The Ideological Impact of Knowledge Claims

Drayfus, H.L. and Rabinow, P. (1982) *Michel Foucault: Beyond Structuralism and Hermeneutics*. Chicago: University of Chicago Press.

Gergen, M.M. and Davis, S.N. (Eds.) (1997) *Toward a New Psychology of Gender*. New York: Routledge.

Ibanez, T. and Iniguez, L. (1997) *Critical Social Psychology*. London: Sage.

Prilletensky, I. (1994) *The Morals and Politics of Psychology*. Albany, NY: State University of New York Press.

Cultural Representations of Identity

Fabian, J. (1983) *Time and the Other: How Anthropology Makes its Object*. New York: Columbia University Press.

Huizer, G. and Mannheim, B. (Eds.) (1979) *The Politics of Anthropology: From Colonialism and Sexism Towards a View from Below*. The Hague: Mouton.

Nencel, L. and Pels, P. (Eds.) (1991) *Constructing Knowledge, Authority and Critique in Social Science*. London: Sage.

Ruby, J. (Ed.) (1982) *A Crack in the Mirror: Reflexive Perspectives in Anthropology*. Philadelphia: University of Pennsylvania Press.

Sampson, E.E. (1993) *Celebrating the Other*. Boulder, CO: Westview Press.

On Social Construction

Abhib, M.A. and Hesse, M.B. *The Construction of Reality*. Cambridge: Cambridge University Press.

Gergen, K.J. (1994) *Realities and Relationships, Soundings in Social Construction*. Cambridge, MA: Harvard University Press.

Potter, J. (1996) *Representing Reality*. London: Sage.

Sarbin, T.R. and Kitsuse, J.I. (Eds.) (1994) *Constructing the Social*. London: Sage.

Shotter, J. (1993) *Conversational Realities*. London: Sage.

Social Construction of Scientific Knowledge

Barnes, B., Bloor, D. and Henry, J. (1996) *Scientific Knowledge*. Chicago: University of Chicago Press.

Danziger, K. (1990) *Constructing the Subject: Historical Origins of Psychological Research*. Cambridge: Cambridge University Press.

Latour, B. (1987) *Science in Action*. Cambridge, MA: Harvard University Press.

McCarthy, E.D. (1996) *Knowledge as Culture*. New York: Routledge.

Pickering, A. (1995) *The Mangle of Practice*. Chicago: University of Chicago Press.

3

DISCOURSE AND EMANCIPATION

[We must] appreciate the power of redescribing, the power of language to make new and different things possible and important – an appreciation which becomes possible only when one's aim becomes an expanding repertoire of alternative descriptions rather than The One Right Description.

Richard Rorty, *Contingency, Irony, and Solidarity*

If language is a central means by which we carry on our lives together – carrying the past into the present to create the future – then our ways of talking and writing become key targets of concern. It is not only our grand languages of self, truth and morality at stake; our futures are also fashioned from mundane exchanges in families, friendships, and organizations, in the informal comments, funny stories and the remainder of the daily hubbub. Informed by a constructionist sensitivity, we are challenged to step out of the realities we have created, and to ask significant questions – what are the repercussions of these ways of talking, who gains, who is hurt, who is silenced, what traditions are sustained, which are undermined, and how do I judge the future we are creating? Such questioning does not proceed effortlessly – with methods tried and true. It is not easy in part because we live these discourses. If I say "I love my children," it is very difficult to suspend this reality and examine it as "only one and possibly problematic way of putting things." Between "is" and "as if" lies the void.

This kind of analysis is also frustrating because firm conclusions will always elude us. At the outset, we find that our analyses themselves are social constructions. That is, when we try to reflect on our discourse we do so in language, and this language is neither a reflection nor a map of our subject. It too constructs its subject as meaning "this" and not "that." If I propose, for example, that "men use more curse words in daily conversation than women," I thereby reify the male/female binary, I propose that everyone would agree on what constitutes a "curse word," and so on. Further, there are no unequivocal answers to the repercussions of any discourse, its uses and abuses, its advocacies and its suppressions. There are always multiple interpretations of how a given form of discourse functions in social life, and there is no ultimate means of grounding a conclusion.

Yet, in spite of these difficulties, there are exciting reasons for forging ahead – contingently, conjecturally. First, reflection on discursive conventions can be liberating. Much was said in the previous chapter about the oppression and injustice sustained by our languages. In such instances critical reflection opens possibilities of reconstruction. If our forms of intelligibility are injurious how can we change them; what alternatives are available; what can we create together? The same holds true in our daily lives. Often our conventional ways of talking – for example, about our feelings or intentions – lock us into unwanted patterns of action: hostile arguments, self-scorn or pity, a debilitating outlook on the future. In reflecting on these "ways of putting things," so do we open the door to new forms of life. In the broadest sense, discerning reflection is the first step to *emancipation* – the opening of new visions and alternative futures.

The emancipatory outcome is coupled with another. Consider what is involved in reflecting on a given way of talking or writing. If I focus, for example, on an inconsequential guy-remark, "He's just trying to get laid," I might question, "that's a curious way I have of talking. Doesn't it treat the woman as just an object of sexual gratification, dehumanizing her?" In this small maneuver I exit one form of discourse – guy-talk – and enter another. My critical remarks in this case are more representative of, let's say, the way many women talk. So as I reflect on a way of talking I essentially bring to the table the voice of another community. The two communities meet within me; I become a conduit for mutual understanding. In effect, in the reflexive appraisal I foster connection among the many communities in which I am immersed, and thus open possibilities for reconstructing the world in a less conflictual or more coordinated way. Reflecting on our discourses, then, may yield a greater knitting of human community.

The passion for provoking dialogues on what we otherwise accept as "just natural" has fired scholarship across the sciences and humanities. In the preceding chapter we glimpsed this process of unmasking in the natural sciences. Elsewhere scholars have created a small tidal wave of reflection and renewal. As a sample, we learn of the socially constructed character of what it is to be a child, an adolescent, or old;[1] the sense of self including emotions, thoughts, memories, and ethnicity;[2] gender differences and sexuality;[3] mental illness such as schizophrenia, anorexia, and multiple personality disorder;[4] the body and physical illness;[5] suicide, murder, and other social problems;[6] along with the news reports and historical accounts that inform us of such matters.[7]

Not all constructionist studies have the same aim, and it is useful to distinguish among some of the major forms. Many studies show how presently unquestioned definitions have actually changed with time and circumstance – for example, how we have come to speak so unreflexively about "mental illness," "mental retardation," "homosexuality," and so on. What social processes have favored the use of these particular terms and not others? These inquiries into the origins and context of *definition*, may be contrasted with other studies concerned with how various people or states of affairs are currently *framed* by such terms. How do schools, medical exams and psychological tests, for example, construct us in their terms; why can't inmates of a mental hospital escape the designation of "ill," or how do we come to experience various sensations as painful, sexual, or enjoyable? Finally, many studies focus on the way in which languages function within the broader scheme of things, how world constructions are at the same time participations in cultural life. In this case we see how discourse helps to *constitute* our lives in ways that we now take for granted – for example, our actions as men and women, black or white, young or old. Words are important in creating our lives in these ways but they gain their significance in the way they are embedded within patterns of action, material conditions, and social institutions.

These three forms of analysis – focused on definition, framing, and constitution – are not always so cleanly separated. However, all are centrally concerned with discourse or the way language creates our worlds. In this chapter we shall explore in greater detail process of linguistic construction. Here it will be helpful to employ three different lenses. First, we shall treat *discourse as structured*, that is, as a set of conventions, habits or ways of life that are stable and recurring. We shall focus specifically on metaphor and narrative as they influence our definitions of ourselves and our world. This kind of analysis can be dramatic, as it reveals the otherwise hidden walls that contain our attempts to describe and explain. We often feel our expressions are free and spontaneous; this analysis suggests that the moment we begin to speak we are already "spoken" by a pre-existing structure. We then consider a variation on the image of discourse as structure, namely, *discourse as rhetoric*. Here the emphasis is on the ways in which conventions or structures of language are used to frame the world and thus achieve certain social effects. The structures are not static in this sense, but used by people to build favored realities. Finally, we abandon concern with structure altogether, and put on the lens of *discourse as process*. In particular, we shall be concerned with the ongoing flow of social interchange, the conversations, negotiations, arguments and other processes by which we are constituted. Here we sense the possibility for continued change, sudden rupture, and the evolution of new ways of life.

Discourse as Structure: Metaphors We Live By

> What, therefore, is truth? A mobile army of metaphors . . .
>
> Friedrich Nietzsche, *On Truth and Falsity in Their Extramoral Sense*

Where reality counts metaphors have a bad reputation. Why? Because we traditionally define metaphors in terms of their contrast with "literal" words. Literal language is essentially "true to fact," "not exaggerated," while metaphors are considered so much literary fluff. As George Eliot once said, "We all of us, grave or light, get our thoughts entangled in metaphors, and act fatally on the strength of them." In the literal/metaphoric binary the first term has long been the privileged. Yet, as the preceding pages make clear, this tradition is flawed. In what sense can a word be "true to fact?" Certainly not because the word mirrors, maps or otherwise captures the essence of its referent. As we found, words gain the sense of being true to fact through long-term usage within a community. If we take a word out of one context of usage and place it within another, however, we now consider it metaphoric. The world is *his oyster*; life is a *bowl of cherries*. The difference between literal and metaphoric words, then, is *essentially the difference between the conventional and the novel*. In this sense, all our understandings can be seen as metaphoric if we but trace them to their origins. For example, we identify ourselves with names – which we take to be literal and precise. I am Ken, you are Sally, and you are Harry. Yet we were not always so – the names are all borrowed words, once literal descriptions of other persons, ripped out of context and deposited on our beings. In a sense, then, we are all metaphors of other people.

George Lakoff and Mark Johnson entitled their popular book *Metaphors We Live By*.[8] In this way they point to the way in which the common words by which we understand our worlds are typically appropriated from other contexts. Because these words also make up our forms of life, tracing their metaphoric base becomes an exciting challenge. It is when we free ourselves from the sense of the literal, as discussed above, that we move toward renewal and reconstruction. Consider: disagreements between people are typically the grounds for argument. However, as most of us find, arguments can often be unpleasant. Voices are raised, insults are exchanged, and instead of resolution there is animosity. These outcomes may be traced to a network of metaphors that inform our understanding of what an argument is. Specifically, as Lakoff and Johnson propose, arguments are equated metaphorically with war. Consider our common ways of talking:

> Your claims are *indefensible*.
> He *attacked* every weak point in the argument.
> Her criticisms were *right on target*.
> He *demolished* her case.
> I've never *won* an argument with her.
> He *shot down* all my arguments.

By equating argument with war in this way, we enter as combatants – it is either win or lose, kill or be destroyed. With the argument-as-war metaphor in place, our roles are clear. If we wish it otherwise it may be useful to develop alternative metaphors for the argument – such as a game, an exploration, or a dance. And if we can elaborate and extend such metaphors, we might change the character of our disagreements.

Metaphors of the Mind

> Facticity is always saturated with metaphoricity
>
> Donna Haraway, *Modest Witness*

I began this book with a deep concern over changing conceptions of the self – who and what we are as persons. The question we must now ask is whether our fundamental conceptions of our minds are not, in the end, derived from metaphors. We believe we possess thoughts, emotions, intentions, and the like. But if we pursue the origins of such terms, do we finally locate the borrowing or the appropriation now transformed into common sense?

Consider first the use of metaphor in the mental health professions, and particularly in Freud's psychoanalytic theory. To put it simply, Freud proposed that we are born with strong erotic desires; at an early age, for example, young boys wish to possess their mothers sexually. However, because these and related desires are unacceptable to parents, subject to severe punishment – the child *represses* them. In effect, the desires are forced out of the realm of consciousness. Individuals then erect neurotic defenses – compulsions, self-defeating actions, etc. – to ensure they are never released. On this view, therapy is an attempt to unearth the unconscious, to reveal the desires, and to help the person gain conscious control over them. For the psychoanalyst, hints of unconscious process can be obtained through dream analysis, slips of the tongue, and peculiar word associations. In effect, psychoanalytic practice derives from this particular conception of the mind.

Perhaps you sense the metaphoric elements in the psychoanalytic view. One of the most prominent metaphors, as Donald Spence describes it, is the *archeological*.[9] The archeologist is one who studies the distant past, and because these early events can never be known directly, makes use of various artifacts (shards of pottery, bones, stone formations) to interpret what must have been. Often this means digging through layers of earth deposits to locate evidence of past lives. This metaphor seems to tie together many aspects of Freudian theory – with its emphasis on the hidden and unavailable dimensions of the unconscious, the early formation of repression, the use of small bits of evidence to draw inferences regarding the unknown. The psychoanalyst serves as the archeologist, whose professional success rests on revealing "new knowledge." Yet, as Spence proposes, "To see the Freudian metaphor more clearly does not make it disappear and need not reduce it to triviality (as in saying 'Well, it's only a metaphor'). Because metaphors are central aspects of our understanding we will always continue to use them; by the same token, we should not be used *by* them."[10] For Spence, as a practicing psychiatrist, to be used by the metaphor is to mistake it for the real, and thus to reduce clinical sensitivity and imagination. It is to "reduce our options to only one."[11] In effect, by recognizing the metaphoric basis of the otherwise real, the way is opened for alternative actions.

All very well about a theory as exotic as psychoanalysis, you may say, but what about my "experience," "thought," and "emotion?" Aren't they real, something other than metaphor? The preceding chapters have certainly raised significant doubts about how we are to comprehend inner realities. A search for metaphors only increases an appreciation of the point. Consider first the concept of experience. The conception of "private experience" relies on a pivotal metaphor of the person in Western culture, one that views the *mind as a form of container* with certain specified ingredients inside (for example, "what's on my mind," "in my thoughts," "my private feelings") and the remainder outside (an "out there" as opposed to an "in here"). Yet, when you stop to locate what precisely is in vs. out, it becomes exceeding difficult to distinguish. Where does the outside stop and the inside begin, on the skin or the surface of the retina, in the receptor nerves, or perhaps the cortex? Consider: if you removed everything we consider "outside" from experience (for example, everything "in the physical world"), would there by anything left over we could identify as experience; and if you removed everything we call inside, would there be any "objects of experience" still remaining? When we try to tease apart what is inner vs. outer, we enter a morass of ambiguity. As scholars also point out, history has also deposited on our doorstep competing metaphors of "the nature of experience." Many accounts in our history view experience as *passive* – a repository of sense data deposited by the passing world – while others hold experience to be *active* – moving into the world to search, sort, and select.[12] In/out, active/passive – borrowed binaries which construct our sense of experience.

One major ingredient of the mind is said to be "thought." Yet, what precisely is thought? How do we identify it; how do we know its expressions? And when we attempt to describe thought will we not be in the thrall of linguistic traditions? Even the careful attempts of empirical psychologists to document the nature of cognition cannot escape the grip of metaphor. One dramatic illustration is offered by Gerd Gigerenzer.[13] As he points out, we typically think of statistical methods as a means by which we test the validity of a hypothesis; statistics then are mere tools for evaluating theories. On the contrary, proposes Gigerenzer, statistical methods have been major sources of inspiration for psychologists in generating metaphors about the mind, and especially cognition. Because statistics became valuable research tools, psychologists began to attribute statistical processes to the mind. For example theories of decision making began to speak about how individuals "test hypotheses," theories of trait attribution argued that people carry with them an "intuitive analysis of variance", and theories of information processing argued for a "Bayesian basis" for problem solving. As Gigerenzer concludes, "Scientists' tools for justification precede the metaphors and concepts for their theories."[14]

The way we understand our emotions also owes a debt to metaphor. There are several basic metaphors that guide much of what we can intelligibly say about our emotions.[15] Because we believe that emotions represent *the animal* in us, we can say, "he bellowed in anger," or "her feathers were ruffled." However, because the animal metaphor is prominent we cannot easily say, "his anger was robotic." We inherit a conception of emotions as *driving forces*, and thus we can say, "He was driven by fear," or "love makes the world go round." We would lapse into nonsense if we said, "He was so joyous that he fell off to sleep." There is a prevalent metaphor of emotion as *biological*, which enables us to say "I have a gut feeling," or "his heart broke from grief." To a lesser degree we also have a tradition of emotions as a *disease of the mind*. Thus, we say, "he was blind with envy," or "she fell madly in love," but not, "his rage is a sign of his maturity." One might say that when we speak of our minds we enter the world of poetry.

Discourse as Structure: Narrative Reality

> I can only answer the question What am I to do? if I can answer the prior question 'Of what story or stories do I find myself a part?' . . .
> Mythology . . . is at the heart of things.
>
> Alasdair MacIntyre, *Beyond Virtue*

Imagine yourself a witness to a crime, and placed on the witness stand. You are asked to describe what happened on the night of June 6? You reply, "blue . . . four . . . shoe . . . I . . . hair" and then go silent. You are questioned again, "No, no no . . . listen carefully . . . tell me clearly what really happened." You repeat yourself, and do so again as the lawyer grows increasingly exasperated. Finally, the judge bellows, "I hold you in contempt of court!" Based on earlier chapters, the judge's actions would seem unjustified. After all, you know that whatever happened on that night doesn't demand or require any particular formation of syllables; words aren't pictures. However, within the Western tradition of "reporting what happened," the judge is perfectly justified. Within this tradition one is required to tell a proper story.

What does telling a proper story mean by Western standards? In the more formal terms, this is to ask about the standards for *narrative construction*. What, by Western standards, are the conventions or rules for constructing an intelligible narrative? There appear to be at least five significant features of what we commonly take to be well-formed narratives. A narrative may be intelligible without meeting all five criteria, but as the ideal is achieved ironically the narrative will seem more "true to life." Among the most prominent criteria for a well-formed narrative by popular standards are the following.

A valued endpoint: An acceptable story must first establish a goal, an event to be explained, a state to be reached or avoided, or more informally, a "point." This point is typically saturated with value; it is understood to be desirable or undesirable. For example, your criminal testimony should be built around the single point: the occurrence of a crime. How did this awful event occur? If you answered the question of what happened on the evening in question in terms of how you tied your shoe, again you would be chastised. The event has no value in this context.

Events relevant to the endpoint: Once an endpoint has been established it more or less dictates the kinds of events that can figure in the account. Specifically, an intelligible narrative is one in which events serve to make the goal more or less probable, accessible, or vivid. Thus, if the point of the story is "the crime," you are expected to tell of events that are relevant to this point. If you said, "I tied my shoe, the dog barked, the light was on, John lay dead on the floor, and my tooth ached," you would still fail as a witness. The "truth and nothing but the truth" is not what is wanted, but a proper story. This means relating events that had specifically to do with John's death. This is to say that "the dog barked" could figure in the account, but connectives would be necessary, such as, "The dog barked at the man I saw jump from John's window."

Ordering of events: Once a goal has been established and relevant events selected, the events are usually placed in an ordered arrangement. The most widely used convention of ordering is that of linear time. In an intelligible story, one understands the events in terms of linear time. Thus you would fail as a witness once again if you said, "The man jumped from the window; a scream occurred, John lay dead on the floor, a shot rang out."

Causal linkages: The ideal narrative provides a sense of explanation. As it is said, "The king died and then the queen died," is only a rudimentary story. But to say, "The king died and then the queen died of grief" is the beginning of a tale. As narrative theorist Paul Ricoeur puts it, "Explanation must . . . be woven into the narrative tissue."[16] Thus, you would receive high marks as a witness if you could tell a tale of John and Harry's argument, causing Harry to become angry and pull out a pistol, which caused John to scream at him, at which point Harry pulled the trigger, which sent John sprawling to the floor, the sight of which caused Harry then to leap from the window. Each event is causally related to the preceding in a seamless tale.

To illustrate the importance of these criteria of good narration, researchers asked participants to either tell a story of an actual occurrence in their lives, or to make up an occurrence.[17] When a group of evaluators were asked to distinguish between the true and false stories they were unable to do so. However, when an analysis was made of those stories the evaluators believed to be true as opposed to false, the results were interesting. Stories believed to be genuine more closely approximated the well-formed narrative as outlined here. Particularly important to the "sense of truth" was evidence of a valued endpoint and causal linkages among events. In telling the truth, life should copy art.

Narratives of the Self

Let us return again to the construction of the self. As we saw, common understandings of our mental life are suffused with metaphor. What is to be said about the place of narrative in understanding self and others? First, consider the way we understand our momentary daily lives in terms of "ups" and "downs," progress and setbacks, fulfillment and frustration. To see life in these ways is to participate in a storied world. To be "up," to progress, or to be fulfilled is to participate in a story. Similarly I understand my writing at this moment not as an isolated act, but as coming from somewhere in the past and leading to something I value in the future. Or as one commentator has put it, "We dream in narrative, daydream in narrative, remember, anticipate, hope, despair, believe, doubt, plan, revise, criti-cize, construct, gossip, learn, hate and love by narrative."[18] The same may be said about the way others respond to us – at least our long-term acquaintances. We are typically treated by them as characters in a story, with a past, present, and future that are causally related, and moving in a direction – good or bad.

Yet, there is another way in which narrative structure informs and contains our lives. Because we are treated by others as storied characters, we are often called upon to "tell our story," to recount our past, to identify where we have been and where we are going. In effect, we identify ourselves through narration. In this sense, narrative structures set certain limits over who we can be. To get a better grasp of the way in which narrative conventions fashion our sense of identity, it is useful to consider major forms of narrative convention. Such forms can be understood best by returning again to the first essential ingredient of the good story, the valued endpoint. To make sense of our lives, we typically posit some kind of endpoint or goal ("how I came to be X," "achieve Y," or "believe in Z"). Given the endpoint, try to envision a two-dimensional space in which all events are arrayed over time in terms of whether they move toward or away from the valued goal. To illustrate, consider two rudimentary narrative forms: the *progressive narrative*, in which the endpoint is positive (a success, victory, etc.), and the story is all about the events that lead up to achieving this valued state; and a *regressive narrative*, in which the endpoint is negative (a failure, loss, etc.) and the story tells about continuous decline. While few of our stories about ourselves are pure examples of progressive and regressive narratives, they often approximate these cases. "How I won the match ... came to this conclusion ... achieved these results" and so on in the former case, and in the latter, "How my romance failed ... I was screwed over ... or ended up on drugs."

Fortunately these are not the only story forms available to us. Other

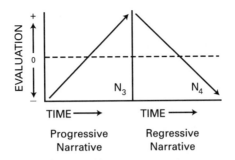

Figure 3.1   *Rudimentary Forms of Narrative*

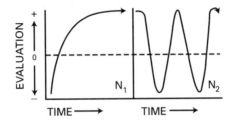

Figure 3.2   *The Happily-ever-after Narrative and the Heroic Saga*

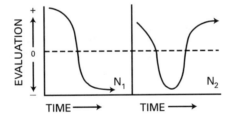

Figure 3.3   *Tragic and Comedy-Romance Narratives*

popular variants of these more rudimentary forms include the *happily-ever-after narrative* ("How after many difficult years, I finally ended up in a profession that is rewarding"), and a narrative that is often very attractive to males, the *heroic saga narrative*. In this case one understands one's life as a series of ups and downs – a struggle, perhaps, to achieve a goal, misfortune sets in, I struggle again toward victory, but again set-backs occur, until finally I win out. Two other popular narratives deserve mention. The first is the *tragedy*, in which someone in high position or at the point of success, falls rapidly into despair or failure. More mundanely, if my computer crashes and takes my manuscript copy with it, and I shout a curse, I am giving expression to a tragic narrative – at the peak of production I am brought low. Finally, almost all prime-time television dramas take the form of what might be called a comedy–romance.[19] In this case a positive state of affairs is interrupted by a calamity (for example, a crime, an error of judgement, a *faux pas*), and the remainder of the story is occupied with a series of events that finally restore order and tranquillity. Perhaps you are one of those many people who understand their daily lives in this way – constructing your world so that you begin strong in the morning, run into problems, snags, and glitches during the day, and then attempt to "dig out" so that by bed-time the day has come to a happy conclusion.

Significant illustration of these ideas is furnished by Donald Spence's groundbreaking book *Narrative Truth and Historical Truth*.[20] When people come to therapy with personal problems, most (but not all) therapists seek to locate the origin of these problems. This search is typically important in the case of psychoanalysis, as relief from distress in this case requires unearthing repressed urges, fears, or memories tied to events long past. Now the analyst confronts an interesting problem – trying to locate the actual events of the past ("historical truth") as opposed to searching the past in a way that will yield a good story ("narrative truth"). The narrative structure is also quite demanding: we have a story ending ("my problem"), and presume there are previous events leading necessarily to this conclusion – in effect a powerful *regressive narrative* is required. As Spence argues, in spite of the analyst's attempts to document the truth, the narrative subtly and necessarily wins out. The accomplishment is facilitated by several factors: the fuzzy recollections of the patient, the incapacity of the verbal report of the patient to match available images of the past, the necessity for selecting from among everything that is recalled, events that will have meaning in the therapeutic relationship, and the commitment to psychoanalytic theory which presumes a regressive narrative of development. There is, then, no free reporting of the past; the therapist and the patient work together to generate a narrative which will inevitably support the presumptions of psychoanalytic theory. This narrative then serves not only as the key to cure but for the patient, it becomes "my life". As Spence concludes, "The construction not only shapes the past – it *becomes* the past."[21] We shall return to the use of narrative in therapy in Chapter 7.

Discourse as Persuasion: the Lens of Rhetoric

> Rhetoric is the art of speaking well – with knowledge, skill and elegance.
>
> Cicero, *De Oratore*

The structural view of discourse tends to emphasize fixity and determination, suggesting that our traditions of discourse constitute a background from which our current constructions of world and self cannot escape.

Although this is a useful metaphor for certain purposes, many scholars reject the deterministic implications. Rather, they are drawn to the way in which discourse is used, abused and transformed by people in the process of their daily interchanges. This concern with the pragmatic process will be fully developed in the next section. However, there is a mid-range of concerns that fall somewhere between structure and process. Here scholars point to the way in which structured traditions are placed in motion; they are used by people to achieve certain ends. More generally this emphasis is identified with rhetoric – or more crudely, the art of persuasion. The discipline of rhetoric has a long and honored tradition, dating to classical Greek civilization when rhetoric was an essential element in the education of promising young men. For centuries afterwards, the works of Aristotle, Cicero, and Quintillian were used to fashion skills in public speaking. Yet, with the growing influence of modernist, beliefs in objectivity, science, and truth, rhetoric suffered the same fate as the concept of metaphor. To convince others by virtue of "pretty talk," cleverness, emotional appeals, and the like was illegitimate. For the modernist logic and factual evidence – expressed clearly and plainly – were the keys to progress.

Yet in recent years the study of rhetoric – like metaphor – has undergone a renaissance. This rekindling of interest grows directly from the soil of critique described in Chapter 1. If modernism is wrong about rhetoric then let us re-consider its potentials. Of particular interest, what can rhetorical study help us to understand of the difference between successful and unsuccessful constructions. Or, to put it another way, if rhetoric is the art of persuasion, then the study of rhetoric is the illumination of power in action. In effect, contemporary inquiry in rhetoric has little interest in the art of effective speaking; rather the hope is to sharpen our critical acumen in the service of emancipation.

Rhetorical unmasking can be turned on any target – the news media, political speeches, court testimony, business policies – any person or group that attempts to exert or exercise power over others. A selection of illustrative works is included at the chapter's end. Perhaps the most significant critique, however, has been directed not against advertising, political persuasion, or religion, but against those who make claims to objective reality. There is already sufficient skepticism of those whose profession is to persuade. More dangerous are those who seem only to be reporting the facts – the world as it is outside anyone's particular prejudice. Rhetorical analysis thus attempts to question the authority of science, policy making, military decision making, economics and indeed all attempts to use "just the facts, mam" to silence other voices. The critique is not motivated simply by the way such claims deny their existence as social constructions. Nor is it that the rhetoric is so common – indeed built into most public school curricula – that we are unconscious of it as rhetoric. Rather, the language of objective reality is essentially used as a means of generating hierarchies of inclusion and exclusion. This is so not only in science, where one of the chief aims of the scientist is to lift his or her own particular constructions into the status of "accepted fact."[22] But it is also the case more generally, where those who don't speak the rhetoric are scorned as "unrealistic," "deluded," "irrational," or "self-deceived." To illuminate these rhetorical maneuvers is thus to challenge the conventions and thereby open a space for all to speak.

The Rhetoric of Reality

> Objectivity is much more than merely the opposite of subjectivity: It is an instrument of disciplinary power that can distinguish science from art and professional knowledge from pre-professional opinion.
>
> W. Natter, T. Schatzki, and J.P. Jones *Objectivity and its Other*

How is it that our discourse succeeds in generating the sense of the "really real" – the taken-for-granted world of atoms, chemical elements, neurons, cognitions, economic processes, social structure and the like? While much has been written on this question,[23] central to the power of words to create "the real" is a single, but widely shared image or metaphor of the person. The metaphor is that of the "mind as mirror," the belief in the mind is inside the head (subjective) and the world is outside (objective). This, you will recall from Chapter 1, is a central presumption in Western modernism. Based on this metaphor, we hold that one is objective when private experience is a perfect reflection of the natural world. One is objective when he/she "sees things for what they are," "is in touch with reality," or "takes a good look at things." Now it was also clear from Chapter 1 that there is no way to separate subject from object, no means of knowing "what's inside the mind," or determining whose mind is reflecting reality more or less accurately. Thus, we see that objectivity cannot refer to a relationship between mind and world; rather, as the rhetorical analyst proposes, objectivity is achieved by speaking (or writing) in particular ways. The common assumption of the mind as mirror enables us to appreciate the particular ways in which reality is achieved. Let's consider three of these.

DISTANCING THE OBJECT: THE WORLD "OUT THERE"   Because reality talk is supposed to be about a "world out there," it is important that a rhetor employs *distancing devices*, that is, discursive means of ensuring that the object in question is not "in the mind" but exists at a distance. At the simplest level, adjectives such as *the, that*, or *those*, call attention away from the agent and place the object(s) at a seeming distance. Distancing may be contrasted with personalization, terms calling attention to the object as a private possession of the mind. "My view," "my perception," "my sense of" are all personalizing. Thus, the scientist is likely to speak of "the apparatus", as opposed, for example, to "my sense of an apparatus," "that experimental chamber" as opposed to "my impression of an experimental chamber", or "those questionnaires," and not "my image of questionnaires." The former phrases create the real, while the latter create suspicion.

The distancing of object from observer can also be achieved through the use of metaphors. Consider, for example, the *metaphor of the hidden continent*, a land out there to be explored. In science one thus finds such phrases as "Smith first discovered the effect," "Jones found that . . .," "Brown detected that . . .," and so on. Terms such as "unearthed" and "brought to light" are similarly used, suggesting a companionate *metaphor of buried treasure*. Consider the unfortunate consequences of some personalized contrasts: "Smith first felt is was so," "Jones also shared this fantasy," and "Brown loved this image of the world."

ESTABLISHING AUTHORITY: EXPERIENTIAL PRESENCE AND ABSENCE   If we believe the mind functions like a mirror, then to establish oneself as an authority on "what exists" one must show that the mirror was indeed in a position to reflect. Experiential presence is often achieved during the initial pages of a scientific report by the use of personal pronouns, such as "I" or "we," or possessives ("my" or "our"). One says for example, "Our attempt was to explore . . ." or "We were concerned with . . ." thus insinuating experiential presence into the scientific finding. Consider, for example, the effects of scientific writing that violated the convention: "I was very busy with my teaching and various conferences during the semester, so I had little time to observe the research process. Smith, my graduate student, actually did all the work, though he did discuss it with me from time to time."

Because the experience of a single person is suspect, it is often useful to show that "other mirrors reflect the same thing." Thus, regardless of the variations in procedures, samples, laboratory environment, time of the research, and so on, the scientific report will write as if the same reflection was found in all the mirrors, "Smith demonstrated that . . .' Brown corroborated it . . ., and Jones found the same effect . . .' More subtle are rhetorical devices suggesting that the mirror of the author is at a special advantage, possibly superior to all others, or at the extreme, a *god's eye view*. This effect is often accomplished through the use of impersonal pronouns. Rather than "I observed . . .," one uses the phrase "One observed . . .," in preference to "I found that . . .," the phrasing shifts to "It was found . . ." More frequently the god's eye view is simply suggested by inference. One writes, "The stimulus was presented . . .," and not "I thought I saw that the stimulus presented . . .," or "The button was pressed . . .," in lieu of "My assistant reported that he experienced the button being pressed . . ."

PURIFYING THE LENS: THE DEATH OF PASSION   The mirror of the mind achieves objectivity when there is no interference, when it possesses no defect that might "distort," or "bias" the image produced by the world. One means of demonstrating that there are no "mirror effects" is to use phrases granting the world an *active power* to create the image (as opposed to characteristics of the mirror itself). Thus, such phrases as "the data spoke for themselves," or "I was struck by" contribute to the sense of the real. On the other hand, it is important to demonstrate the *absence of internal states* – such as the emotions, motives, values, and desires – in creating the reflection. One can say, "We recorded a mean of 5.65 . . .," "It was observed that the subjects were ill at ease . . .," or "The results demonstrated ..." without impunity. However, should affective states be inserted into the same phrases, the effects would be debilitating. Consider: "My heart was set on finding a mean of over 5.00 and I was overjoyed when I got it . . .," "Given that the research would be virtually unpublishable if we didn't get positive results, we sought evidence that the subjects were ill at ease. Lo, they proved to be so . . .," or "I fell in love with this research subject and it is thus a pleasure to share her insights." To admit one's passions is to see through a glass darkly.

This purging of the mirror has an interesting side-effect on social science writing. While such writing should be fascinating – as it attempts to "explore the depths" of human existence – it is typically dull, flat and antiseptic. One reason for this tendency is that emotional or colorful descriptions suggest biases in the mind's mirror. In contrast, passionless technical description suggests a neutral – and thus objective – standpoint. We learn, for example, that the research subjects were college males, or women aged 40–60, or black school children from the inner city. In contrast, there is no mention of such matters as sexual attractiveness, off-putting obesity, cloying superficiality, charming manners, stupefying ignorance, enviable clothing, repulsive pimples, and so on. To write about such matters would subvert the sense of objectivity.

To demonstrate that objectivity is not a state of mind but of rhetoric functions to replace gullibility with reflective pause. It enables other voices to enter the conversation than those laying claim to the real. However, this is not to argue for abandoning the rhetoric. Rather, the rhetoric of reality plays a very important role within communities. Often it is vital in achieving trust, community, and results. For example, when space scientists use this rhetoric they ask their colleagues to trust that they are using the language in the same way and for the same purposes as the remainder of the community. They are "calling a spade a spade" in terms of the community's standards, and as a result humans can walk on the moon. The same holds for doctors, military strategists and economic planners; and without such rhetoric there would be nothing we could call "truth" in courtroom testimony. The rhetoric of the real may be essential to effective community functioning; problems result primarily when the internal realities are treated as universal or "really real."

Discourse in Use: the Pragmatic Dimension

So far we have focused on discourse as both a fixed and mobile structure, either acting as a background constraint on forms of construction or used by people to achieve particular ends. Although these forms of analysis are very useful in demonstrating how forms of language may define and frame our actions, they are insufficient. Specifically they fail to recognize the continuous, unsystematic, hurly-burly of everyday meaning making, the tensions, negotiations, and sudden turns in conversation that constitute the world for what it is. Fascinated with language in action, many scholars devote their attention to the way discourse is used by people in the course of daily life – how words are variously deployed, how conversations develop or fail, and how realities are often held together by a delicate to and fro of relationship. To appreciate the pragmatics of everyday discourse we shall first touch on the seminal work of Erving Goffman and Harold Garfinkel. This will set the stage for a more detailed discussion of the conversational creation of the self.

The Legacy of Goffman and Garfinkel

Much contemporary work in pragmatics owes an enormous debt to the writings of Erving Goffman and Harold Garfinkel. For Goffman, language must be understood as a form of social action. Language includes not only the words we use to define what is real and good, but includes all our gestures, dress, bodily markings, personal possessions and so on. As Goffman explored in perhaps his major work, *The Presentation of Self in Everyday Life*,[24] we are constantly giving off signals that define who we are to others. One of Goffman's favorite quotes deliciously illustrates the point: the novelist William Sansom describes Preedy, an Englishman, making his first appearance on the beach of his summer hotel in Spain.

> But in any case he took care to avoid catching anyone's eye. First of all, he had to make it clear to those potential companions of his holiday that they were of no concern to him whatsoever. . . . If by chance a ball was thrown his way, he looked surprised; then let a smile of amusement lighten his face (Kindly Preedy) . . . looked around dazed to see that there were people on the beach, tossed it back with a smile . . . But it was time to institute a little parade of the Ideal Preedy. By devious handlings he gave any who wanted to look a chance to see the title of his book – a Spanish translation of Homer, classic thus, but not daring, cosmopolitan too – and then gathered together his beach-wrap and bag into a neat sand-resistant pile (Methodical and Sensible Preedy), rose slowly to stretch at ease his huge frame (Big Cat Preedy), and tossed aside his sandals (Carefree Preedy, after all.)[25]

For Goffman, perhaps our primary task in social life is to create a sense of public identity, that is, an image of ourselves as an acceptable person. "When an individual plays a part he implicitly requests his observers to take seriously the impression that is fostered before them."[26] For every relationship, however, there is a *back region*, a domain of action hidden from the observer, but knowledge of which would discredit the public performance. For many students, relations at college serve as a back region in terms of the way they present their identity at home; meanwhile their parents' bedroom talks serve as a back region in terms of their relationship with their son or daughter. In effect, when parents and offspring are together they create a set of local identities that they ask to be taken seriously by each other – yet in some sense, a sham for the moment. Goffman's approach is called *dramaturgical*, in that it paints a picture of social life as a stage, where we all perform for each other, knowing at the same time that what we seem is scarcely who we are.

In spite of its fascination, for many constructionists Goffman's dramaturgy is deeply unsettling. What kind of a world, after all is Goffman constructing in this analysis, and if we take it seriously, what follows in social life? Goffman's analysis suggests that just beneath the surface of our actions there is a manipulative agent who is continuously conning others. Sincerity itself is just another con, which might even succeed in duping the actor. To accept such a view leaves us with an enormous distance between ourselves and others, a prevailing sense of distrust, a doubt in all support, gratitude, or affection. Nor, in the end, can we trust or accept ourselves, for our finest hour would be that in which we could successfully fool the greatest number of people.

In a second line of groundbreaking work, spawned by sociologist Harold Garfinkel, many of these problematic elements are avoided. In his signal volume *Studies in Ethnomethodology*,[27] Garfinkel moved the focus from the way single individuals manage social life to the ways in which people work together to achieve a sense of order and understanding. Specifically, proposed Garfinkel, our interchanges are deeply reliant on a range of *ethnomethods* – primarily linguistic expressions – used to achieve what we take to be a rational or taken-for-granted order. Ethnomethods are not the possession of private individuals attempting to impress; rather they are public resources from which we draw and create together a visibly rational world.

Consistent with earlier discussions, Garfinkel points out that we treat words as if they match the objects to which they refer. On the contrary, he proposes, we are always borrowing words and phrases from other contexts and "making do" with them in our present circumstances. In Garfinkel's terms, we use words *indexically*, that is, to point or name *for all practical purposes*. It is largely through indexicals that we create the sense of rational order from what is otherwise ambiguous or chaotic. Consider, for example, the case of suicide. We typically treat some deaths as "natural," and others as "suicide." However, when you consider more carefully you quickly realize that it is exceedingly difficult to distinguish between the two. To qualify as suicide, one must intentionally choose to end one's life. But recalling Chapter 1, how do we ever know another's true intentions; how do we even know our own? What if we believe we "freely intend", but we are actually conditioned to think this way; what if we are unconsciously driven, and simply don't have control; do we ever genuinely know what pushes and pulls us to act as we do? And what about natural death? If you truly wanted to live as long as possible chances are you would lead a very different life, avoiding all junk food, avoiding all crowds and the alien bacteria, seeking frequent health exams, taking no chances in athletics, and so on. Of course, most of us are more carefree. Does this mean that in a certain sense, every natural death is a small suicide? When we step away from specific contexts we see that whether a death is *really* a suicide is undecidable in principle.

Now consider the task facing an official team of investigators attempting to determine for the courts, the police and extended kin whether a given death is a suicide. As Garfinkel shows, such teams do not engage in endless debate. Rather, they develop specific rules and procedures – ways of talking and reporting – or more formally, a set of indexicals into which the world's events are poured. For example, in Los Angeles inspecting agents must sort all deaths into some combination of four elementary possibilities – *natural death, accident, suicide,* and *homicide*. All the available evidence, questions asked of friends and neighbors, the background investigation, and the like are subsequently used by the team to achieve the sense that one of the categories is rational and correct. As Garfinkel puts it, the participants rely on a set of *routine grounds* – themselves unquestioned – to convert chaos to order. Without our ordinary unnoticeable conventions of indexing the world, we would come face to face with a meaningless existence.

This last phrase is certainly overdramatic. But before recoiling in suspicion consider some cases in which the routine grounds of the real and the rational are violated. As a class exercise Garfinkel enlisted his students to break the unspoken rules of everyday life and report on the consequences. Specifically, they were to question the adequacy of a common indexical, that is, to challenge whether the linguistic vehicle being used to generate "common sense" was truly applicable. Here is the account of a student's report on his interchange with a member (A) of his car pool who is telling him (B) about a flat tire of the previous day:

A: I had a flat tire.
B: What do you mean, you "had a flat tire?"
A: [*Momentarily stunned, replies hostily*] What do you mean, "What do you mean?" A flat tire is a flat tire. That is what I meant. Nothing special. What a crazy question.

In a second case, an acquaintance (A) of the student (B), waved his hand and said:

A: How are you?
B: How am I in regard to what? My health, my finances, my school work, my peace of mind, my . . .?
A: [*Red in the face and out of control*] Look! I was just trying to be polite. Frankly, I don't give a damn how you are.

Another student questioned his fiancee for approximately a minute and a half on the precise meaning of what she was saying. She then began to reject the questions, and finally became nervous and jittery, her face and hand movements uncontrolled. "She appeared bewildered and complained that I was making her nervous and demanded that I 'Stop it' . . . She picked up a magazine and covered her face . . . When asked why she was looking at the magazine she closed her mouth and refused any further talk."[28] As these vignettes suggest, if we challenge the taken-for-granted ways of indexing our world – even momentarily – the social fabric quickly unravels.

The Conversational Construction of the Self

> Universally developed individuals . . . are not products
> of nature, but of history.
>
> Karl Marx, *Grundrisse*

Although the work of Goffman and Garfinkel continues to inspire contemporary scholarship, emphases and interests have expanded considerably over the years. In particular, constructionist scholars have become increasingly interested in the emancipatory potential of discourse analysis, that is, inquiry which causes us to reflect critically and creatively on our common ways of life. In this vein, constructionist scholars have carried out an enormous range of fascinating and far-reaching work. For example, there is substantial work on the ways discourse is subtly used to maintain power relations, to derogate certain groups of people, and to silence those who might upset the status quo. Scholars particularly concerned with politics have exposed the ways unnoticed moves in language sustain particular ideologies, obscure shortcomings in various policies and programs, and perpetuate structures of privilege. There is also significant inquiry into the use of discourse in controlling others – students in classrooms, patients in a medical interview, clients in therapy. Still other work focuses on discourse use as it generates misunderstanding and conflict among people. Although some of this work will make its way into this volume, the interested reader should take advantage of the resources listed at the end of the chapter.

In this context let's return to the recurring theme of the self. The earlier discussions of metaphor and narrative both suggested a fixedness to the self, ways in which the traditions of discourse force us into inescapable boxes. In the present context we concentrate on fluidity, the ways in which precisely who one is depends on the moment-to-moment movements in conversation. Here we understand identity as precariously situated, subject to subtle shifts of word, intonation, and gesture. There is no final fixing of this process, as pragmatic uses are continuously evolving in society. Here let us focus on three aspects of self-construction.

Creating Ontology, Ethics, and the Self

> By the blending of breath
> From the sun and the shade,
> Equilibrium comes to the world.
>
> Lao Tzu, "The Way of Life"

At the most fundamental level, what is required in order for us to go on together? Putting aside issues of personality, ideology, gender and so on, what is essential for a relationship to occur? In the present context, this question can be answered in terms of *ontology* and *ethics*; that is, we must have a set of shared understandings – even if primitive – of what exists ("the real") and of what constitutes proper conduct ("the good"). More concretely a shared ontology is largely the byproduct of a common language. At the extreme, if you communicate to me only in Chinese and I can reply only in English, we shall scarcely be able to generate a relationship. Or more locally, if your world is made up of angels, divine spirits, and evil powers, and mine is composed of neurons, synapses, and endorphins, our mutually exclusive ontologies will make it difficult for us to communicate. Ideally, we should employ similar words on similar occasions – such that if you are a surgeon working with your team, your assistant will not respond to your demand for a "scalpel" by offering you a "stick of gum." As the Russian literary theorist Mikhail Bakhtin might put it, our relationships are subject to a *centripetal force*, that is, a tendency for our practices of communication to become singular – repetitive and conventional. Some might put this in terms of the tendency for relationships to become routinized, dull and dead; more positively one might point to the tendency toward smooth, efficient, and effective connection. A certain legitimacy inheres in both interpretations.

The lurch toward a common reality also lays the groundwork for establishing a rudimentary ethics. That is, as we come to coordinate our talk and actions within various contexts, so do we establish the conditions for disruptions, glitches, or failures. The establishment of pattern creates the context for its violation. At the most basic level, the disruption of the pattern functions as a threat to the accepted reality and all those patterns of action into which this reality is woven. Married couples are often jarred when they disagree on a story of the past; academics are often shunned if they shift to a new theoretical paradigm; and many have been martyred for unconventional religious convictions. "Evil" lurks in the disruption of the accepted patterns.

It is also important to note here the commonalty of such evil in any reasonably complex society. To the extent that people participate in multiple and broadly distributed relationships – with friends, spouses, colleagues at work, siblings, parents, children, neighbors, club members and the like – so will a multiplicity of local realities emerge – myriad ways of talking and being. As we move from one relationship to another so do we transport the residues. In this sense we carry with us enormous potential for evil, for unsettling existing ontologies. Even the word "ontology" cannot simply be uttered anywhere; it is as dangerous as the word "shit" in threatening certain established orders. It is here that Bakhtin's metaphor of *centrifugal force* is useful. The centripetal tendency toward order in relationships is coupled with a tendency toward disorder, a tendency for new words and actions to enter spontaneously into any relationships, possibly threatening, possibly transforming.

How do issues of ontology and ethics apply to the self? In the former case, persons typically figure within the emerging ontology. Thus, who I am and the nature of my actions come to be negotiated and defined within relationships. From the moment I am given a name at birth and assigned a gender my existence as an individual person begins to figure in a communal ontology. As I talk about "myself," my "thoughts," "feelings" or "beliefs," so do I create the reality of the single agent, "me." As you call me by name, or treat me in various ways, so may this reality become solidified. And, all such words and actions will carry with them a moral force – variously constructing me as good or evil.

To illustrate some of these ideas, consider Paul Willis' controversial analysis of how British adolescents come into their identity as working class.[29] As Willis proposes, it is all too easy to look at economic betterment as a natural drive: everyone wants to make more money. And with this assumption in place it is typical to see the working class as oppressed, as people who have no choice but to remain in the lower economic ranks of society. However, through extensive field work in schools and the workplace, Willis challenges these common beliefs. As he finds, working class boys join together to construct a world in which they are different from and better than the upper classes. Here, for example, they define their school teachers:

Joey: They're bigger than us, they stand for a bigger establishment than we do . . . and [we] try to get [our] own back.
Eddie: The teachers think they're high and mighty 'cos they're teachers, but they're nobody really.[30]

These dispositions also permeate the boys' classroom behavior. Willis describes:

As the 'lads' enter the classroom or assembly, there are conspiratorial nods to each other . . . [they] specialize in a caged resentment which always stops just short of outright confrontation . . . During class a mouthed imaginary dialogue counterpoints the formal instruction: 'No, I don't understand, you cunt'; 'What you on about, twit?'; 'Not fucking likely . . .' At the vaguest sexual double meaning giggles and 'whaos' come from the back . . . If the secret of the conspiracy is challenged, there are V signs behind the teacher's back, the gunfire of cracked knuckles from the side, and evasive innocence at the front. Attention is focused on ties, rings, shoes, fingers . . . anything rather than the teacher's eyes.[31]

This ontology of "us" vs. "them" is also supported by implicit ethics: "we and our way of life are valuable." Particularly worthy is the group and commitment to its standards:

Joey: . . . when you're dossing on your own, it's no good, but when you're dossing with your mates, then you're all together, you're having a laff and it's a doss . . .

Fred: We're as thick as thieves, that's what they say, stick together.[32]

The value placed on their way of life is revealed in the boys' characterizations of students who act in all the socially approved ways. These "ear'oles," as they were called (the ear being a symbol of passive reception) are the subject of continuous derision. Consider:

Derek: [The ear'oles] are prats like, one got on his report he's got five As and one B . . .

Spanksy: I mean, what will they remember of their school life? What will they have to look back on? Sitting in a classroom, sweating their bollocks off, you know, while we've been . . . I mean look at the things we can look back on, fighting on the Pakis, fightin on the JAs [Jamaicans]. Some of the things we've done on teachers, it'll be a laff when we look back on it.

Joey: [The ear'oles] are still fucking childish, the way they talk, the way they act like . . . they've got it all to come. I mean look at Tom Bradley, have you ever noticed him? I've always looked at him and I've thought, well . . . we've been through all life's pleasures and all its fucking displeasures, we've been drinking, we've been fighting, we've known frustration, sex, fucking, hatred, love and all this lark, yet he's known none of it. He's never been with a woman, he's never been in a pub.[33]

It is in just such conversations as these that "the lads" help to create a world of differences, a world populated by different groups and individuals, and each laden with moral value. One must ask in this case – and perhaps all – whether these realities may not be imprisoning.

Social Accounting: Identity and Responsibility

"How could you do that . . ."
"You were a jerk . . ."
"Don't you remember our agreement . . ."
"I don't really appreciate what you said . . ."

These familiar phrases are samples from the enormous compendium of correctives at our disposal. From the scoldings received as children to the silences and cold stares we endure as adults, to be corrected is simply to live in organized society. The criticisms, attacks, stares and the like are all means of sustaining order; they are relational ethics in action. At the same time, as sociologists Scott and Lyman point out, a major feature of common talk is "its ability to shore up the timbers of fractured sociation, its ability to throw bridges between the promised and the performed, its ability to repair the broken and restore the estranged."[34] In effect, while leading complex lives inevitably means violating the implicit ethics of our relationships (the centrifugal tendency at work), so have we also developed means of restoring order as we go. These restoration practices are often called *social accounting*.

A helpful context in which to consider social accounting comes from the domain of *conversation analysis*. One of the most important concepts to emerge from studies of informal conversation is the *adjacency pair*.[35] The concept refers to the strong tendency of conversation to proceed in terms of ordered pairings, with the action of the first speaker calling forth a particular kind of response from the second. Perhaps the most obvious example of the adjacency pair is the *greeting-greeting*, where a warm greeting on the part of one person virtually demands a similar action in response. In the same way, if someone confronts us with a *question*, we are inclined to respond with an *answer*; an *invitation* with an *acceptance* (or *rejection*); a *request* with *compliance* (or *denial*), and so on. In this context we find that social accounts figure as the second entry in an adjacency pair. They are largely responses to acts of *blame* – accusations, disappointments, shaming, or other forms of discrediting. These initial acts essentially challenge one's identity within the relationship, as a "member in good standing" within the circle of meaning making. The typical reply is some form of *reparation* – an indication that "I am still one of you," (in agreement with the way "our family," "our organization," or "the two of us," for example, have constructed the world).

Centuries of language usage deposit at our doorstep an enormous range of responses to such accusations. Often these replies are collected under two rubrics: *excuses* and *justifications*.[36] This distinction is important as it calls attention to differing logics and functions of reply. In the former case, most excuses rely on a logic of individual agency. That is, they presume the modernist vision of the self – with conscious agency at its center. Thus, although the individual's behavior may be "out of line," the more important question is whether the internal core – the self at the center – has abandoned the relationship. Excuses are assurances that the core is still in place. "I didn't mean to," "It wasn't my fault," "I wasn't thinking straight," "I let my emotions get the best of me," "I was drunk," "They made me do it," and so on. In each case, the message is: "It wasn't the real me." Restoration is thus set in motion. But notice, the excuse does not challenge the order; it primarily informs the accuser that "You may think I was deviating, but I was not. I am the same. Everything remains as is."

In the case of justification, however, both the logic and the result are different. Consider the following justifications:

"He deserved everything he got."
"It's the nature of the business . . ."
"It's a question of my own self-realization . . ."
"It was self-defense . . ."
"If I didn't do it I would lose all credibility . . ."
"We live in a free country."

One common element in these responses is their appeal to a commonly accepted reality. They draw on intelligibilities not necessarily central to the relationship in question ("our marriage," "our family" etc.), but which are commonly shared by the participants. For example, our relationship as lovers may not be based on the concept of "free country," but because we are participants in the broader culture these words have a certain rhetorical power. In effect, justifications remove from the table the question of one's identity ("Am I in good standing?"), and replace it with the question of the relationship itself ("Are we in good standing with respect to everything else?"). They remind the accuser of the broader world of ethics, rules, and conventions in which life is carried out. In this respect, justifications can have the effect of modifying the relationship and the identities of the members. For example, the justification of "freedom" often has the effect of distancing participants in a love relationship and possibly destroying the definition of the bond. In apologizing, excusing and justifying we create the kinds of relationship in which we live.

Reflection

I have found so much of the work in this chapter intellectually exciting and personally useful – liberating, practical, generative – that I have written without much critical reflection. There is much that can be said in this regard, but perhaps the most important for me is the unfortunate tendency toward *linguistic reductionism*. This relentless foregrounding of discourse blurs the significance of the background – from whence it derives its potency. Here I am referring, first, to the scarcity of attention in this analysis to *non-verbal signals* – facial expressions, gaze, gestures, posture and the like. How words function in a relationship depends so very much on the way they are embodied. I had a friend who could tell me things about myself I did not want to hear, but because of his warm smile and soft voice, I could listen without resentment. Second, I have said almost nothing about what we might call the *material context*. My clothing, for example, can add or subtract significance from my words; so can the object in my hands (a bouquet of flowers, a book, a knife), the space in which we talk (a classroom, a pub, a forest), or the shape of the weather (bright sun, rain, a snowstorm). All impart or deny significance. Finally, the focus on discourse suppresses the importance of the *communication medium.* Wedding vows communicated by telephone or e-mail would scarcely count as serious; the "power of the written word" depends importantly on its being written (as opposed, for example, to shouted over a loudspeaker, or uttered by a stranger on a street corner.) Or as the technology guru Marshal McLuhan once put it, "the medium is the message." So the bottom line for me is to underscore the limitations and partialities of all analyses. I think we gain most if we appreciate these analyses not as reports on objective truth, but as "frames" or "lenses" on our world – to shake us up, reconstruct, give further dimension, and open new vistas of action. There is always more to say – for which we should be thankful.

Notes

1 See for example Kessen, W. (1990) *The Rise and Fall of Development.* Worcester, MA: Clark University Press; Hazan, H. (1994) *Old Age, Constructions and Deconstructions.* Cambridge: Cambridge University Press. Shweder, R. (Ed.) (1998) *The Social Construction of Middle Age.* Chicago: University of Chicago Press; Gubrium, J., Holstein, J.A. and Buckholdt, D. (1994) *Constructing the Lifecourse.* Dix Hills, NY: General Hall; Rosenblatt, P.C. (1994) *Metaphors of Family Systems Theory.* New York: Guilford.

2 See for example Harré, R. (Ed.) (1986) *The Social Construction of Emotions.* Oxford: Blackwell; Coulter, J. (1979) *The Social Construction of Mind.* Totawa, NJ: Rowman and Littlefield; Graumann, C.F. and Gergen, K.J. (1996) *Historical Dimensions of Psychological Discourse.* New York: Cambridge University Press; Sarbin, T. (Ed.) (1984) *Narrative Psychology,* New York: Praeger; Said, E. (1979) *Orientalism.* New York: Random House; Sarbin, T.R. and Kitsuse, J.I. (Eds.) (1994) *Constructing the Social.* London: Sage.

3 See for example Lorber, J. and Farrell, S.A. (1991) *The Social Construction of Gender.* Thousand Oaks, CA: Sage; Kitzinger, C. (1987) *The Social Construction of Lesbianism.* London: Sage; Gergen, M.M. and Davis, S.N. (Eds.) (1997) *Toward a New Psychology of Gender.* New York: Routledge; Butler, J. (1990) *Gender Trouble: Feminism and the Subversion of Identity.* New York: Routledge; Tiefer, L. (1995) *Sex is Not a Natural Act.* Boulder, CO: Westview.

4 See for example Hacking, I. (1995) *Rewriting the Soul: Multiple Personality and the Sciences of Memory.* Princeton, NJ: Princeton University Press; Boyle, M. (1991) *Schizophrenia: A Scientific Delusion.* London: Routledge; Rose, N. (1990) *Governing the Soul.* London: Routledge; Gordon, R.A. (1990) *Anorexia and Bulimia, Anatomy of a Social Epidemic.* Cambridge, MA: Blackwell.

5 See for example Kleinman, A. (1988) *The Illness Narratives.* New York: Basic Books; Lorber, J. (1997) *Gender and the Social Construction of Illness.* Thousand Oaks, CA: Sage; Hartley, G.M. and Gregory, S. (Eds.) (1991) *Constructing Deafness.* London: Pinter; Clay, C.J. (1995) *The Social Construction of AIDS.* Sheffield: Sheffield City Polytechnic; Frank, A.W. (1995) *The Wounded Storyteller.* Chicago: University of Chicago Press.

6 See for example Jenkins, P. (1994) *Using Murder: The Social Construction of Serial Homicide.* New York: A. de Gruyter; Hutson, S. and Liddiard, M. (1994) *Youth Homelessness: The Construction of a Social Issue.* Houndemills, UK: Macmillan;

Goode, E. (1994) *Moral Panics: The Social Construction of Deviance*. Cambridge, MA: Blackwell; Atkinson, J.M. (1977) *Discovering Suicide: Studies in the Social Organization of Sudden Death*. London: Macmillan.

7   See for example Bond, G.C. and Gilliam, A. (1994) *The Social Construction of the Past: Representation as Power*. London: Routledge; Barrett, E. (Ed.) (1992) *Sociomedia: Multimedia, Hypermedia, and the Social Construction of Knowledge*. Cambridge, MA: MIT Press; McCormick, C. (1995) *Constructing Danger: The Mis/representation of Crime in the News*. Halifax. NS: Fernwood.

8   Lakoff, G. and Johnson, M. (1980) *Metaphors We Live By*. Chicago: University of Chicago Press.

9   Spence, D. (1987) *The Freudian Metaphor*. New York: Norton.

10   Ibid., p. 7.

11   Ibid., p. 8.

12   See Bruner, J. and Feldman, C.F. (1990) Metaphors of consciousness and cognition in the history of psychology. In D. Leary (Ed.) *Metaphors in the History of Psychology*. New York: Cambridge University Press.

13   Gigerenzer, G. (1996) From tools to theories: discovery in cognitive psychology. In C.F. Graumann and K.J. Gergen (Eds.) *Historical Dimensions of Psychological Discourse*. New York: Cambridge University Press.

14   Ibid., p. 36.

15   Averill, J.R. (1990) Inner feelings. In Leary (Ed.) *Metaphors in the History of Psychology*; Gergen, K.J. (1995) Metaphor and monophony in the twentieth-century psychology of emotions. *History of the Human Sciences*, 8, 1–23.

16   Ricoeur, P. (1981) *Hermeneutics and the Human Sciences*. New York: Cambridge University Press, p. 278.

17   Bennett, L.W. and Feldman, M.S. (1981) *Reconstructing Reality in the Courtroom*. New Brunswick, NJ: Rutgers University Press.

18   Hardy, B. (1968) Towards a poetics of fiction: an approach through narrative. *Novel*, 2, 5–14.

19   This term derives from Aristotle's classic theories of narrative, in which he distinguishes between the comedy and the romance on the grounds of their specific content. However, because both Aristotelian types share the same narrative form they are here allied.

20   Spence, D. (1982) *Narrative Truth and Historical Truth*. New York: Norton.

21   Ibid., p. 175.

22   Latour, L. and Woolgar, S. (1979) *Laboratory Life: The Social Construction of Scientific Facts*. Beverly Hills, CA: Sage.

23   See for example, Potter, J. (1996) *Representing Reality*. London: Sage.

24   Goffman, E. (1959) *The Presentation of Self in Everyday Life*. Garden City, NY: Doubleday.

25   Sansom, W. (1956) *A Contest of Ladies*. London: Hogarth.

26   Goffman, *Presentation of Self*, p. 17.

27   Garfinkel, H. (1967) *Studies in Ethnomethodology*. Englewood Cliffs, NJ: Prentice-Hall.

28   Ibid., p. 42.

29   Willis, P. (1977) *Learning to Labour*. Westmead: Saxon House.

30   Ibid., p. 11.

31   Ibid., pp. 12–13.

32   Ibid., pp. 23–4.

33   Ibid., pp. 15–16.

34 Scott, M.B. and Lyman, S.M. (1968) Accounts. *American Sociological Review*, 33, 46–62.
35 Sacks, H. (1992) *Lectures on Conversation* (2 volumes, Ed. G. Jefferson). Oxford: Blackwell.
36 For a classic overview of these myriad forms of excuse and justification see Semin, G. and Manstead, A.S.R. (1983) *The Accountability of Conduct: A Social Psychological Analysis*. London: Academic Press.

Further Resources

General

Van Dijk, T.A. (Ed.) (1985) *Handbook of Discourse Analysis*, vols. I–IV London: Academic Press.
Van Dijk, T.A. (Ed.) (1997) *Discourse as Structure and Process*. London: Sage.

On Metaphor

Lakoff, G. and Johnson, M. (1980) *Metaphors We Live By*. Chicago: University of Chicago Press.
Leary, D. (1990) *Metaphors in the History of Psychology*. New York: Cambridge University Press.
Olds, L.E. (1992) *Metaphors of Interrelatedness*. Albany, NY: State University of New York Press.
Soyland, A.J. (1994) *Psychology as Metaphor*. London: Sage.

On Narrative

Gergen, M.M. (in press) *Impious Improvisations*. Thousand Oaks, CA: Sage.
Hinchman, L.P. and Hinchman, S.K. (Eds.) (1997) *Memory, Identity, Community: The Idea of Narrative in the Human Sciences*. Albany, NY: State University of New York Press.
Josselson, R. and Lieblich, A. (Eds.) (1993) *The Narrative Study of Lives*, V.1. Thousand Oaks, CA: Sage.
Rosenwald, G. and Ochberg, R. (Eds.) *Telling Lives*. New Haven: Yale University Press.
Sarbin, T.R. (1986) *Narrative Psychology, The Storied Nature of Human Conduct*. New York: Praeger.

On Rhetoric

Billig, M. (1996) *Arguing and Thinking, A Rhetorical Approach to Social Psychology*. Cambridge: Cambridge University Press.
McClosky, D.N. (1985) *The Rhetoric of Economics*. Madison, WI: University of Wisconsin Press.
Myerson, G. (1994) *Rhetoric, Reason and Society*. London: Sage.
Simons, H.W. (Ed.) (1989) *Rhetoric in the Human Sciences*. London: Sage.
Simons, H.W. (Ed.) (1990) *The Rhetorical Turn, Invention and Persuasion in the Conduct of Inquiry*. Chicago: University of Chicago Press.

On Discourse Pragmatics

Antaki, C. (Ed.) *Analyzing Everyday Explanation: A Case: A Casebook of Methods.* London: Sage.

Buttny, R. (1993) *Social Accountability in Communication.* London: Sage.

Coulter, J. (1979) *The Social Construction of Mind.* London: Macmillan.

Coupland, N. and Nussbaum, J.F. (Eds.) (1993) *Discourse and Lifespan Identity.* Newbury Park, CA: Sage.

Edwards, D. and Potter, J. (1992) *Discursive Psychology.* London: Sage.

Harré, R., Brockmeier, J. and Muhlhausler, P. (1999) *Greenspeak: A Study of Environmental Discourse.* London: Sage.

Hazan, H. (1994) *Old Age, Constructions and Deconstructions.* Cambridge: Cambridge University Press.

Lupton, D. and Barclay, L. (1997) *Constructing Fatherhood.* London: Sage.

Potter, J. (1996) *Representing Reality, Discourse, Rhetoric and Social Construction.* London: Sage.

Wagner-Pacifici, R. (1994) *Discourse and Destruction.* Chicago: University of Chicago Press.

Wetherell, M. and Potter, J. (1992) *Mapping the Language of Racism: Discourse and the Legitimation of Exploitation.* London: Harvester Wheatsheaf.

Wilkinson, S. and Kitzinger, C. (Eds.) (1995) *Feminism and Discourse, Psychological Perspectives.* London: Sage.

4

HORIZONS OF HUMAN INQUIRY

> Extricating ourselves from the debilitating pessimism accompanying
> the failure of modernist straight-line trajectories seems to involve
> some creative wandering . . . This means reenchanting, redoing, and
> reenlightening the fields of inquiry we have inherited from the past.
>
> Barbara Maria Stafford, *Good Looking: Essays on the Virtue of Images*

Recently I received a request from a top administrator at my school for a
brief description of "my program of research." Here was an unremarkable
request. Over and above our teaching, all of us in the sciences are expected
to have research programs. Our *raison d'être* is to accumulate new knowledge, and there are recognized methods, procedures, and publishing
outlets for achieving this goal. At least, this was my world prior to social
constructionism. Now the request left me lost in reverie. What now is a
"program of research," "the nature of knowledge," "an objective method"
or a "scientific report?" These are not easy questions, and there are no
definitive answers. However, constructionist dialogues do raise two significant challenges. First, if we abandon our commitment to a tradition in
which systematic methods are supposed to grind out truth like so many
sausages, then what is to be done? What can we justifiably carry with us
from this tradition? Second, what new doors are opened for the constructionist? Already we have glimpsed the profusion of inquiry into discourse
and its societal implications. However, are such efforts sufficient? What
other lines of exploration are opened by constructionist dialogues?

These questions frame the content of this chapter. First we shall take a
closer look at the tradition of empirical research within the human sciences. We shall have a look at constructionist critiques of its central
assumptions, and thereby open the door to alternative ventures. The
remainder of the chapter will explore some of these new vistas. First we
shall consider new forms of inquiry into contemporary societal life, ways
of exploring human action in today's world. We shall then turn to inquiry
that illuminates our present condition by probing its contrasts, namely in
other cultures and historical climes. In this case we shall again return to
the topic of the self.

Empirical Research in Question

Traditional research in the human sciences is at one with the tradition of Western modernism, and is heavily reliant on the network of interlocking assumptions treated in Chapter 1. Recall the emphasis on the individual knower, the promise of objective truth, and progress through research. The phrase *empirical research* means literally to be "guided by experience" in a re/searching of the world. In this light, consider some of the chief criteria of research excellence in the empiricist tradition; consider too the constructionist critique.

Remain dispassionate: The aim of good empirical research is to reflect the world as it is. Thus, the scientist must experience the world directly; biases should not be allowed to creep in to cloud one's observations. Scientists with emotional feelings toward the subjects under study, strong ethical or political motives, or deep religious interests are under suspicion. The scientist must keep a dispassionate distance between self and subject.

The constructionist replies: Scientists seldom carry out research for no reason; typically they have investments in some vision of the good, some benefit that will derive from their work. These investments enter into the research at every point, from the words selected to frame the problem to the description of the subjects' actions. It is disingenuous to cloak these investments in the language of neutrality. Even when such investments are unclear, scientific explanations can have significant societal consequences – for good or ill; the mantle of value neutrality blinds scientists to such effects. And finally, what are the societal effects of this quest for dispassion? What is it for professionals to inform the world that we know most about each other when we care the least, when we are cool and distant? Is this a good model for our relations with each other?

Control the conditions: Most empirical research is based on a model of cause/effect. For every event there are preceding causes. Thus, in the human sciences all human actions can, in principle, be traced to antecedent conditions (environmental, psychological, hereditary, etc.) An effective program of research will give an increasingly precise account of the specific conditions giving rise to specific actions. Such precision is most likely when the scientist can gain control of the antecedent conditions. With control of the antecedents, the scientist can systematically vary conditions and observe the variation in consequences. To systematically control the antecedents and observe the consequences is the basis of the experimental method. Experimentation is said to be the most effective methodology for tracing causal sequences.

The constructionist replies: The idea of cause/effect is a social construction; "causes" and "effects" are not located in nature but "read into" observations. Similarly, to divide the world into precise segments – "events," "stimulus conditions," "actions" – is again an *a priori* commitment, a fore-structure of understanding as opposed to a derivative from the world as it is. And the societal consequences of such a commitment are scarcely neutral. If the cause/effect model becomes accepted as truth, then we foreclose on the concept of human agency along with the humanist tradition which it supports. People are by implication reduced to robots – of no intrinsic value and with little capacity for creative deliberation. It is not that constructionism holds agency to be true, but there are very good reasons for nurturing this vulnerable tradition.[1] Further, to echo earlier concerns, what is it for professional scientists to inform the society that the most effective means of gaining knowledge of others is to manipulate conditions and observe their responses? Would we wish to live with others oriented in this way? Finally, when scientists do secure results through this means, the findings are chiefly of value to those in power. If I carry out research to demonstrate what kinds of television ads are most effective in boosting sales, it is the large corporation that can best make use of the results. Controlled research too often benefits those in a position to control.[2]

Convert observations to numerals: Empirical researchers typically view verbal languages as clumsy devices for capturing the nuances of observation. If accounts of the world can be converted to a system of numbers, high precision can be achieved. For example, we can move from rough concepts like "more" and "less" to fine gradients of change. Numbers also represent the most neutral language of description. Unlike many theoretical terms they do not carry subtle connotations of good and bad. And, of prime importance, when observations are converted to numerals, we open the way for sophisticated statistical analysis. With a high degree of confidence we can estimate the strength and reliability of cause/effect relations. Fortified by statistical results we can begin to make reliable predictions of the future.

The constructionist replies: When our language of description is converted to numbers, we do not thereby become more precise. Numbers are no more adequate "pictures of the world" than words, music or painting. They are simply a different translation device. This translation device also throws out most of what we hold to be valuable or significant about persons. To learn of a friend who has been raped or robbed is deeply engaging; we are moved and motivated to action; when such events are converted to crime statistics we are removed from the scene, distanced from those we care about. As one research participant remarked, "Statistics are human beings with the tears wiped off."[3] Further, statistical language is an expert language, and those who speak it can use it in many subtle and ingenious ways. When the truth is announced to the public in this language, those without expertise are left voiceless. Because they cannot discern the manipulations necessary to produce a given result, they cannot raise questions. Statistics, then, often function as silencing devices.

Search for *the* answer: Because of its realist commitment to one objective world, empirical research strives to reveal the one true answer to any question. Good science will replace mixed opinion with the single, clear solution. It is the investigator's task to winnow through the competing claims to determine what is truly the case.

The constructionist replies: Whatever the nature of the world, there is no single array of words, graphs, or pictures that is uniquely suited to its portrayal. Further, each construction has both potentials and limits, both scientifically and in terms of societal values. Thus, in its efforts to abandon all voices save one, there is an enormous suppression of potential. And when it is the investigator's voice that will finally reign supreme, the voices of all those under study are silenced.

Separate truth from practice: It is the aim of empirical research to produce empirically grounded theories of broad scope. The highest ambition is to render accounts of fundamental processes, thus offering theories of universal and transhistorical significance. Research on very specific practices is of little scientific value; it has little generality or durability. However, with fundamental processes revealed, practitioners can apply the knowledge under any and all conditions. With truth in hand, practice can proceed most effectively.

The constructionist replies: Data can never prove a theory true or false; whatever counts as data, and how it is credited, requires an interpretive forestructure. And because this interpretive stance is embedded within a particular community, the desire to generate universal and transhistorical truths constitutes a form of cultural imperialism. "My truth is truth for all." Finally, because theories are developed within a community of scientists, and gain their meaning within their particular forms of life, their applicability outside this community is problematic. There is no means of deriving from an abstract theory any application to a particularistic circumstance. An abstract theory of aggression, for example, never tells us what specific actions count as aggression. Any action can be constructed as aggression or not, depending on one's interpretive stance. Even speaking can be seen as aggression if you see it as dominating others.

Fruits of Empirical Research

Given these critiques of the empirical research tradition, what are we to conclude? Is this to argue for a wholesale abandonment of all experimentation, data collection, statistics, general theories and the like? Should we simply cast away the vast domain of empirical literature – journals, handbooks, monographs treating all aspects of human action? Not at all. Recall that it is not the aim of constructionism to establish the truth, against which all competitors – such as empiricism – are silenced. Constructionism makes no claims for its own truth, and all traditions or ways of life sustain certain values and useful intelligibilities. The empiricist tradition is no exception. There are, however, two major hopes that many constructionists share. First, it would be highly desirable to abandon the prefix "is true" typically attached to or implied by empirical research. If empiricist researchers could recognize their endeavors as historically and culturally located, and enter the world with contributions to a conversation as opposed to desires for the "the last word," there would be far less resistance to such work. Second, there is much to gain by removing the imperialist claims ("truth for all") and recognizing the very specific ways in which empirical research can be useful to the society. In particular:

Empirical findings can generate vivid illustrations of a perspective: While not themselves proving (or disproving) a theory, empirical results can provide powerful illustrations. They can inject life into an idea in a way that helps us to appreciate its significance and plausibility. In this sense good research in the human sciences can function like photographs in journalism or eye-witness accounts on television news. We are moved and absorbed. My introduction to Skinnerian theories of reinforcement was precisely of this sort. Although prepared to resist the theory on intellectual and political grounds, as I watched the professor use food pellets to bring the random movements of a pigeon under his complete control – speaking all the while of reinforcement contingencies, operant responses, and the like – I could not escape the power of that perspective. Its plausibility will never be lost from me.

Empirical findings can vitalize deliberation on moral and political issues: Debates cast in abstract theoretical terms often become dry and smack of irrelevance. However, empirical results can speak with a powerful voice; we can literally visualize the issues in "real life" terms. I think here of the classic laboratory experiments on obedience by Stanley Milgram.[4] Here an experimenter commanded subjects to deliver what appeared to be harmful electric shocks to another human being; although seemingly in deep turmoil about their actions, most of them continued to deliver the shocks even after it appeared that the victim was unconscious. The study proved nothing in general, but in the way the research echoed the atrocities of Nazi concentration camps, for example, it continues to incite discussion on the nature of responsibility and obedience.

Empirical findings can be used to generate useful predictions: Although much experimental research is limited to studying trivial behavior (for example, how people fill out questionnaires, press buttons, rate ambiguous situations), empirical methods can be used to generate predictions of broad social utility. So long as local agreements can be reached on what constitutes an event, how various actions are to be labeled, and moral and political implications, then traditional methods can be pressed into useful service. Just such methods are used by political parties to predict election returns, by insurance companies to gauge the probability of an auto accident, and by prison probation boards to determine probable recidivism. They can also be used to determine the mental health care needs of a community, or the likely success of students in an educational program. Again, the success of such studies does not thereby prove the descriptive and explanatory constructions of the findings; nor should the success of such research suppress dialogue on its societal implications (consider programs of school prognostication). However, such work does carve out an important place for empirical research in contemporary society.

Exploring Contemporary Life: the Qualitative Explosion

> Over the past two decades, a quiet methodological revolution
> has been taking place in the social sciences.

> Norman K. Denzen and Yvonne S. Lincoln, *Handbook of Qualitative Research*

We now find that the empirical tradition is not Science with a capital S, but rather, only one possible tradition among many, with both potentials and limitations. Because of the long-standing dominance of the empiricist tradition in the human sciences, this realization has been a breath of fresh air. It now operates as an invigorating invitation to new departures. Given the shortcomings of the tradition, can we envision new vistas of inquiry? What kinds of practices might be opened? Attempts to answer such questions are now everywhere in evidence; developments are mushrooming even as I write. Often these developments are indexed as *qualitative research*, drawing from an early distinction between quantitative (tough) and qualitative (tender) research. The binary itself grows from the soil of modernism (privileging the former as opposed to the latter term), and should ultimately be abandoned. By the same token, not all of the emerging departures solve all of the problems posed above. Each has its advantages; all have their limitations. Let me touch on three forms of research I find particularly exciting.

Narrative and the linking of lived worlds

> Pure unstoried action, pure unstoried existence in the present, is impossible.

> William Lowell Randall, *The Stories We Are*

The empiricist tradition honors the investigator who "discovers" or "reveals" the true nature of things. Resultingly, the investigator's voice dominates; all competitors are either suppressed or shown to be wrong. And too, the discourse of scientific description is that of the profession, a "sacred" discourse as opposed to the "profane" language of the street. As an alternative to the professional domination of the text, researchers now seek means of extending the platform, of admitting more voices to the conversation, and generating understanding through exposure to the first-hand accounts of people themselves. There are many variations on narrative based inquiry. Personal accounts have long been used by investigators wishing to avoid the manipulative and alienating tendencies of experimental research. Feminist works, such as Gilligan's *In a Different Voice*,[5] and Belenky et al.'s *Women's Ways of Knowing*,[6] are classics in the effective use of first-hand accounts. Other investigators have centered on autobiography, with the hope that people's life stories can illuminate the economic and political forces affecting a society; and still other researchers have used family stories, oral histories, journals, and letters.[7]

A subtle shift in the use of such writings has occurred as constructionist dialogues have become increasingly pervasive. Much of the early work used personal narratives for purposes of vindicating or illustrating an abstract idea. For example, abortion stories told by adolescent girls were used by Gilligan to make a virtually universal argument about women's moral decision making. The stories were employed in the service of scientific ends. However, more recent work tends to place greater emphasis on *emancipation* and *empathy* – either exploring narratives in order to generate alternatives to the status quo, or for generating a sense of first-hand understanding of the other. In both cases the research interests are tied more closely to the concerns of the society as opposed to intellectual issues.

A good illustration of the emancipatory interest at work is furnished by Mary Gergen's exploration of gendered narratives.[8] The research was stimulated by Mary's concern with the gender imbalance in the top echelons of business, government, the university and the like. If we live out our lives within narrative, she reasoned, is it possible that the dominant male narratives differ from those of women? Men may see themselves in a story where high level achievement is presumed ("What else is life all about?"), where women infrequently entertain such narratives for themselves ("Why should I want to do that?"). Do women need to expand the range of possible life stories? To explore these possibilities Mary examined autobiographies of men and women of high accomplishment. The results were unsettling: the successful men did describe their lives in far different terms, but with what seemed an inhumane narrowness. There was little concern for family, friends, emotions or their bodies. Consider:

- Richard Feynaman, Nobel prize-winning physicist reporting on his return to his work in Los Alamos after his wife's death:
  "When I got back (yet another tire went flat on the way), they asked me what happened. 'She's dead. And how's the progam going?' They caught on right away that I didn't want to moon over it."
- Lee Iacocca, CEO of Ford and Chrysler, after recalling his wife's death by heart attack:
  "Above all, a person with diabetes has to avoid stress. Unfortunately, with the path I had chosen to follow, this was virtually impossible."
- John Paul Getty describing the drilling of his first great oil-well:
  "The sense of elation and triumph . . . stems from knowing that one has beaten nature's incalculable odds by finding and capturing a most elusive (and often dangerous and malevolent) prey."

In contrast to the men, the women seemed more diffuse in their goals and more deeply wedded to their relations with others. Consider:

- The opera diva Beverly Sills talking about her early career:
  "I began reevaluating whether or not I truly wanted a career as an

opera singer. I decided I didn't . . . I was twenty-eight years old, and I wanted to have a baby."

- Tennis star Martina Navratilova describing her first win at Wimbledon:

"For the first time I was a Wimbledon champion, fulfilling the dream of my father many years before . . . I could feel Chris patting me on the back, smiling and congratulating me."

- Business executive Nien Cheng recounts her relations with a spider during her years as prisoner of the Cultural Revolution:

"My small friend seemed rather weak. It stumbled and stopped every few steps. Could a spider get sick, or was it merely cold . . . when I had to use the toilet I carefully sat well to one side so that I did not disturb its web."

So much more appealing were the women's stories, that Mary Gergen's concept of accomplishment began to shift. Why should women wish to appropriate more forthrightly directive narratives of success? The world might benefit far more from men expanding their repertoires of narrative connection, and for the emphasis on heroic accomplishment to be reduced to folklore.

Narrative research with a more empathic orientation often attempts to give voice to the unheard and marginalized in society, to generate understanding through sharing first-hand experience. People are encouraged to "tell their story" in their own terms, with the hope for increased appreciation and sensitivity.[9] A radical illustration is furnished by the development of *autoethnography*.[10] In autoethnographic research investigators weave their own stories into their work, revealing often intimate details that bear on the issues at stake. For example, in her essay "A Secret Life in a Culture of Thinness," Lisa Tillmann-Healy tells of the fears and the pain of growing up as a bulimic. Here she describes – using three narrative voices – her first attempt to tell a lover of her practices:

"Douglas?" *my strained voice calls out.*
"Umhmm . . ."
"There's something I need to tell you."
Probably not a good opening line.
"What's that?" he asks.
"I know I should have told you this before, and I hope you won't be upset that I didn't." Deep breath. Swallow.
It's okay. You're doing fine.
"What is it?" he asks, more insistent this time.
Looooong pause. "Lisa, what is it?"
He's getting nervous. Spit it out.
"Oh, god, Douglas. I don't . . . I . . . shit!"
You've come too far. Don't fall apart. Just say it, Lisa. Say the words.
"To one degree or another . . . I have been . . . bulimic . . ."
Fuck! I hate the sound of that word.

"... since I was 15."
It's out there. You said it.
Douglas asks several questions about who else knows of the problem, and then queries,
"Well, how bad is it now?"
"It's been much worse."
"That's not what I asked."
"It's not that bad."
Liar.
"Have you done it since you met me?"
If you only knew.
"A couple of times, but I don't want you to be concerned."
Oh, please. Please be concerned.
"You must know what that does to your body."
Believe me, I know. I know everything.
"I'm really glad you told me," he says as I start to cry.
"I love you, Lisa. Tell me how I can help you. Please."
You just did. You can't imagine how much.
He pulls me close, stroking my hair until I go to sleep.
I am 22 years old.

In these lines the writer draws the reader into the experience as lived, revealing bulimia from the inside; she also gives hope to others in this situation. And, by discussing her experiences in the context of the "culture of thinness," she helps us to see her particular problem as an outgrowth of our culture. At this point we must also ask about our own part in maintaining this culture. The common prejudice against fatness furnishes the supportive chorus for the anorexic.

Collaborative Inquiry

Empiricist research typically separates the investigator from the subjects of study. The subjects' lives are revealed to the investigator, but the investigator remains distant and opaque to the subjects. The investigator uses the data for his/her professional purposes; the subjects' desires are largely irrelevant. Subjects' actions are treated as predetermined (caused by antecedents), while the investigator appears as self-determining. One alternative to this orientation is to join with subjects to carry out research collaboratively. The attempt is to join together in achieving mutual goals, and in this way subjects reveal themselves for purposes they value. They help to determine the research directions, and thus retain their agency. Collaborative inquiry may take many forms; there are no rules because each form will depend on the conjoint aims and hopes of the participants. In one case, for example, mid-life women joined together with a psychologist to discuss the conventional construction of menopause and its relevance (or irrelevance) in their lives;[11] in other instances therapists have joined with their clients in writing professional papers about their particular problems and the efficacy (or inefficacy) of therapy;[12] and in still other instances, feminist scholars have worked with women on the possibility of reconstructing the meaning of emotion for more productive purposes.[13]

One impressive example of collaborative inquiry is contained in Patti Lather and Chris Smithies work *Troubling the Angels*. The volume is the result of their collaboration with 25 women with HIV/AIDS. The work emerged over a period of several years in which the women met to discuss their personal lives, common problems, and the potential of making their insights available to others. The hopes were not only to use the interchange itself for mutual support, a way of giving meaning to life under continuous threat; but ultimately to provide support and information to other women with HIV/AIDS, along with their friends and families, and to inspire them to advocacy. The work itself offers a fascinating, multi-vocal pastiche. Most prominently are the voices of the women themselves. For example, Linda B tells one of the groups:

> I'm more alone now than I've probably ever been in my whole life. Some of it is self inflicted; a lot of it is the fear of being rejected. I'm better off being by myself alone and being sad, rejection is the hardest thing a person has to go through.

Lori immediately responds:

> I think it is possible to have relationships. When you're ready, you take a chance on somebody.[14]

Following is a lengthy discussion in which the women share stories and insights on how to tell someone you are infected, starting relationships, safe sex and the like. The participants learn and share experiences on possibilities, dangers, and ways to go on.

In addition to these voices, both the investigators contribute their own feelings, doubts, and hopes to the mix, sometimes revealing personal issues, at others theoretical insights. Also included is relevant scientific information, statistics and research reports on HIV. Finally, in a self-reflexive mode, participants look back on their work and comment on its successes and failures. Researchers in this case don't have the last word. They work together with the research participants to generate a multi-hued world of possibilities.

Action Research: Social Change in Motion

> Research and action, even though analytically distinguishable,
> are inextricably intertwined.
>
> William Torbert, *Creating a Community of Inquiry*

Empiricist research typically conveys an aura of value neutrality, misleadingly suggesting that its outcomes are free of moral or political investment. The contrary to such disingenuousness is to wear one's values on one's sleeve, to carry out research that celebrates its political agenda. Perhaps the most visible research of this kind is called *participatory action research*. For many, action research sprang to life in the political storms of the 1960s; however it is a movement of many hues – with different emphases and ideological interests across various nations and ethnicities.[15] There is universal agreement among action researchers that it must be collaborative. The ultimate aim of the researcher is to empower those with whom he/she works to improve their condition. At the same time, the researcher typically enters the collaboration with particular political ideals or goals; the collaboration is typically intended to further this agenda. Or in Fals-Borda's terms, "This experiential methodology emphasizes the acquisition of serious and reliable knowledge upon which to construct power, or countervailing power, for the poor, oppressed and exploited groups and social classes."[16]

To illustrate, a group of African descendants in the community of Villarrica in rural Colombia had become increasingly dependent on electrical power for maintaining their way of life.[17] However, during a period of economic decline community members began to find their electrical bills altered in ways that favored the public service utility responsible for their electricity. Individual complaints to the company were typically ignored, and the utility's demands for payment were accompanied by threats of cutting off electricity. Feelings of frustrated exploitation and hopelessness were rampant in the community. With the assistance of action oriented organizations from outside, a Villarrica Users Committee was formed. This group initiated a series of community-wide meetings in which people could give voice to their frustrations, and begin to generate a sense of solidarity. Further, these meetings were used to collect stories that detailed the picture of exploitation. A grassroots initiative was then formed to collect copies of individual bills for purposes of documentation. With additional assemblies a strategy for action was developed. The community demanded that the public service utility negotiate, and when this demand was backed up by a threat from the community to pay no more bills, meetings began. The ultimate result was not only a vast improvement in the service, but the creation of a politically energized grassroots democracy.

These adventures – into narrative expression, collaborative inquiry, and action research – only sample the explosion in research practices of recent decades. Guides to additional work are included in the resources listed at the end of the chapter. However, realize that these are primarily forms of inquiry into the here and now of societal life. We turn now to additional work that plays a significant role in constructionist inquiry, in this case however, exploring life in other times and cultures. To place this inquiry more squarely into our discussion, we shall focus on the construction of the self.

Historical and Cultural Exploration: the Self in Question

How do you really feel about me? Do you remember the night? What are you thinking about? How much do you want the job? What is your opinion on this? What was your real intention?

Such questions are the stuff of everyday life, unremarkable to be sure, but so much depends on how we answer – what we say about our feelings, thoughts, opinions, and the like. So why do we say what we do when asked such questions? Why do we answer in one way as opposed to another? Perhaps you want to respond: "For the most part I try to answer as genuinely as I can – to say what I am feeling, or thinking, or what I want." This is a reasonable answer by contemporary conventions, but consider some of the problems raised in Chapter 1: If you try to answer "genuinely" how do you know what you truly feel, or think, or want? How can you "look inward" to find an answer? With what sensory device would you be looking – an inner eye? And what would you be looking at? What is the size of a thought, the color of a want, or the shape of an opinion? How would you recognize an "intention" as opposed to a "need," or distinguish between a "feeling" and an "opinion?" And if you could accomplish such feats of recognition, what language would you use to report on them? A private language will not do under these circumstances. No one would understand if you said you felt "fluzzy" or "mumby" for example. You must necessarily use the common language to be understood. But why should we suppose that the common language of "feelings," "opinions," or "wants" is an accurate picture of our inner states? Talking about our inner states is not a matter of accurate reporting. If someone asks "How do you feel about me?," there is no looking inward to locate the answer.

An appreciation of why we might answer these questions as we do began to emerge in the preceding chapter. Here we found it possible to locate both questions and answers within conventions of discourse. We explored the use of metaphor and traditions of narrative, along with rhetorics of reality-making. And we took account of the micro-social processes in which personal identity is contested, negotiated, and defended. This discussion of self was embedded in a larger concern. As argued, one of the chief aims of constructionist scholarship is reflexive and emancipatory. By reflecting critically on our taken-for-granted worlds, and the way in which our lives are affected by these constructions, we may be freed to consider alternatives. This same emancipatory quest serves as a stimulus to additional kinds of inquiry. Rather than focusing on the conventions of the here and now – how we currently talk and act – we turn to the historical and cultural context in which these conventions are embedded. To appreciate that which differs temporally and geographically from our taken-for-granted commonplaces is to generate the possibility of change and/or renewal. Let us first consider the historical lodgment of the self, and then turn to cultural considerations.

Historical Vicissitudes of the Self

> Each cultural form, once it is created, is gnawed
> at varying rates by the forces of life.
>
> Georg Simmel, *The Conflict in Modern Culture*

We have already glimpsed the way in which contemporary beliefs in the self-contained individual took shape within Western history. Largely born of Enlightenment critiques of totalitarian regimes – crown and cross – we have come to place great value on the rational, self-directing individual – bounded and autonomous, integrated and self-knowing, and with conscience and emotions rooted in the natural order. Although we found such a conception to be deeply problematic, to it we must largely credit our institutions of democracy, public education, and justice. Regardless of our evaluation, we must view this conception as a cultural achievement. That is, this conception of the self is not guaranteed by "what there is." Required is intense effort – dialogue, negotiation, and poetic invention on the one hand, and argument, devaluation, and suppression on the other. Constructed realities are always born of a price and precariously situated. The present chapter is scarcely the place for a full review of the self in Western history.[18] However, to appreciate the ways in which constructions of the self develop, change, and succumb over time, let us focus on two particular inquiries: bodily sensation, and human development. These will also serve to illustrate the significance of historical work in a constructionist frame.

SENSING THE WORLD – OR MAKING SENSE?

> The eye, after all, is not only a part of the brain, it is a part of tradition.
>
> E.W. Eisner, *Objectivity in Educational Research*

What is clearer than the fact of our five senses: sight, smell, taste, sound, and touch? Is it not through our physiologically based sensory capacities that the world makes itself known to us? But is this so clear? Doesn't such a view repeat all the problems of dualism – with an internal mind separated from an external world – discussed in the first chapter? If we lived a dualistic existence how would we ever know – or even guess – that there was an "external world?" We should simply live in our own private experience, confronting "one damn thing after another." Consider an alternative possibility: what if "sensing" is not the transfer of information from an external world (via the nervous system) to an internal one, but a communally constituted action? By this I mean an action that has been created as meaningful within a cultural tradition. To illustrate, there is nothing about fermented grape juice that would seem to draw people naturally to it. For many people the taste is indeed disgusting.

However, consider the small community of professional wine tasters – those who evaluate the qualities of fine wines. This community possesses its own vocabulary of taste, a vocabulary that would scarcely be understood by the uninitiated. The wine does not, then, simply demand a response from the senses. Rather, the professionals are engaging in a communally shaped act of evaluation. Surely the wine is an important component; so is one's body. But the pleasureful taste is a byproduct of a social tradition.

This strand of argument opens a fascinating line of inquiry into the historical lodgment of the senses, how people in various historical eras "experience" their worlds. Moreover, by understanding the senses in terms of their communal base we are invited to consider their social function, how the dimensions of sensory experience are suffused with values, politics, social class, religion, and so on – why it is that a rose is not a rose is not a rose. Alain Corbin's *The Foul and the Fragrant* was one of the first significant explorations of this kind.[19] As Corbin's study of French history indicates, the smells of individual persons was a minor aspect of social life until roughly the eighteenth century. At this time the scientific study of gasses (vapors and associated odors) grew into prominence. Of particular interest were the smells given off by decomposing matter (or petrification). As the theories of Pasteur later suggested the air is a carrier of bacteria. Over time, then, Corbin argued, illness and death became associated with particular smells and these smells carried the threat of affliction. As the nineteenth century approached, systematic attempts were made both to rid cities like Paris of putrid materials (feces, slaughterhouse leavings, garbage) and to eliminate the associated smells as well.

On the social level, there were two important results of these developments. First, on the day-to-day level odorlessness became a positive value; the lack of odor signified purity and cleanliness. This attitude carries down to the present, and sparks the pervasive use of body deodorants. Further, the smell of musk and other animal secretions used to make perfumes moved into a negative register. Their smell came to be vile and intrusive. Indeed, musk has only slowly made its way back to popularity within the present century. However, you may appreciate the point by considering the way the once welcomed smells of cigarette and pipe tobacco have now become "stenches."

A second result of bacteria theory was broader in social implication. Because putrification was so often located within the poorer sections of the city, there was an increased sensitivity among the wealthier classes to the smell of the poor. The bourgeois, the peasant, and the courtesans, for example, were thought to emit different kinds of smells. As Corbin writes, "The absence of intrusive odor enabled the [bourgeois] individual to distinguish himself from the putrid masses, stinking like death, like sin, and at the same time implicitly to justify the treatment meted out to them. Emphasizing the fetidity of the laboring classes, and thus the danger of infection from their mere presence, helped the bourgeois to sustain his self-indulgent, self-induced terror, which dammed up the expression of remorse."[20] Remnants of this posture remain today. The conclusion slowly emerging in such work is that the human senses are deeply social in character. There is little of "human nature" that is outside relationship, outside culture.

THE PROBLEM OF PAIN   You may well doubt this last conclusion. After all, regardless of the arguments there seem to be some psychological states that are simply there, beyond interpretation. And surely the most compelling of these is pain. Who would doubt the universality of agony at the touch of a torch to the skin, or the dentist's drill to a raw nerve? In her provocative book *The Body in Pain*, Elaine Scarry proposes that pain is a universal, prior to and beyond social construction. For Scarry, "Physical pain does not simply resist language but actively destroys it, bringing about an immediate reversion to a state anterior to language, to the sounds and cries a human being makes before language is learned."[21]

Yet, it is just this sort of essentialism that stimulates the constructionist scholar. Is pain simply pain, regardless of history or culture? Here the constructionist first looks to variations in the construction of pain in contemporary culture. For example, research suggests significant variations in the constitution of pain across different ethnic groups; Italian and Jewish patients, for example, often evidence far more pain than the more stoic New England Yankee culture.[22] Such variations should come as little surprise when we consider the joy that boxers, American football players, and masochists find in receiving blows from which most of us would recoil in agony. Historical inquiry permits the same conclusion. Prior to the development of modern anesthetics, many people were able to consciously endure the repair of severe wounds and extensive surgical procedures. In medieval Christendom, pain was often welcomed as an expression of religious devotion. To be in pain was to absolve oneself of sin and to approach the suffering of Christ on the cross.[23]

This view of pain as culturally constructed has profound potential for the common experiences of daily life. Pain is a common feature of cultural life; the management of pain is one of the central challenges of the medical and therapeutic professions. From the constructionist perspective our experiences of pain are not simply given – as objects to endure. Rather, pain requires interpretation, and the way we subsequently live our lives depends significantly on this interpretation. For example, in his far-reaching work *The Wounded Storyteller*, Arthur Frank reports on the experience of serious illness – including his own cancer.[24] As Frank proposes, there are several major narratives we can tell when we are suffering. There is the *restitution narrative*, in which we see our bodies as temporarily disabled, and our major task is to return the body to its normal state of well-being. This narrative gives us purpose and direction, but it creates a sense of pain as a noxious attack. In the *chaos narrative*, the illness makes no sense – it was not anticipated, and there is no direction to be taken. All one can do in this case is listen and be respectful of the teller. The third alternative, preferred by Frank, is the *quest narrative*. Here one understands suffering as a teacher; through this experience one gains a more profound grasp of the nature of things – life, love, and nature. Through suffering, one acquires the sense of personal morality, and becomes one whose testimonies can teach and guide others. Pain as an experience is significantly refigured, it redeems rather than attacks.

THE PAST NOW SPEAKING US: THE DEVELOPING CHILD   The taken-for-granted world of today echoes the voices of previous generations – often far removed. Consider in this respect the commonly accepted idea of human development. Parents are typically concerned about the development of their children, teachers about the ways they can help children to grow mentally, and indeed most of us in terms of whether we are fulfilling our potential. This same image of the individual as moving from a primitive or ground-zero state, to a condition of full maturity, rationality, or actualization also pervades the psychological sciences. Psychologists have been deeply engaged in the task of characterizing, documenting, and measuring the stages of child, adolescent and adult development. What is "the path of normal development;" how can therapists help people realize their potentials; what conditions deter development? All are major research questions.

Yet, why do we presume there is human development – a direction or a goal toward which we are travelling? We cannot simply "see" development occurring in the burst of a child's momentary actions. Doubts grow when you realize that the idea of development approximates a narrative – and specifically, the progressive narrative form (see pp. 70–71) in which there is continuous movement toward a valued goal. The story we tell about our children – and indeed ourselves – over time seems to be one in which we are (or should be) moving toward some ideal. But why this narrative in particular? It is not one shared by the Hindus, for example, who hold human life to be in a continuous state of repetition. Nor was it a significant feature of early Greek culture, when historical narratives – either personal or cultural – were scarcely evidenced.

Several discerning scholars answer this question by locating the assumption of development in early Judaeo–Christian theology.[25] In particular, they see the biblical saga of creation, fall and redemption as the major source of our common beliefs today. This story is one in which God created the heavens and earth, culminating in the creation of the human being (Adam and Eve). They are perfect beings until they succumb to the temptation of evil, at which point they are cast from Eden into a state of sin, evil and suffering. In this sense they are at ground-zero, a state of nothingness, or emptiness. Yet, they must not remain so. Christ's birth is a sign that God has promised redemption for sin. They are not destined to remain in this degraded condition, but may become blessed. Notice, however, that the act of redemption itself is displaced into the future; it is something that must be achieved; we must demonstrate that we are worthy of redeeming. In effect, we are born into sin; it is our natural state. However, by living virtuous lives we approach a state of ultimate redemption. As this story becomes a cornerstone of religious belief, so does it inform us that our beginnings in infancy are meager, that life is a linear trajectory, and that with proper effort and support we may move toward a positive conclusion. In effect, our common conceptions today – indeed our practices of child rearing and psychological research – bear the faint echoes of ancient mythology.

In an interesting elaboration of this view, Suzanne Kirschner has explored the specific characteristics of recent psychoanalytic theories of development.[26] Here the strong emphasis is placed on the psychological problem confronted by the infant in separating from the mother. The developmental challenge is to leave the security of feeling "at one" with the nurturing agent, and developing a firm sense of self, autonomous and creative. This view cannot be derived from observation, argues Kirschner. Is it possible that it, too, has its roots in early religious beliefs? A possible answer is found in religious mysticism emerging several centuries after Christ's death (neo-Platonist), and later modified in nineteenth century romantic texts. In this branch of Christianity, Adam and Eve's fall from grace is equivalent to a break in a divine unity – man with God. The individual is now cast out, alone, helpless, dejected. Salvation is achieved through transcending this state, by re-establishing a connection with the Holy One – "a rebirth within the soul of the spark of God."[27] Indeed, it is this very achievement of "reunification at a higher level" that is evidenced in the psychoanalytic writings. As analysts propose, to achieve a full and creative sense of autonomy, the child must internalize the mother into itself, comprehend the mother as both distinct and yet retained within one's own being. The highest level of development entails estrangement as a prelude to reconciliation – first separation from and then reunification with mother (the Holy Unity). In spite of the attempt by psychoanalysts to claim they are a science as opposed to a religion, here we find that the line is quite blurred. To "develop" as human beings, we can scarcely escape the religious roots of Western culture.

Exploring Other Cultures, Understanding Our Own

> Every version of an "other" . . . is also the construction of a "self."
>
> James Clifford, *Writing Culture*

Some years ago I had the privilege of traveling in Morocco. Perhaps the most dramatic experiences there resulted from excursions into the Medinas of Marrakech and Fez. The Medina is the ancient quarter of the city, a complex tangle of narrow streets and walkways – open shops, unlighted dwellings, craftsmen, working children, open sewers, laden donkeys, exotic sounds and smells, and the continuous jostling on the crowded streets – all concatenating into an overwhelming sensory experience. For me this truly was a "foreign culture," and it was unceasingly fascinating. I was particularly interested in the fact of my own safety. I was clearly an alien in their midst – a literal infidel – carrying a camera that was probably worth a year's wages to many. And I was clearly unfamiliar with my surrounds, wandering, unsure of my direction. Why wasn't I robbed, or worse? Who would ever discover the crime; and would it even be a crime in their eyes? These musings then gave way to startling reflection: why did I find my safety such a matter of curiosity? What was this fact saying about me, and my home culture? Did it not suggest that I lived in a culture of pervasive distrust, where economic differences were resented, and where there was insufficient community to unite around a vision of the good?

It is just this form of reflection that constructionist inquiry is designed to encourage. Earlier we found that our explorations of the past can be used to draw us into deliberations on our present – helping us to assay our inheritance, consider its sustainability, and give us purchase on creating new futures. In a similar vein, explorations of other cultures draw us into questions of similarity and difference. We are fascinated by what we share, and the ways in which we are alien. However, all such distinctions are drawn from our own vernaculars, the conventions of construction with which we attempt to make sense of the other. And such distinctions are necessarily saturated with the values they sustain. Thus every telling of similarity and difference – every assay of the other – is not so much a reflection of the real as it is a reflection of our own modes of being. To read the other is to make manifest our own existence – how it is we construct the world and with what end. And herein lies opportunity to move beyond.

As in the case of historical scholarship, relevant research is voluminous. Let us narrow the focus again to the construction of selves, and particularly to the emotions.

EMOTIONALLY SPEAKING

> All you need is love.
>
> The Beatles

If queried about the most important things in life to you, chances are the emotions would play a major role. Many therapists, for example, treat our capacity to love as central to self-fulfillment; others propose that if we don't express our emotions – our anger and fear among them – our sense of well-being will suffer. As ethologists tell us, the emotions are basic to the make-up of the human species. Further, we are not the only animal species to inherit an emotional constitution. As Charles Darwin wrote confidently in his *The Expression of Emotions in Man and Animals*, "Even insects express anger, terror, jealousy, and love by their stridulation."[28]

This view of the emotions as "just natural" is thrown into question by constructionist inquiry. First consider the intellectual problems, and especially the attempts to identify the emotions over the centuries, to locate what kind and how many there are. For example, Aristotle identified *placability, confidence, benevolence, churlishness, resentment, emulation, longing,* and *enthusiasm,* as emotional states no less obvious than *anger* or *joy.* Yet, in their twentieth century studies, neither Sylvan Tomkins[29] nor Walter Izard[30] – both scientific experts – recognize these states as emotions. Thomas Aquinas believed *love, desire, hope,* and *courage* were all central emotions, but all these states go unrecognized in the recent theories of Tomkins and Izard. Thomas Hobbes identified *covetousness, luxury, curiosity, ambition, good naturedness, superstition,* and *will* as emotional states, but none qualifies as such in contemporary psychology. Tomkins and Izard agree that *surprise* is an emotion, a belief that would indeed puzzle most of their predecessors. However, where Izard believes *sadness* and *guilt* are major emotions, they fail to qualify in Tomkins' analysis; simultaneously, Tomkins sees *distress* as a central emotion, where Izard does not.

This kind of disagreement is not uninteresting. Why is it so difficult for expert scholars to reach agreement after centuries of study? Consider more carefully: how would you go about identifying an emotional state, or counting how many different kinds of emotions you possess? Rapidly you realize the dimensions of the enigma: how would we go about "looking inward," what would we be "looking at," and what sort of senses would be registering these states? These are the knotty questions of self-knowledge raised in the opening chapter. If we were left to identify our own psychological states it is not even clear that we would come up with the idea of emotion. Further, when we consider how we identify emotions in others – and how psychologists and biologists identify emotions in various creatures – we find they must rely on "expressions" or manifestations. Never do they confront "the real thing." Why should we, then, be so certain that there are indeed emotions inside people's heads or lodged in their biological make-up.

These are not merely academic questions. Emotion terms are socially and politically loaded. That is, such terms are used as subtle means of evaluation. We use them as if they describe actual events within the person, while their effect is often to evaluate the person. Consider but two ways in which this is so. Feminist scholars note the following cluster of common binaries in western culture:[31]

rational	emotional
cultured	natural
strong	weak
effective	ineffective
responsible	irresponsible

Notice two aspects of the binaries. First, the former term is often privileged over the latter. It is better to be rational than emotional. Second, the former term is more often associated with men than women. Although the linguistic terrain is far more complicated, these stereotypic ways of talking do seem to place women at a disadvantage, and they do so without our capacity to identify the actual existence of the states. Scholars also suggest that these discursive tendencies may reflect power differences; they suggest ways in which masters or colonizers characterize themselves as opposed to their servants or the colonized.[32] "We are natural, cultured and strong, while they are emotionally expressive and ineffectual." This explanation also accounts for a second common tendency, speaking of emotions as dangerous and combustible, as urges that must be kept in check. As commonly said, "You must get a grip on your emotions," or "Try to rise above those feelings." Within most professional circles, being known as a highly emotional person is usually a prelude to failure.

EMOTION IN CULTURAL CONTEXT   Given the problems of identifying the emotions, and given the political uses of emotion talk, we are prepared to appreciate emotion as a cultural construction. That is, we may understand emotion not as a feature of our biological make-up, a constitutional urge that drives our actions, but as a component of cultural life. The work of cultural anthropologists helps us to appreciate this possibility and its many implications. Scanning a broad sample of ethnographic work yields three broad conclusions.

1.   *Cultural variations are enormous*: Consider but two cases unfamiliar to us in the West:

(a) In the highlands of New Guinea, otherwise normal men in their mid-twenties may occasionally explode into patterns of "wild pig behavior." The "wild pig" will break into local dwellings, loot, shoot arrows at bystanders, and generally make an abysmal nuisance of himself. After several days he will disappear into the forest, where he destroys what he has taken (usually inconsequential objects.) Afterwards, he again enters the village, unable to recall his actions and seldom reminded by the villagers. If he returns to the village in his wild state, a ceremony is performed, one that resembles a ritual used to "redomesticate" actual pigs that have gone wild.

(b) In Southeast Asia, and most frequently in Malaysia, a native man may withdraw from the normal course of daily life, meditate for some time, and then suddenly leap up, grab a sword or knife, rush into the street and commence slaughtering any living creature – person or animal – unfortunate enough to be in the vicinity. The people flee, racing through the village with cries of warning – "amok, amok." When the individual who has "run amok" has completed his killing spree, he turns his weapon on himself and begins to stab and gash himself until he finally succumbs.[33]

2.   *Cross-cultural translations are troublesome*: Although we are inclined to see the above cases as demonstrating differences in emotion, cultural

study complicates the picture. Yes, we do recognize these as differences, but differences in what? Why the emotions, and not let's say, motivation, cognition or spirit? The problem is that we have no way of understanding how to translate across cultures, of knowing whether a smile or a frown, for example, mean the same thing in one culture as they do in another. Are emotions universal? Without the capacity to translate across cultures, we cannot answer.

A good illustration of the problem is furnished by Michelle Rosaldo's work among the Illongots, a group of hunters and gatherers in Northern Luzon in the Philippines.[34] For them a man is judged on the basis of his possession of *liget*. But what precisely is *liget*; do we possess such a state and simply call it something else? Consider: for the Illongots *liget* issues from the organ of the heart, and is equated with all that is vital, potent, energetic, and intense. *Liget* is the basis of violent action and confusion; it can be triggered by slights and insults. Yet, it is also the source of passivity and loss of will. None of this means that it is negatively evaluated; on the contrary, *liget* is highly desirable. It is the basis of concentration and industry, and perhaps most important, the primary motive for taking the heads of warring tribesmen. Following the head hunt, there is a great celebration in the tribe. So should you celebrate your *liget* or not? We shall return to this issue in a later discussion of hermeneutics (Chapter 6).

3. *Emotions are culturally constituted*: Realize one of the unsettling consequences of this last argument. If we cannot in principle translate emotion terms across cultural contexts, then how can we be certain that people in other cultures have emotions; or for that matter, how can we know that emotions exist within our own? The entire concept turns strange. As an alternative to identifying emotions as internal conditions of the mind, many anthropologists turn attention to the cultural constitution of meaningful action. Can we, they propose, describe for a Western audience (in this case) a composite of actions that we might index with the term emotion? To paraphrase, "We don't know what precisely goes on inside the head, but let us tell you about some forms of life that we in the West might call emotional." What we call emotions on this account are not so much possessions of individual minds, but forms of public performance specific to a given culture. We shall return to this way of conceptualizing mental states in Chapter 5. But a preliminary illustration will be helpful.

As a result of her field work on the small island of Ifaluk in the South Pacific, Catherine Lutz described a range of actions that we might call emotional, but would also be quite *unnatural* to us in the West. Among these "emotions" is *fago*. In certain respects *fago* seems akin to liking or love; "I *fago* him because he gives me things," "You *fago* someone because they do not misbehave," "You *fago* them because they are calm," Lutz was informed. At the same time, sexual relations are not contexts where *fago* is relevant. *Fago* is also a term that suggests pity; a person who is shamed by others or who has no kinfolk deserves *fago*. At the same time, the term suggests admiration; if someone acts in an exemplary, intelligent or leaderly way, they too deserve *fago*. Sometimes the term suggests grief, as islanders speak of *fago* when another is absent or dead. Yet, *fago* is not simply grief for a lost loved one, for it is also actively displayed in ongoing relations, particularly toward those who are weak or incapacitated. In this sense it seems more like compassion. Lutz goes on to speculate about the origins of this emotion. Rather than viewing it as genetically inherent – the universalizing view of the West – she turns to the environmental and social conditions that might favor *fago*-like actions. For example, *fago* is favored as a form of cultural life by virtue of the precarious interdependency of the Ifaluk people. The tiny atoll is threatened by typhoons; there is also over-population and scarcity; strong social ties are necessary for survival. It is *fago*, reasons Lutz, that facilitates this survival. "Food sharing, adoption, the treatment of visitors, relations between brothers and sisters, forms of and attitudes toward authority, and the system of health care are all examples of central features of everyday life that take their importance and character in part from the ideological charter provided by the concept of *fago*."[35] *Fago*, thus, is not just a word, it is an action fissured to an entire way of life.

Reflection

For me, the discussion of emotion in this chapter has special significance. I grew up an emotional realist; not only were the emotions very real "things" but they were among the most important things in my life. To feel was to be. When I was ten years old I was swept away by Southern Baptism, a passionate faith. We received periodic communion in which we were to symbolically drink Christ's blood and eat his flesh, a drama that for me was only slightly diminished by their materialization as grape juice and wafers. However, we were warned that we could not partake in this sacred rite unless we truly believed. But how was I to know whether I "truly" believed; what if I were fooling myself? Perhaps a budding empiricist, I presumed that my emotions wouldn't lie, and that while I waited for my turn at the altar I could measure my emotions by the amount of moisture my hands would deposit on "the glass of blood." This was an excruciating exercise, and reverberated down the years. For example, courting years were replete with the usual dramas and upheavals, and not infrequently I was asked "what I truly felt," "was I really in love." Panic. How could I tell; what evidence was trustworthy? My wife, Mary, finally taught me the living value of the constructionist perspective. "Saying 'I love you' is not about reporting on your internal condition," she pointed out. "It's a way of being with another person, and it's a good way of being." And so it is with the entire range of emotional performances; they are ways of being, historically provided ways of life. We need not measure them, wait for them to move us, or be concerned that we feel more than is "natural". Rather, like forms of dress or moves in a game or a dance, they are vocabularies of action, and life will be filled or emptied according to how we press them into action.

Notes

1 Slife, B.D. and Williams, R.N. (1995) *What's Behind the Research, Discovering Hidden Assumptions in the Behavioral Sciences*. Thousand Oaks, CA: Sage.
2 Argyris, C. (1980) *Inner Contradictions of Rigorous Research*. New York: Academic Press.
3 Linda B, as quoted in P. Lather and C. Smithies (1997) *Troubling the Angels: Women Living with HIV/AIDS*. Boulder, CO: Westview Press. p. xxvi.
4 Milgram, S. (1974) *Obedience to Authority*. New York: Harper & Row.
5 Gilligan, C. (1982) *In a Different Voice*. Cambridge, MA: Harvard University Press.
6 Belenky, M., Clinchy, B.M., Goldberger, J.N.R. and Tarule, J.M. (1986) *Women's Ways of Knowing*. New York: Basic Books.
7 See for example Bertaux, D. (1981) *Biography and Society*. Beverly Hills, CA: Sage.
8 Gergen, M.M. (1992) Life stories: pieces of a dream. In G. Rosenwald and R. Ochberg (Eds.) *Storied Lives*. New Haven, CT: Yale University Press.
9 Exemplary work includes Josselson, R. (1995) *Exploring Identity and Gender: The Narrative Study of Lives*. Thousand Oaks, CA: Sage; Rosenblatt, P.C., Karis, T.A. and Powell, R.D. (1995) *Multiracial Couples: Black and White Voices*. Thousand Oaks, CA: Sage.
10 Ellis, C. (1995) *Final Negotiations: A Story of Love, Loss, and Chronic Illness*. Philadelphia, PA: Temple University Press.
11 Gergen, M. (1999) *Impious Improvisations: Feminist Reconstructions in Psychology*. Thousand Oaks, CA: Sage.
12 cf. Karl, Cynthia, Andrew and Vanessa (1992) Therapeutic distinctions in an on-going therapy. In S. McNamee and K.J. Gergen (Eds.) *Therapy as Social Construction*. London: Sage.
13 Crawford, J., Kippax, S., Onyx, J., Gault, U., and Benton, P. (1992) *Emotion and Gender: Constructing Meaning from Memory*. London: Sage.
14 Lather and Smithies (1997) *Troubling the Angels*, p. 103.
15 See Further Resources for this chapter.
16 Fals-Borda, O. (1991) Some basic ingredients. In O. Fals-Borda and M.A. Rahman (Eds.) *Action and Knowledge*. New York: Apex. p. 3.
17 de Roux, G. (1991) Together against the computer: PAR and the struggle of Afro-Colombians for public services. In Fals-Borda and Rahman, *Action and Knowledge*.
18 See Further Resources.
19 Corbin, A. (1986) *The Foul and the Fragrant*. Cambridge, MA: Harvard University Press.
20 Ibid., p. 143.
21 Scarry, E. (1985) *The Body in Pain*. New York: Oxford University Press. p. 4.
22 Classic is the work of Zborowski, M. (1952) Cultural components in responses to pain. *Journal of Social Issues*, 8, 16–30. Also see Bates, M.S. (1996) *Biocultural Dimensions of Chronic Pain*. Albany, NY: State University of New York Press.
23 Cohen, E. (1993) Towards a history of physical sensibility: pain in the later

middle ages. Paper presented at the Israel Academy of Sciences and Humanities.

24 Frank, A. (1995) *The Wounded Storyteller*. Chicago: University of Chicago Press.

25 Kessen, W. (1990) *The Rise and Fall of Development*. Worcester, MA: Clark University Press; White, S. (1983) The idea of development in developmental psychology. In R. Lerner (Ed.) *Developmental Psychology: Historical and Philosophical Perspectives*. Hillsdale, NJ: Erlbaum.

26 Kirschner, S. (1996) *The Religious and Romantic Origins of Psychoanalysis*. New York: Cambridge University Press.

27 Ibid., p. 128.

28 Darwin, C. (1873) *The Expression of Emotions in Man and Animals*. New York: D. Appleton. p. 850.

29 Tomkins, S. (1962) *Affect, Imagery and Consciousness*, vol. 1. New York: Springer-Verlag.

30 Izard, W.E. (1977) *Human Emotions*. New York: Plenum.

31 cf. Shimanoff, S. (1993) The role of gender in linguistic references to emotive states. *Communication Quarterly*, 30, 174–179.

32 cf. Lutz, C.A. (1990) Engendered emotion: gender, power, and the rhetoric of emotional control in American discourse. In C.A. Lutz and L. Abu-Lughod (Eds.) *Language and the Politics of Emotion*. Cambridge: Cambridge University Press.

33 For further description see Averill, J. (1982) *Anger and Aggression*. New York: Springer-Verlag.

34 Rosaldo, M.Z. (1980) *Knowledge and Passion*. New York: Cambridge University Press.

35 Lutz, C.A. (1998) *Unnatural Emotions*. Chicago: University of Chicago Press. pp. 153–4.

Further Resources

On Problems of Empirical Research

Danziger, K. (1990) *Constructing the Subject: Historical Origins of Psychological Research*. Cambridge: Cambridge University Press.

Gergen, K.J. (1993) *Toward Transformation in Social Knowledge*, 2nd edn. London: Sage.

Slife, B.D. and Williams, R.N. (1995) *What's Behind the Research? Discovering Hidden Assumptions in the Behavioral Sciences*. Thousand Oaks, CA: Sage.

Alternative Practices of Inquiry

Denzin, N.K. and Lincoln, Y.S. (1994) *Handbook of Qualitative Research*. Thousand Oaks, CA: Sage.

Dunaway, D.K. and Baum, W.K. (Eds.) (1996) *Oral History*. Thousand Oaks, CA: AltaMira.

Ellis, C. and Bochner, A.P. (Eds.) (1997) *Composing Ethnography, Alternative Forms of Qualitative Writing*. Thousand Oaks, CA: Sage.

Fals-Borda, O. and Rahman, M.A. (Eds.) (1991) *Action and Knowledge: Breaking the Monopoly with Participatory Action Research*. New York: Apex.

Gergen, M., Chrisler, J.C. and LoCicero, A. (1999) Innovative methods: resources for research, teaching and publishing. *Psychology of Women Quarterly*, 23, 431–456.

Kvale, S. (1996) *InterViews*. Thousand Oaks, CA: Sage.

Polkinghorne, D.E. (1988) *Narrative Knowing and the Human Sciences*. Albany, NY: State University of New York.

Van Maanen, J. (1988) *Tales of the Field, On Writing Ethnography*. Chicago: University of Chicago Press.

The Self in Historical Context

Badinter, E. (1980) *Mother, Love, Myth and Reality*. New York: Macmillan.

Carrithers, M., Collins, S. and Lukes, S. (Eds.) (1985) *The Category of the Person*. Cambridge: Cambridge University Press.

Danziger, K. (1997) *Naming the Mind*. London: Sage.

Graumann, C.F. and Gergen, K.J. (1996) *Historical Dimensions of Psychological Discourse*. New York: Cambridge University Press.

Hacking, I. (1995) *Rewriting the Soul. Multiple Personality and the Sciences of Memory*. Princeton, NJ: Princeton University Press.

Miller, W.I. (1997) *The Anatomy of Disgust*. Cambridge, MA: Harvard University Press.

Morss, J. (1991) *Growing Critical. Alternatives to Developmental Psychology*. London: Routledge.

Onians, R.B. (1988) *The Origins of European Thought*. Cambridge: Cambridge University Press.

Spacks, P.M. (1995) *Boredom, The Literary History of a State of Mind*. Chicago: Chicago University Press.

Taylor, C. (1989) *Sources of the Self*. Cambridge, MA: Harvard University Press.

The Self in Cultural Context

Bachnik. J.M. and Quinn, C.J. (1994) *Situated Meaning*. Princeton, NJ: Princeton University Press.

Heelas, P. and Lock, A. (Eds.) (1981) *Indigenous Psychologies: The Anthropology of the Self*. New York: Academic Press.

Kirkpatrick, J.T. (1983) *The Marquesan Notion of the Person*. Ann Arbor, MI: University of Michigan Press.

Levine, G. (Ed.) (1992) *Constructions of the Self*. New Brunswick, NJ: Rutgers University Press.

Lutz, C.A. and Abu-Lughod, L. (Eds.) (1990) *Language and the Politics of Emotion*. Cambridge: Cambridge University Press.

Morris, D.B. (1991) *The Culture of Pain*. Berkeley, CA: University of California Press.

Radley, A. (1993) *Worlds of Illness: Biographical and Cultural Perspectives on Health and Disease*. London: Routledge.

5

TOWARD RELATIONAL SELVES

In the beginning is the relationship.

Martin Buber, *I and Thou*

In the preceding chapters I have tried to make a strong case for reflexive inquiry, that is, forms of investigation that help us to reflect critically and appreciatively on our condition, our traditions, institutions, and relationships. If we create our worlds largely through discourse, then we should be ever attentive to our ways of speaking and writing. Through reflexive inquiry on our ways of constructing the world, and the practices which these sustain, we open doors to emancipation, enrichment, and cultural transformation. We must now press further. While reflexive inquiry is much to be prized, in the end it is insufficient. It is one thing to explore and ponder, and quite another to generate alternatives. Such inquiry brings us to the border of new frontiers, but how are we to cross over and with what resources? It is precisely at this juncture that constructionist dialogues make another significant contribution.

Generative Theory

Patterns of action are typically intertwined with modes of discourse. To say "I care deeply for you" implies that a particular pattern of action will follow (for example, maintaining contact, supporting), and other actions will not (for example, avoidance, hostile remarks). Thus, if we wish to change patterns of action one significant means of doing so is through altering forms of discourse – the way events are described, explained or interpreted. In certain respects this means of change is already ingrained in daily practices. From friendship circles to national politics, we use gossip, snide remarks and ridicule to alter the image of the target, and thus redirect people's actions. However, constructionism substantially raises the stakes. In the case of daily practices we typically move within the accepted realities. We use the language readily available and change is thus minimal. For more significant change we must break significantly with the conventions.

It is useful to illustrate this point in terms used in Chapter 1. As we found, word meaning could be understood in terms of a structure of binaries, and these binaries often invited us into polarities: for example, up/down, in/out, smart/dumb. If we attempt to use the traditional binaries for purposes of cultural change, reinscribing the world or persons in their terms, transformation is only superficial. The "old way" remains in the wings, always readied for return. When we use our traditional vocabularies to demonstrate that "good people" (for example, the president, judges, police) are in reality "bad" (corrupt, biased, unjust), or the reverse, we continue to operate within the system of a good/bad binary. To say "they are bad" reinstantiates the system of talk in which people are divided into these polar categories, and simultaneously sets in motion the grounds for arguing the reverse. Or as feminist critic Andre Lorde has put it, "You can't destroy the master's house with the master's tools." The more radical move is to generate ways of talking in which the entire binary is suspended or rendered irrelevant. Can we imagine moving beyond the good/bad polarity in speaking of others and self?

Although increasing the fluidity of action, binary breaking doesn't succeed in "building new houses." New departures in construction, new ways of putting things, new metaphors and narratives, and new forms of description and explanation are needed. In effect, we require *generative theory*, that is, *accounts of our world that challenge the taken-for-granted conventions of understanding, and simultaneously invite us into new worlds of meaning and action.*[1] Freud's theoretical work was surely generative, challenging as it did the traditional assumption of consciousness as the center of action, sexuality as a minor aspect of human functioning, and morality as an essential good. Marxist theory was similarly generative in questioning the "naturalness" of economic class differences, and the wage differences between management and labor. B.F. Skinner's behaviorist theories – holding individual action to be a product of reinforcement contingencies – flew in the face of accepted views of human agency (free will) and the importance of psychological process. In each case there were substantial repercussions – including the creation of the psychiatric profession, the Russian revolution, and the overhauling of educational practices. This is not to approve of the consequences of these formulations, nor to argue that they remain generative today. However, it is to recognize that one of the major routes to social change is through audacious theorizing.

It is important to realize the radical nature of what is being proposed here. From the traditional realist standpoint, the task of the scholar is to furnish accurate accounts of reality, to map or picture the world as it is. In research informed by this tradition there is a strong incentive to use a language of description that is broadly acknowledged as objective or realistic. Thus, if we are confronted with the problem of crime, we carry out research on modes of prevention. By conventional standards it is taken for granted that crime has causes and should be prevented. Thus, to approach an issue *realistically* is to sustain our conventions along with associated ways of life. In effect, little is changed. The move to generative theory, however, invites us to suspend the traditions, and to experiment with new ways of inventorying the world, describing and explaining. What if street crime is viewed as a manifestation of societal ills, for example, or a means toward enhancing self-esteem, or a construction created by certain classes of people to punish those outside the class? Each of these alternatives opens the way to new forms of inquiry, and possible ways of going on in the world. In a sense, generative theorizing is a form of *poetic activism*. That is, it asks us to take a risk with words, shake up the conventions, generate new formations of intelligibility, new images, and sensitivities.

The present chapter treats but a single expedition into generative theory. In focussing on a single case, my hope is to furnish a sense of the challenge, its complexities, the promises and possible shortcomings. The case will also allow us to extend the preceding focus on the self. How can we transform our understanding of selves through language. How can we subvert a tradition of many centuries duration, and give new meaning and dimension to our lives through inscription? These are the challenges. The particular attempt will be to replace the traditional assumption of individual selves with a vision of self as an expression of relationship. Before exploring this vision we must consider more closely the rationale.

Individualism and Ideology

> None of us lives without a reference to an imaginary
> singularity which we call our self.
>
> Paul Smith, *Discerning the Subject*

It is comfortable to believe in the centrality of private experience and ourselves as conscious decision makers, masters of our own action. However, beginning with the first chapter of this book such comfortable assumptions have also been placed in question. Up till now the problems have primarily been conceptual in nature – incoherencies, conundrums, impasses. Recall our problems in Chapter 1 with separating mind from world, understanding how mind could mirror nature, and identifying precise states of mind. In the subsequent chapters we found that individual selves were socially defined – both in micro-social relationships and again in the mass media. And in the chapter preceding this we found that concepts of the self vary significantly both across culture and historical era. In effect, the assumption that we privately think, feel, desire, intend, and the like is not demanded by "what there is," but is essentially optional.

Given the wobbly set of assumptions on which we rest the conception of individual selves, we must now turn attention to issues of societal value. No set of assumptions is without weaknesses; there are no ultimate justifications for any of our beliefs. If we had to locate feckless foundations for our ways of life, we could scarcely go on. The more important question is, what are the implications for cultural life of putting things in the ways we do? Or in the present case, what do we gain and what do we lose by sustaining the tradition of private, individual selves as the wellspring of action? I suspect that most of us would agree that such a conception has made a positive contribution to Western culture. As indicated earlier the assumption of private, individual thought is essential to the institution of democracy. Closely coupled with our commitment to democracy, the value we place on public education derives from the belief that it will cultivate independent minds. As often argued, the stronger the minds of individuals, the more effective the democratic process. Further, without a belief in individual agency, our institutions of moral adjudication begin to crumble. It makes sense to hold each other responsible for our actions – both in daily life and courts of law – in so far as we believe people are capable of individual choice. Clearly, we owe an enormous debt to this, the *individualist tradition*. We would scarcely wish to strike the discourse from the cultural vernacular. However, we must also free our curiosities to wander the dark side.

In recent years discontent with individualism – and its companion discourse of individual minds – has accelerated at a rapid rate (see Chapter 1). As inhabitants of the Western tradition we have tended not only to presume its truth, but its universal application. Yet, as the globalization process is increasingly extended, and the challenge of difference mounts in magnitude, what are the implications of our Western commitments? Who gains and who is crushed? Can individualism see us successfully through the twenty-first century? Should we seek to cultivate alternatives? There are many who believe that individualism is a form of cultural ideology. Although its history has been a promising one, this *ideology of the self-contained individual* is also deeply problematic in its consequences. Consider the following lines of critique.

The Problem of Isolated Souls

If what is most central to me is within – mine and mine alone – then how am I to regard you? At the outset, you are fundamentally "other" – an alien who exists separately from me. I am essentially alone, I come into the world as an isolated being and leave alone. Further, you can never fully know or understand that which I am, for it is never fully available to you, never fully revealed. There can never be another who fully understands me in my isolation. By the same token, if what is most significant about you – what makes you tick – lies always "behind the mask," then I can never be certain of you, can never know what you are hiding from me, what you truly want. Even in our most intimate moments I cannot know what you are truly feeling. In effect, our mutual isolation is locked arm in arm with distrust. Because we cannot be certain, no words or actions are fully trustworthy, then suspicion always lies just over the shoulder. If this is our dominant orientation to life, what is the fate of close and committed relations, and how can we build cooperative relations on a global scale?

Narcissism and Others as Instruments

> I celebrate myself.
>
> Walt Whitman, "Leaves of Grass"

The prevailing sense of isolation, alienation and distrust also feeds a second problem deriving from individualist ideology. If self is the center of one's existence, and one can never fully know or trust another, then our primary mission must be to "look out for number one!" This is only natural; to expend effort on behalf of others is unnatural. Regarding others, one must continuously ask the question "how do I gain by this; what is lost?" More broadly, this orientation is labeled *instrumentalist* (or alternatively, *utilitarian*). Here one discounts doing things for their intrinsic worth; rather, actions are only rational if they are instrumental to achieving self-gratification of some kind. Thus, the ideology of individualism may favor altruism, but typically because altruism will bring one rewards – praise, gratitude, a better community, etc. Christopher Lasch's *The Culture of Narcissism*[2] is one of the most condemning statements of the "me-first" attitude engendered by the individualist impulse. For Lasch, when we are instrumentalist in our orientation, then we reduce to trivia emotional relationships and sexual intimacy. If one engages in love and sexual intimacy only to achieve self-gratification, then the traditional value of these actions is undermined. Similarly, scholarly research conducted only to "help my career," and political activism designed "to help me win" are also emptied of their deeper worth.

Relationship as Artifice

Consider some common phrases: "We need to work on our relationship," "This relationship is falling apart," "We must develop better teamwork," "He really helped build the organization." All of these phrases are lodged in the premise of individualism: if we believe that selves are primary – that society is made up of individual actors – then relationships must be built, made, or repaired. In effect, the self is the primary reality; relationships are artificial, temporary, and desirable primarily when one cannot function adequately alone. In the celebrated volume *Habits of the Heart*,[3] Robert Bellah and his colleagues propose that in its emphasis on self expression, freedom, self-development, and fulfillment, the individualism of today works at cross purposes with the kinds of social institutions that are central to a viable society. For example, "If love and marriage are seen primarily in terms of psychological gratification, they may fail to fulfill their older social function of providing people with stable, committed relationships that tie them into the larger society."[4] On the individualist account, if one finds that marriage frustrates one's desires for freedom or self-expression there is little reason to remain in the marriage. Self is the essential unit, and if marriage is an uncongenial companion then it must go. Similarly, Bellah and his colleagues are concerned with the potentials of communities to govern themselves, and indeed people's willingness to engage in public life, institutions, and politics. Because these activities typically require time and energy, they may seem inimical to self-development and personal gain. The individualist, then, is likely to "look on bonds as restraints, values as opinions or prejudices, and customs as impositions."[5]

The Tragedy of All Against All

In his famous work *The Leviathan*, the seventeenth century political philosopher Thomas Hobbes developed a strong case for civil law and a strong central government. As he saw it, humans in their natural state prefer themselves above all others. Thus, the underlying condition of human existence is a "war of every man, against every man." In this state of things, human life is "solitary, poor, nasty, brutish, and short." As a result of this condition, both civil law and central government are essential for our well-being. In important degree, Hobbes' vision of the individual remains central to present day individualism – whether in daily life, or in our institutions of government, education, and business. The pervasive view is that our fundamental condition is one of isolation and distrust. When "push comes to shove," what is there to do but "look out for number one?" No one can be fully trusted; everyone is primarily motivated by self-gain.

In slightly different terms, individualism invites us into a posture of competition. We enter a college classroom, and we are typically thrust into competition – only a handful will emerge with top marks. We enter the workplace, and again we traditionally find ourselves in competition: only a few will rise to the top. Both education and the workplace are individualism in action. As Marxist critics propose, the capitalist market is also allied with individualist ideology. The economic world, as we understand it, is made up of individual agents each attempting to maximize his/her own gain and minimize losses. In a world of limited resources this means that we are each pitted against the other in a dog-eat-dog world. We must ask, then, is the sense of continuous embattlement desirable; must we necessarily build institutions that embody this view; and if this view is extended into global relationships, what kind of future can we anticipate?

The Power Problem

"Divided we fall . . ."

In large measure we have followed the Hobbesian view of governance. That is, because we see ourselves as isolated, untrustworthy, self-serving and competitive, we establish institutions to keep us in check – organizations of surveillance, evaluation, punishment, incarceration, and eradication. Once these organizations are set in motion, however, they often come to have a life of their own – unmonitored and unchecked by those who have brought them into being. The KGB and the CIA are good illustrations from the past; even government officials were placed in fear by their uncontrollable powers. It is not simply the suspicion of the untrustworthy individual that is at stake here. In addition, it is through an individualizing process that overarching powers increase their control. Foucault has proposed that in earlier periods of Western history there was little demand that written books be attached to the names of single authors. Writing was not viewed as the expression of an originary mind. The concept of the author as origin came into prominence, proposes Foucault, when the French royalty became fearful of political tracts critical of their governance. By making it unlawful to publish written materials without the name of an author attached, the means for control was secured. Likewise, many are concerned today with the quantification of the individual, and the ways in which massive amounts of information about a person are now assembled and available on the internet. As Rosy Stone argues, we have become *fiduciary* subjects, on whom a numerical value is placed by others and who can be identified and called to answer at any time.[6] Resistance to individualization is essential in order to sustain a free society.

Systemic Blindness

Because we believe in self-contained individuals – who think, feel, weigh evidence and values, and act accordingly – we also inherit a handy way of understanding bad action – weirdness, crime, harassment, bigotry, and so on. In all cases we are led to suspect fault in the internal functioning of the individual. Weirdness is traced to "mental illness," we see crime as the outcome of a decrepit "sense of right and wrong," harassment and bigotry are traced to "deep seated prejudice," and so on. In effect, we locate ways of saying "the buck stops here." Individuals cause problems and individuals must be repaired – through therapy, education, imprisonment and so on.

But consider again. Does anyone's action entirely originate within the self – independent of any history or circumstance? If I am prejudiced, did this prejudice spring naturally from within? It is difficult to imagine such a possibility. Yet, if we are deeply immersed in the world – in relationships, jobs, physical circumstances and the like, why do we select the individual mind as the source of problematic behavior? If my job is boring and my boss a tyrant, why should I be treated for my feelings of depression? Why not change the workplace? In broader terms the individualist presumption operates like a blinder. It is a crude and simplistic way of reacting to problems. We fail to explore the broader circumstances in which actions are enmeshed, and focus all too intensely on the single body before our eyes. Not only is the individualist option highly limited, but if the broader circumstances of individual lives are not addressed it may be disastrous.

In summary, despite its salutary contribution to valued traditions, we also find the presumption of individual selves deeply flawed. When the self is the essential atom of society, we find invitations to isolation, distrust, narcissism, and competition; we find relationships reduced to inessential artifice and our freedoms threatened; and we find an obtuse simplification of our ills. In all these ways we might wish for more promising alternatives, new conceptions of self that might render and social life less chilling – and possibly create a more promising global future. Can we develop generative alternatives to carry us into the emerging century? It is to this possibility that we now turn.

Self as Relationship: First Steps

> In this disrupted moment, the ability to tolerate and the will
> to encourage fluid and multiple forms of subjectivity is an imperative
> and fully ethical position.
>
> Jane Flax, *Multiples*

We must be clear about what is being proposed: if we inherit a strong reality of the individual self – a self that senses, thinks, feels, and directs action – and we find this construction of the person flawed, can we set out to reconstruct reality in a different key? And toward what kind of alternative should we strive? In what way can we conceptualize persons such that the individualist ills are not duplicated, and the possibilities for more promising forms of societal life are opened? Although we should not foreclose other avenues of departure, one promising possibility emerges uniquely from social constructionist dialogues.

As outlined in the preceding chapters, social constructionism traces commitments to the real and the good to social process. As proposed, what we take to be knowledge of the world grows from relationship, and is embedded not within individual minds but within interpretive or communal traditions. In effect, there is a way in which constructionist dialogues celebrate relationship as opposed to the individual, connection over isolation, and communion over antagonism. Yet, the question remains, can we compellingly reinscribe what it is to be a person in a way that moves us away from the individualist premise and toward the relational? This is not an easy task because the language we inherit from the past is so deeply embedded in individualism. We have over 2000 terms in the English language that refer to ("make real") individual mental states, and very few that refer to relationships. Even the concept of relationship itself, as we inherit it, presumes that relationships are built up from the more basic units of single individuals. It's as if we have become enormously sophisticated in characterizing individual pawns, rooks, and bishops, but have little way of talking about the game of chess. How, then, can we embark on a generative form of theorizing without a ready vocabulary at hand?

Because we cannot start from scratch, generating meaning without relationship to any tradition, steps toward a relational understanding benefit from a closer examination of the past. Specifically, if we scan our traditions can we find pockets of intelligibility that offer resources for the future? Indeed, we do find riches at our disposal. Let us consider three significant roads toward relational being: symbolic interaction, cultural psychology, and phenomenology. Let us also consider ways we might wish to press beyond these traditions.

Symbolic Interaction: Inter-subjective Selves

> Selves can only exist in relationship to other selves.
>
> George Herbert Mead, *Mind, Self and Society*

Since the 1930s the discipline of social psychology has been committed in most respects to an individualist view of the person. Laboratory experiments are used to manipulate *stimulus conditions* in the environment, to which the individual – based on processes of cognition, motivation, emotion and the like – *responds* with more or less aggression, altruism, prejudice, attraction and so on. Relationships, on this account, are the byproduct of independent individuals coming together. Because relationships are thus derivative of individual minds, they have ironically been less than interesting to most social psychologists. Not only is individual functioning the center of research attention, but most theories in social psychology also demonstrate a strong animus toward the intrusion of others in one's life. That is, other persons are typically treated as disruptions in or deviations from optimal functioning of the individual. It is "other people", in the social psychological tradition, who demand that one conform to erroneous beliefs, who elicit obedience to inhumane directives, or who cause independent thought to deteriorate ("group think").

This condition of social psychology could have been otherwise – both in terms of research emphasis and in the value placed on the presence of others in our lives. A significant alternative was generated in 1934, with the publication of George Herbert Mead's classic work *Mind, Self and Society*.[7] As Mead proposed, there is no thinking, or indeed any sense of being a self, that is independent of social process. For Mead, we are born with rudimentary capacities to adjust to each other, largely in response to gestures – with the hands, vocal sounds, facial expressions, gaze, and so on. It is through others' response to our gestures that we slowly begin to develop the capacities for mental symbolization; or in effect, our gestures and the reactions they elicit from others come to be represented mentally.

Language becomes possible when people share a common set of mental symbols, for example, when words call forth the same symbols in both parties to a conversation. The development of common symbols is vitally enhanced, for Mead, by what he views as a natural tendency for *role-taking*. That is, as others respond to our gestures, and we experience these responses within us, we are able to gain a sense of what the other's gesture symbolizes for him or her. If, as a child, I scream at my father and he raises his hand in a threatening way, I become fearful and stop my screaming. In doing so, however, I also gain a sense that for my father my screaming is unacceptable. By taking his role in the situation, I understand that in his symbolic world, he can't tolerate my screams.

As Mead also proposes it is through role-taking that I become conscious of myself. By taking the role of the other, as he or she responds to my actions, I come to understand who and what I am. Over time I come to develop a sense of a *generalized other*, that is, a composite of others' reactions to me across situations. It is out of the sense of the generalized other that I develop a coherent sense of self, or "what I truly am." Because each of us draws our sense of self from others, we are thus thoroughly inter-related. For Mead, "No hard-and-fast line can be drawn between our own selves and the selves of others, since our own selves exist and enter as such into our experience only in so far as the selves of others exist and enter as such in our experience also."[8]

Although largely disregarded in social psychology, Mead's work did give rise to a small but vital movement called *symbolic interactionism*. Symbolic interactionists have taken a special interest in the ways both social order and deviance come about. Of major importance is the concept of *social role*. From the symbolic interactionist perspective, social life is played out in the roles we acquire, invent, or are forced into.[9] In this sense, if you look ahead in life you can see stretched out before you a structure of roles – teacher, therapist, manager, and the like, or wife, father, homosexual. Even the deviant from mainstream society – the drug addict, the thief or the "mentally ill" – can be viewed as playing out scripts that are largely determined before we ever arrive on the scene. You can also appreciate the close relationship between symbolic interactionism and the dramaturgic perspective developed by Erving Goffman (Chapter 3) and others.

It is also clear that symbolic interactionism makes a substantial contribution to an appreciation of human interdependency. From this perspective, thinking, knowing, believing, and self-understanding, all have their origins in social interchange. Mind, in effect, is inseparable from social process. Yet, in spite of its intellectual significance, symbolic interactionism fails as a fully adequate replacement to individualism. The problems are several. First, in spite of the relational emphasis, symbolic interactionism retains a strong element of individualism. For Mead, one is born into the world as a private subject, and as a private subject must come to "experience" others, and then, mentally "take the role of the other," in order to develop processes of higher thought. Private subjectivity is never really abandoned in the formulation. Communication is from one individual sub-jectivity to another. Further, symbolic interactionism poses the intractable problem of explaining how it is a person is able to grasp others' states of minds from their gestures. If I am a child, and my father raises his hand, how do I know what this gesture means to him? This is the problem of "knowing other minds" that we encountered in Chapter 1. Finally, there is a strong flavor of social determinism in symbolic interactionism. For Mead there is a "temporal and logical pre-existence of the social process to the self-conscious individual that arises in it."[10] That is, how we think about the world and self is ultimately determined by others; without their having views of us, we could have no conception of ourselves. The deterministic view also haunts the analysis of social roles: are we simply determined to play out the roles already laid out for us? The complaint here is not the tra-ditional one that this kind of social determinism will eradicate the concept of human choice or agency. This would be the individualist's lament. Rather, it is to ask whether any mechanical view of human relations – in which each of us determines the actions of others – is optimal in its impli-cations for social life. Isn't the very notion of cause and effect in human rela-tions one that – by implication – divides and alienates us? If you are "causing my behavior," are you not then both separate from me and have power over me? Optimally we might wish for a formulation that would dis-pense altogether with the binary of free will vs. determinism. This is a sig-nificant intellectual challenge, and will continue to demand our attention.

Cultural Psychology: Carrying On

> Speaking/thinking (a dialectical unity) is social-cultural activity.
>
> Lois Holzman, *Schools for Growth*

As we have seen, social psychology could have developed in directions that emphasized relationship over the individual, but did not. There is a similar story to be told about developmental psychology. Developmentalists might well have come to see human development primarily as a social process. However, in the main they have followed the direction of the social psy-chologists, defining human development in terms of the self-contained individual. In the main, developmentalists have based their work on either one or two major metaphors of the person: the machine or the flower, or what are often called the *mechanistic* and the *organismic* conceptions of development.[11] In the mechanistic case, the infant is largely viewed as an input–output machine, that is, as an organism whose development – or behavioral output – is largely shaped by environmental conditions (the input). Here investigators trace, for example, the influence of early stimu-lation on the infant's intelligence, or the impact of different child rearing patterns on the child's attachment, or feelings of self-esteem. In effect, child behavior is the output resulting from machine (environmental) inputs. The mechanistic orientation to development is often called *behaviorist*. In contrast, the organismic theorist stresses the genetic basis of development. Like a developing daffodil, the direction and stages of development are predetermined – inherent in the nature of the organism. Here the work of Piaget is illustrative, emphasizing as it did the way in which the child's capacities for thought develop naturally – from rudimentary sensory reactions in infancy to abstract conceptual skills in later childhood. In both the mechanistic and organismic case the child is fundamentally separate from his/her surrounds.

The history of developmental inquiry could have been otherwise. In 1930s Russia, the work of Lev Vygotsky began to offer a bold alternative to the dominant conceptions. For Vygotsky, individuals are inextricably related, both to each other and their physical surrounds. To separate the individual – either as a machine or a flower – from the surrounds can only be accomplished analytically – as an exercise in theory – for in truth, they are inseparable. Of particular interest for Vygotsky, were the "higher mental functions" such as thinking, planning, attending, and remembering. Psychologists typically view these functions as universal: research is devoted to the "nature of cognition" in general, and almost never to cognition within, let us say, differing ethnic or religious traditions. Yet, for Vygotsky, these higher processes are lodged within relationships: "Social relations or relations among people genetically underlie all higher (mental) functions and their relationships."[12] In effect, mental functioning reflects social process.

In the same way that George Herbert Mead's work gave rise to symbolic interactionism, Vygotsky's theories have sparked the development of what is called *cultural psychology*. One of its chief proponents, Jerome Bruner, has proposed the stimulating idea that the everyday accounts of why people act as they do, what we often call *folk psychology*, reflect the essential elements of thought. As we explain others' actions in terms of their desires, beliefs, goals, and passions, for example, we are engaged in folk psychologizing. And these are the terms in which we think. As Bruner argues, without our sharing a folk psychology we would scarcely know how to carry out relationships. Society as we know it would come to an end. For Bruner, folk beliefs are carried within the mind as narratives; that is, we understand others by thinking in narratives. We think, for example, "Alex became angry because he wanted the prize, and Suzie won; that's why he isn't speaking to Suzie." Further, proposes Bruner, these mental narratives organize the way we experience the world, and regulate our feelings. Because of our narrative knowledge we understand which feelings are appropriate on a given occasion and which are not. "Indeed the very shape of our lives – the rough and perpetually changing draft of our autobiography that we carry in our minds – is understandable to ourselves and to others only by virtue of (our) cultural systems of interpretation."[13]

Cultural psychology is an important development not only for intellectual reasons but practically as well. The cultural view has particularly important implications for educational practice.[14] Traditional education has centered on improving the mind (reason, knowledge, understanding) of the individual student. The student is exposed to educational materials and expected to learn. From the cultural standpoint, however, the focus of the educational process moves from the mind of the individual student to relationships – between teacher and student, and among students themselves. For Vygotsky, in particular, the site of learning is within a matrix of relational action; required is a "doing with." In carrying out activities with others, one metaphorically steps outside the self and takes on some aspect of the other. One of the most radical illustrations of the cultural view in education can be found in the Barbara Taylor School in Brooklyn.[15] For these children (ages 4–14) there is no fixed curriculum, nor strict age grading of classes. The curriculum essentially emerges through a process of relationship among the students and with the teacher. Rather than passively mastering a fixed body of material, the learning process centers on activity – learning by working together. This often means the development of mutual-learning relationships; with the teacher joint projects are developed; students often work in groups, and at times learning projects take students outside the schools and into the community (to shops, museums, political sites).

Yet, in spite of the contributions of cultural psychology, we must once again ask whether this is a satisfactory place to terminate our quest for the relational? You may already suspect the limitations. The reasons are largely foreshadowed in the discussion of symbolic interactionism. Like Mead, the cultural psychologist confronts the intractable enigma of explaining how the cultural understandings are incorporated into the individual mind. If we understand the world, and what others tell or show us, through higher mental processes (or narrative thought in the case of Bruner), then how did we ever come to understand the culture prior to possessing these capacities? As infants – with no understanding – how could we comprehend the words or actions of our parents? If we are not born with self-contained cognitive processes, how could we make sense of our parents' scoldings, pleadings, and appreciations? And if we are born with such processes, then cultural psychology cannot be telling us the whole story. Further, there remains the problem of social determinism. If all thought is the result of enculturation, is the individual anything more than society's robot? And, if culture does give birth to individual minds, then what is the origin of culture? Let us press further.

Phenomenology and the Other

A third significant contribution to a relational view of self emerges in an unlikely quarter: continental phenomenology. Why is this unlikely? Because phenomenological study is generally concerned with describing and analyzing conscious experience – or the nature of individual awareness. In effect, phenomenology seems to be an individualist enterprise par excellence. However, the conventional split between the conscious subject and the object of awareness has never been a happy one for phenomenologists. Of special relevance, the philosopher Edmund Husserl (1859–1938) proposed that all experience is *intentional*. By this he meant that our experiences are always directed toward or absorbed by some pattern (object, person, etc.) in the external world. Thus, conscious experience is fundamentally relational; subject and object – or self and other – are unified within experience. Or to paraphrase, my experience requires you in order for it to have content; you exist for me only in so far as I bring experience to bear on you. It remained, however, to Husserl's successor, Alfred Schutz to elaborate the social dimensions of personal experience.[16]

As Schutz proposed, our experience of the world is governed by a *natural attitude*. By this he means that our sense of the orderly and understandable world around us is a byproduct not of the world as it is, but of what we take for granted. Your hands, torso, feet, shoulders and eyes may all move as you smile, but I do not register all such passing events. Rather, I understand only that "you smiled." Our natural attitude is largely composed of *typifications*, that is, assumptions about classes of events. Thus, I may see hundreds of different smiles, and your smile may never be quite the same from one of our meetings to the next, but I tend to experience only the typification of "a smile." And, for Schutz, most of our typifications are implanted through language. Thus, as we learn the word "smile," for example, we essentially incorporate a class name; we don't have words for all the many different qualities of smiles we confront in daily life. We tend only to say "she smiled," and sometimes qualify with "big," "slight," "superficial," and the like. Thus, as we learn language we come to experience the world in ways that effectively "blind" us to its nuances. Our experiences are inevitably colored by the social – and most directly – the linguistic world in which we are immersed.

It is this latter point that makes phenomenological writings especially significant in the development of the relational standpoint. For what Schutz is proposing is essentially that what we take to be most uniquely personal – our conscious experience – is largely derived from the social interchange. Or more dramatically, the private cannot be separated from the public. This is indeed a challenging view, and resonates nicely with that of cultural psychology. However, it is also a view with important consequences in action. In particular, the phenomenological view has been warmly received among therapists who variously view themselves as humanistic, wholistic, and existential. Such therapists have wished to separate themselves from more manipulative, mechanistic, and regimented forms of therapy – seeing them as dehumanizing. Phenomenological theory advances this cause in its placing the client's personal experience center-most. For phenomenologists there is a deep valuing of the experience of the other; good therapy will enable the client to give full expression to his/her experience. Qualities of genuineness, warmth, acceptance, and growth are all prized within these circles.[17]

Yet, in spite of its contribution to cultural life, the phenomenological view also shares in the same difficulties we confronted earlier. To whit: if language is the primary vehicle through which we understand the world – how did we ever come to understand language? How could it mean anything to us as young children to hear a particular pattern of syllables? With no categories for experiencing such language "as something," presumably it would be nothing. A second problem follows closely on the heels of the first: how is it that by incorporating a particular array of syllables into our vocabulary our experience of the world is transformed? How does learning words change the actual shapes and colors of objects that we see?[18] Finally, in its continuing commitment to subjective experience, the phenomenological standpoint does not give us all that we might wish in a relational account of the person. Because phenomenological analysis holds subjective experience as its primary subject matter, it never fully gives up the individualist heritage. Language may furnish the individual with the means of understanding, but it is the character of this private world that is ultimately central to the phenomenologist.

Relational Being: the Emerging Vision

> I look for the way
> things will turn . . .
> not so much looking for the shape
> as being available
> to any shape that may be
> summoning itself
> through me
> from the self not mine but ours.
>
> A.R. Ammons, "Poetics"

The preceding discussions – on symbolic interaction, cultural psychology, and social phenomenology – are similar in one major respect: they presume that the psychological is fashioned from the social. As proposed in each case, there is a social world and it preexists the psychological; once the social world has made its mark on the psychological, the self exists independently of society. In this sense, each of these formulations continues to draw from the family of familiar binaries, self/other, inner/outer, individual/society. If we are to locate a successor to individualism, it seems, we must achieve a more radical departure. We must undermine the binaries in which we find ourselves subject to others' influence but fundamentally separated. We must locate a way of understanding ourselves as constituents of a process that eclipses any individual within it, but is simultaneously constituted by its individual elements. How can such a view be made intelligible? One important overture lies in the work of the Russian literary theorist Mikhail Bakhtin.

Bakhtin and Dialogism

> No speaker is, after all, the first speaker, the one who disturbs
> the eternal silence of the universe.
>
> Mikhail Bakhtin, *Discourse in the Novel*

Although deeply concerned with Russian literary and cultural life, Bakhtin's work was in many ways antithetical to the dominant political order of 1930s Russia – sufficiently so that he was sentenced to five years' imprisonment early in his career and never did achieve significant scholarly standing in his country. Nor until recently did his work demand significant attention outside the former Soviet Union. Yet, for many contemporary scholars, discovering Bakhtin has been akin to locating a long-lost family member. Excitement abounds. Bakhtin's writings are substantial and complex and we shall here be concerned with only one central ingredient. It is also a corpus of work that defies clarity of interpretation. And indeed, the incapacity of scholars to "fix its meaning" could be viewed as a central ingredient of its content. For Bakhtin was deeply concerned with the oppressive character of *monologue*, that is, the capacity of a single authority to monopolize meaning, to rule out all competing voices. Bakhtin's critique extended to the oppressive forces of the totalitarian regime under which he lived, thus contributing to his imprisonment. This antipathy should also apply to anyone claiming to have the "single correct interpretation" of his work today.

It was this resistance to monologue that served as a major motivating force for one of Bakhtin's most important contributions, namely his emerging theory of dialogue (or *dialogism*, as it is often called). While in certain respects dialogue is an ideal to be achieved – a way of relating that might replace the monologue – it is also possible to derive from this work an account of the self as inextricably woven into relationship. That is, for Bakhtin, persons are born into meaning through dialogue. How is this so? Here it is helpful first to consider Bakhtin's concept of *heteroglossia*, or diversity of language within a culture. For Bakhtin, the language of a culture is never pure, a product of a single unified tradition, but represents a mixed stew. This is not only owing to the fact that the language of most cultures bears traces of many other traditions with which it has been in contact. English, for example, carries elements of Greek, Latin, Norse, German and more. In addition, the language of a culture is in continuous motion. The meaning of words is subtly altered in each new context of usage, and new words may be coined at any time.

Thus, as Bakhtin saw it, when we communicate with each other we inevitably draw from an enormous and diverse repository of words. When we speak or write, we draw from the past and place it in motion in what Bakhtin calls *the utterance*. The utterance not only carries with it fragments from a diverse heritage, but as well carries with it significance derived from its present context and its form of intonation. Thus, the free-standing sentence, "It is good" tells us nothing; however, when said by Ivan to Peter, as they drink wine and stare into the fire late one evening, it is now a significant entry into a dialogue. And if Peter responds, "It is good," the meaning of the words is now altered. The words now signify an agreement, perhaps a bond. They have been born into meaning by the preceding utterance. In this sense, all utterances are *double-voiced*, carrying the voice of the past but spoken into an ongoing dialogue.

For present purposes, there are two important accomplishments of this analysis: first, we find that the meaning of utterances is generated in a dialogic relationship. There is no meaning that is not derived from relationship itself. In this sense Bakhtin's formulation extends the Wittgensteinian image of meaning as a byproduct of language games (Chapter 2). Second, we find that the ability of the individual to mean anything – to be rational or sensible – is owing to relationship. The self cannot in this sense be separated from the other. Self and other are locked together in the generation of meaning. "Consciousness is never self sufficient," writes Bakhtin, "it always finds itself in an intense relationship with another consciousness."[19] Or in brief, "To be means to communicate."[20]

Relational Being

The Bakhtinian vineyard offers a rich harvest for those pursuing relational ways of understanding our lives. Here we find a vision of human action in which rationality and relationship cannot be disengaged, in which our every action manifests our immersion in past relationships, and simultaneously the stamp of the relationship into which we move. However, you should also notice that traces of individualism still remain at the center of the account. It is the individual who carries past dialogues into the present, who thinks in dialogue, and is born afresh within ongoing dialogue. As Bakhtin writes, "when the listener perceives and understands the meaning (the language meaning) of speech, he simultaneously takes an active, responsive attitude toward it."[21] In effect, the individual mind remains central to the production and interpretation of meaning. Can we, then, retain the catalytic vision of persons as embedded within relational flows, but cut our moorings from individual thought? This is not to propose eradicating the mental talk so central to our daily lives: "I feel . . .," "I think . . .," "I need . . ." and so on. Rather, it should be to view such expressions as themselves constituents of relationship. Desired, then, is an account that draws from the Bakhtinian riches, but which places the relationship at the center. How can this be accomplished? Let's consider two theoretical steps in this direction and then turn to practice.

1.   *Psychological discourse as performative*: This first move follows quite naturally from arguments in preceding chapters. As we have seen, there is no way of understanding such utterances as, "I love you," or "I am angry" as reports on an inner state of mind or the neurons (Chapter 1). However, the utterance, "I love you" can be a powerful statement within

a relationship, possibly drawing the other into greater intimacy or commitment, or in some cases, sending the other person running. In effect, the utterance functions as an important part of the relationship; it creates the relationship as one kind of thing and not another. In this sense near synonyms to "I love you," – phrases such as "I care," "I adore . . ." or "I am mad about you" – are not other ways of saying the same thing, nor are they each tagged to a different mental state. Rather, each functions in a slightly different way, to modify or adjust the relationship in subtle ways. "I care . . .," for example, has a way of transforming a passionate relationship to possibly a friendship. "I'm mad about you," is more stylized, echoing relationships in film or on the stage, and thus removes some of the sense of sincerity often carried by "I love you." The variation in expressions of affection, then, enriches the range of possible relationship.

It is important to realize that we are not dealing here with "mere words," used by people to "get what they want from the other." As you will recall from Chapter 2, utterances serve a *performative* function. That is, in the very saying of something, we are also performing an action within a relationship. You can see this most easily in the case of oaths ("Damn you!"), ritual ceremonies ("I now pronounce you man and wife"), or games ("On your mark, get set . . ."). It is not the specific content of such utterances that is important so much as the way it functions within various relationships. Even statements of fact – "the hydrogen molecules were extracted" – are performances within some social group, serving let us say to establish hierarchies, set agendas, welcome one form of action as opposed to another. The same may be said about our language of psychological states, our expressions of love, anger, hope, desire, and so on. Such statements are typically embedded within full-blown performances – including not only word intonation, but gestures, gaze, and posture. For example, if spoken in a faint voice, eyes on the floor, and with a smile, the words "I am angry" have very little performative value. We wouldn't be certain what the person was saying. In order to perform anger properly within Western culture, voice intensity and volume are often useful; a stern face and a rigid posture may be required. We gain much by replacing the image of private "feelings" with public action; it's not that we *have* emotions, a thought, or a memory so much as we *do* them.[22]

It is important to realize that in saying that psychological language is performative does not lead to the conclusion that our expressions are either superficial or calculating. Think of your own actions in the midst of a heated sports event – running, jumping, excited, fully engaged. You would scarcely say about your actions that they are contrived, artificial or merely done to achieve an effect. Yet, the game itself is a cultural invention – "only a game" we say. Much the same can be said about performances of which psychological discourse is a part. In doing anger, love, memory and the like we may be fully engaged, "doing what comes naturally," even if these doings are born within cultural history and intelligible only by virtue of the rules they obey.

2. *Performance as relationally embedded*: If it is reasonable to view psychological discourse as performative, we are now positioned to ask two significant questions. First, from whence the performance? If there is no animating origin lying behind the expression of emotion, for example, what does give rise to the performance? Here the preceding chapter's account of emotions in cultural and historical context is relevant. Recall the way in which our expressions gain their intelligibility from a cultural history. In the same way I cannot make sense if I use a word that I myself have made up, my actions will not make sense if they do not borrow from a cultural background. Thus, when I perform I am carrying a history of relationships, manifesting them, expressing them. They inhabit my every motion. A second significant question follows the first: performances for whom? To extend the metaphor of theater, who is the audience for one's performances? As Bakhtin pointed out, when we speak about psychological states ("I want . . .," "he feels . . .," "she thinks . . .,") we are always addressing someone – either explicitly or implicitly – within some kind of relationship. To say that the performances are addressed is also to say that they are fashioned with respect to the recipient. One's expressions of anger, for example, are not likely to be the same when addressed to one's children as opposed to one's peers or one's parents. The other enters the expression, then, in its very formulation.

We now find that one's performances are essentially constituents of relationship; they are inhabited not only by a history of relationships but as well by the relationships into which they are directed. By making these two theoretical moves, treating psychological discourse as performative and embedding performances within relationships, we are now positioned to see the entire vocabulary of the mind as constituted by and within relationship. There is no creation of an independent mind through social relationships, as in the earlier accounts. We don't have to worry about how the social world gains entry into the subjective world of the individual. Rather, from the present standpoint there is no independent territory called "mind" that demands attention. There is action, and action is constituted within and gains its intelligibility through relationship.

In this sense theorists propose that thinking is not a private event, but that we attribute thought or reason to people depending on the way they talk and otherwise act. Reason, then, is not distinguishable from effective rhetoric;[23] thinking is essentially the ability to argue well.[24]

You may be suspicious at this point; is this analysis denying our subjectivity, all that we do privately and alone? Surely we are doing something privately in our prolonged gaze into the distance as we prepare to write a term paper, or ponder the meaning of another's harsh words. Why aren't these specifically *psychological* processes, differing in significant ways from social action? Let us consider: when we are preparing a term paper, for example, in what kind of process are we engaged? Are we not readying ourselves to put meaningful arguments on paper, that is, preparing to engage in a social action? Similarly, being rejected by a friend is only meaningful within particular traditions of relationship. Thus, we may be doing something privately – which we might want to call reasoning, pondering, or feeling – but from the present standpoint these are essentially public actions carried out in private. To illustrate, consider the actress preparing her lines for a play. These lines are essentially nonsense independent of their placement within the play; that is, they require a relationship to be intelligible. Yet, the actress can rehearse the lines in private, speaking loudly in her empty room, or she can sit quietly and let the words form without voicing them. In the latter case we might say she was "imagining," or "thinking them through." But essentially she is carrying out a public action, only without audience and full performance.[25]

Let us illustrate this orientation toward relational being in action. Specifically we can turn to processes of memory and emotion.

COLLECTIVE REMEMBERING

> "Do you remember the time that . . . ?"
> "What is the square of the hypotenuse?"
> "Can you describe the events that took place on the night of March 5?"

Questions of memory are always with us, and how we respond may sometimes change the course of our lives. Psychologists and neurologists thus set out to study, for example, the conditions of memory loss, how memory can be improved, and the neurological basis of aphasia. At the same time our common conceptions of memory – and indeed the conceptions that ground this scientific work – are quintessentially individualist. That is, they presume that the word "memory" stands for a specific kind of process inside the head of the individual, a process that is neurologically based and universal in its functioning. We have explored the conceptual and political problems inherent in this orientation. The challenge we now confront is generating an understanding of memory as a relational phenomenon. Following the preceding line of reasoning, let us first consider the word "memory" in its performative role. It makes little sense to view the phrase "I remember" as a report on a particular psychological or neurological condition. What kind of condition would we be reporting on, how would we be able to "look inside" and recognize when we had a memory as opposed to a "thought" or a "desire." Rather, as John Shotter has put it, "Our ways of talking about our experiences work not primarily to represent the nature of those experiences in themselves, but to represent them in such a way as to constitute and sustain one or another kind of social order."[26]

In this sense it may be said that memory is not an individual act but a collective one. Consider the following conversation fragment recorded in a group of British students discussing a movie (E.T.) they had seen together:[27]

Diane: it was so sad
Lesley: that little boy was a very good actor
Diane: he was brilliant he really was
Tina: especially at the end when he . . .
Karen: he was quivering, wasn't he
John: how many didn't cry at it
Lesley: [*emphatically*] I didn't and I'm proud of it too
Diane: tell you what got me the bit when he didn't get on the space ship right
            at the beginning . . . the actual story line was really boring wasn't it
Karen: yeh
Lesley: yeh dead boring
Tina: it was the effects that did it
Paul: it has some incredible little funny bits in it when he got drunk and
            things like that
Lesley: yeh

There is a virtual infinity of ways the film might have been described by the group, but what we find here is that the students are highly selective in what they talk about. And as they talk they generate an account of "what happened." As they come to agree on the sadness, the good acting, and the boring plot so do they prefigure what may later be said if someone asks, "Did you see *E.T.*? What was it like?" Similarly, if a child at school is asked "what does 3 times 3 equal?," the answer "nine" is not a report on an inner condition of memory, but an action that has been fashioned within a complex relational history. And when the family gathers at a reunion, the stories of yore are not pictures of their minds, but forms of conversation that have typically been incubated in a long history of conversation. In their study of how people recall political events – such as wars or revolutions – Spanish colleagues conclude, "Every memory, as personal as it may be – even of events that are private and strictly personal and have not been shared with anyone – exists through its relation with what has been shared with others: language, idiom, events, and everything that shapes the society of which individuals are a part."[28]

Another way of talking about memory and other mental processes as collective is to say that they are *socially distributed*. What does this mean? Consider the child who is being taught the alphabet. The mother asks, "Laura, what comes after F?" The child is silent for a moment, and the mother says, "good, goose . . . gravy . . ." to which the child immediately responds "G!" In this case the production of "the correct memory" is essentially distributed between the mother and the child; the child reports but the mother's prompt is essential to the performance. As scholars propose, memory is very often distributed in this communal way. For example, what is recalled about a historical figure or event in a given nation may be distributed not only across a range of conversations, but across textbooks, newspapers, television productions, and film.[29] In this sense, history is crafted by a collectivity, and as every savvy politician knows, thereby always subject to reconstruction.

In the same way we might say that rationality is socially distributed. As Mary Douglas proposes, because rational decisions emerge from a multiplicity of conversations within organizations, we can justifiably say that "organizations think."[30] Stupid decisions are not the result of any single mind; they are a byproduct of the entire group – including the way they speak together, and who is included or excluded from the conversation. In this context, important research has explored the crew of large aircraft who must work together in close coordination to generate "intelligent decisions" concerning flight paths, weather conditions, landings, and so on.[31] Obviously these coordinations are of life and death consequence. As the research suggests, a significant number of air catastrophes can be traced to cases in which the advice of a junior ranking crew member is unheeded by a senior. It is the defect in collective reasoning that brought death.

EMOTIONAL SCENARIOS We tend to think of emotions as "natural givens," simply part of human nature. Mothers generally assume their infants are born into the world with fully functioning emotions.[32] The child's cry is taken as a sign of anger, her smile as an expression of happiness. Psychologists try to locate the physiological basis of emotion, and argue for its universality.[33] The argument for universality is appealing on one level, as it suggests that human understanding is part of human nature. We are innately prepared, for example, to appreciate another's fear or love or joy. Yet, it is also a dangerous assumption, in as much as what we assume to be "natural" is typically the emotions of our own culture. What the Ifaluk call *fago* or the Japanese call *mayae*, for example, we in the West simply delete from the universal vocabulary of emotion. This problem of cultural imperialism is further buttressed by the host of intellectual problems discussed in preceding chapters.

How can we understand emotional expressions, then, as relational performances? Here it is helpful to use the concept of a *scenario*, that is, a scripted set of interdependent actions such as we might find in a play.[34] Each action in the scenario sets the stage for that which follows; what follows gives intelligibility to that which has preceded. In effect, the performance of each actor is required to give the play its coherent unity; each performance depends on the others for its intelligibility. In these terms, we can view emotional performances as constituents of culturally specific scenarios – parts of a play in which others are required. This is to propose that the angry shout or the sluggish expression of depression only make sense by virtue of their position in a relational scenario. That is, such expressions cannot take place anywhere and anytime, but only within a culturally appropriate sequence. You cannot easily jump to your feet in the middle of family dinner and shout, "I'm mad as hell;" such behavior would seem preposterous by normal Western standards. But if someone insults you publicly, the same expression would not only seem fitting, but if you did not display any sign of anger you might be judged personally deficient ("What kind of wimp are you, anyway?"). More generally, we might say that there are times and places where it is appropriate to perform an emotion.

Further, once an emotion is performed the relational scenario also prescribes what follows. Thus, if a friend tells you that he fears he has a fatal disease, certain actions are virtually required by the cultural scenarios and others prohibited. You may properly respond with sympathy and nurturance, but it would be tasteless to reply with a silly joke or talk about your vacation. Further, like good stories, many emotional scenarios also have *beginnings* and *endings*. If it is late at night and your electric power is suddenly lost, that is the beginning of a scenario in which expressions of fear (as opposed, let's say, to jealously or ecstasy) would be appropriate. In contrast, if someone is telling you of her sorrow, you may continue to give her nurturance and support until she smiles. At that point the scenario is terminated, and you may be free to make a silly joke or speak of your vacation.

From this perspective, emotions are not the private possessions of the individual mind, but are the property of relationships. "Your joy" is not yours but "ours," "my anger" is "our anger," and so on. The implications of this shift in understanding are substantial. Consider the case of depression, for example, a "mental disorder" that is now said to strike one in ten people. From the present standpoint depression is not an individual disorder; an individual "does depression" as a culturally intelligible action within a context of relationship. Therapeutic attention thus moves outward from the individual mind ("what is wrong with him?") to the relational scenarios in which the person is engaged. In what kinds of relationship is the depression invited, with whom, and under what conditions? Are other moves in these relationships possible? Similarly, spouse abuse is not from this standpoint a natural eruption of anger, but is more likely to be embedded within subtle forms of interchange – with family members and others outside or in the past. It has a time and a place when it "feels natural," but the important question is how to abort such scenarios altogether.

On the more positive side, the relational orientation suggests that all our pleasures – the joy of tastes, smells, colors, eroticism and the like – are not the result of individual biology. Rather, we owe all pleasures to our existence in relationships. I never liked opera till there was Shirley; I never enjoyed scotch whisky till there was Mike; baseball was a bore till there was Stan . . . I could go on. Perhaps you could as well.

IN CONCLUSION   Finally, we must ask whether this emerging concept of relational being moves us beyond the problems of the self-contained individual described above. Surely the conception of relational being reduces the debilitating gap between self and other, the sense of oneself as alone and the other as alien and untrustworthy. Whatever we are, from the present standpoint, is either directly or indirectly with others. There is no fundamental reason to be "self-seeking" or to treat others as instruments for self gain. We are made up of each other. Nor do we find ourselves confronting the problem of the earlier relational theorists, to whit, the self is the product of others, a mere *effect* of the social surrounds. From the present standpoint there is no cause and effect; we are mutually constituting. So far so good. In the following chapters we shall explore further consequences of relational conceptions.

Reflection

As you may realize, I am very excited about the idea of the relational self. In part my excitement is generated by the sense that we in Western culture may be on the verge of a major transformation in our way of conceptualizing ourselves. It is like taking part in the development of a second Enlightenment. And if the first period of the Enlightenment – which solidified the concept of the self-contained individual – brought forth democracy, public education, and human rights, then what flowering of practices may now be anticipated? Yet, it is also clear that the attempt to understand ourselves as relational beings is only in its infancy. Significant expansions are essential. One of the most important of these for me, is that of transcending what might be called "the privileging of the social." That is, in developing the concept of relational self, the presumption is that relations are social – carried out by human communities in the process of generating meaning. However, if we circumscribe relations in this way, we contribute to binaries such as social/non-social, or culture/nature, community/environment. And as we speak of processes intrinsic to the first term of the binary, so do we suppress the significance of the second. Most directly to the point, we lose sight of the existence of persons within their natural habitats. What is sorely needed, then, is an expansion of the concept of relation to include the world of the non-social, and particularly the natural environment. Could we generate a new family of metaphors, narratives, images and the like that can reconstitute meaning as a byproduct of persons within environments?

Notes

1 For a more fully developed account of generative theory see my book, Gergen K.J. (1993) *Toward Transformation in Social Knowledge*, 2nd edn. London: Sage.
2 Lasch, C. (1979) *The Culture of Narcissism*. New York: Norton.
3 Bellah, R.N., Madsen, R., Sullivan, W.M., Swidler, A., and Tipton, S.M. (1985) *Habits of the Heart*. Berkeley, CA: University of California Press.
4 Ibid., p. 85.
5 Wallach, M. and Wallach, L. (1983) *Psychology's Sanction for Selfishness*. San Francisco: Freeman. p. 11.

6   Stone, A.R. (1996) *The War of Desire and Technology at the Close of the Mechanical Age*. Cambridge: MIT Press. Interestingly, as a commentator on internet technology, Stone champions the development of multiple identities on the internet as a means of resisting individualization.

7   Mead, G.H. (1934) *Mind, Self and Society*. Chicago: University of Chicago Press.

8   Ibid., p. 164.

9   Interesting examples of research and theory in this domain include Hochschild, A. (1983) *The Managed Heart: Commercialization of Human Feeling*. Berkeley, CA: University of California Press; Turner, R.H. (1978) The role and the person. *American Journal of Sociology*, 84, 1–23; Matza, D. (1969) *Becoming Deviant*. Englewood Cliffs, NJ: Prentice-Hall.

10 Mead, *Mind, Self and Society*, p. 186.

11 The classic discussion of this distinction is that of Overton, W.R. and Reese, H.W. (1973) Models of development: methodological implications. In J.R. Nesselroade and H.W. Reese (Eds.) *Life-span Development Psychology: Methodological Issues*. New York: Academic Press.

12 Vygotsky, L. (1981) The genesis of higher mental functions. In J.V. Wertsch (Ed.) *The Concept of Activity in Soviet Psychology*. Amronk, NY: M.E. Sharpe. p. 163.

13 Bruner, J. (1990) *Acts of Meaning*. Cambridge, MA: Harvard University Press.

14 See for example, Moll, L.C. (1990) (Ed.) *Vygotsky and Education*. Cambridge: Cambridge University Press.

15 See Holzman, L. (1997) *Schools for Growth*. Mahwah, NJ: Erlbaum.

16 See especially Schutz, A. (1970) *On Phenomenology and Social Relations*. Chicago: University of Chicago Press. Schutz's work also plays a pivotal role in one of the first important books on social construction, namely Peter Berger and Thomas Luckmann's *The Social Construction of Reality* (New York: Doubleday, 1966).

17 For further discussion of this contribution see Schneider, K.J. (1998) Toward a science of the heart: Romanticism and the revival of psychology. *American Psychologist*, 53, 277–89.

18 The idea that language influences our perceptions of the world is often called "the Whorf hypothesis," after the writing of the linguist Benjamin Lee Whorf. (*Language, Thought and Reality*, Cambridge, MA: MIT Press, 1956). However, even within linguistics no compelling explanation has yet been made as to how this could occur.

19 Bakhtin, M. (1984) *The Problems of Dostoevsky's Poetics* (Ed. and trans. C. Emerson). Minneapolis, MN: University of Minnesota Press. p. 26.

20 Ibid., p. 287.

21 Bakhtin, M.M. (1986) *Speech Genres and Other Late Essays* (trans. by V.W. McGee) Austin, TX: University of Texas Press. p. 68.

22 Also see Roy Schaeffer (1976) *A New Language for Psychoanalysis*. New Haven, CT: Yale University Press.

23 Myerson, G. (1994) *Rhetoric, Reason and Society: Rationality as Dialogue*. London: Sage.

24 Billig, M. (1996) *Arguing and Thinking*, 2nd edn. Cambridge: Cambridge University Press.

25 For further discussion of this point see Harré, R. (1979) *Social Being*. Oxford: Blackwell.

26 Shotter, J. (1990) The social construction of remembering and forgetting. In D.

Middleton and D. Edwards (Eds.) *Collective Remembering*. London: Sage. pp. 122–3.

27   Middleton, D. and Edwards, D. Conversational remembering: a social psychological approach. In D. Middleton and D. Edwards (Eds.) (1990) *Collective Remembering*. London: Sage. pp. 31–2.

28   Iniguez, L., Valencia, J. and Vasquez, F. (1997) The construction of remembering and forgetfulness: memories and histories of the Spanish civil war. In J. Pennebaker, D. Paez, and B. Rime (Eds.) *Collective Memory of Political Events*. Mahwah, NJ: Earlbaum. p. 250.

29   See for example Schudson, M. (1992) *Watergate in American Memory*. New York: Basic Books.

30   Douglas, M. (1986) *How Institutions Think*. London: Routledge & Kegan Paul.

31   See for example Engestrom, Y. and Middleton, D. (Eds.) (1996) *Cognition and Communication at Work*. Cambridge, Cambridge University Press.

32   See Gergen, K.J., Gloger-Tippelt, G., and Berkowitz, P. (1990) The cultural construction of the developing child. In G. Semin and K.J. Gergen (Eds.) *Everyday Understanding*. London: Sage.

33   For useful discussion see Lillard, A. (1998) Ethnopsychologies: cultural variations in theories of mind. *Psychological Bulletin*, 123, 3–32.

34   See also Gagnon, J. and Simon, W. (1973) *Sexual Conduct*. Chicago: Aldine.

Further Resources

Deliberations on Individualism

Bellah, R.N., Madsen, R., Sullivan, W.M., Swidler, A., and Tipton, S.M. (1985) *Habits of the Heart*. Berkeley, CA: University of California Press.

Sampson, E.E. (1993) *Celebrating the Other: A Dialogic Account of Human Nature*. London: Harvester–Wheatsheaf.

Symbolic Interactionism

Denzin, N. (1992) *Symbolic Interaction and Cultural Studies: The Politics of Interpretation*. Oxford: Blackwell.

Hewitt, J.P. (1994) *Self and Society*. Boston, MA: Allyn & Bacon.

Cultural Psychology

Bruner, J. (1990) *Acts of Meaning*. Cambridge, MA: Harvard University Press.

Cole, M. (1996) *Cultural Psychology*. Cambridge, MA: Harvard University Press.

Moll, L. (1990) *Vygotsky and Education*. New York: Cambridge University Press.

Social Phenomenology

Berger, P. and Luckmann, T. (1967) *The Social Construction of Reality*. London: Allen Lane.

Owen, I.R. (1995) El construccionismo social y la teoria, practica e investicacion en psicoterapia: Un manifesto de psicologia fenomenologica. *Boletin die Psicologia*, 46, 161–86.

Polkinghorne, D. (1988) *Narrative Knowing and the Human Sciences*. Albany, NY: State University of New York Press.

Wagner, H. (1970) *Alfred Schutz: On Phenomenology and Social Relations*. Chicago: University of Chicago Press.

Bakhtinian Theory

Hermans, H.J.M. and Kempen, H.J.G. (1993) *The Dialogical Self*. New York: Academic Press.

Morson, G.S. and Emerson, C. (1990) *Mikhail Bakhtin, Creation of a Prosaics*. Stanford, CA: Stanford University Press.

Shotter, J. (1993) *Conversational Realities*. London: Sage.

Wertsch, J.V. (1991) *Voices of the Mind*. Cambridge, MA: Harvard University Press.

Relational Self

Bakhurst, D. and Sypnowich, C. (Eds.) (1995) *The Social Self*. London: Sage.

Burkitt, I. (1993) *Social Selves*. London: Sage.

Edwards, D. (1997) *Discourse and Cognition*. London: Sage.

Gergen, K.J. (1994) *Realities and Relationships*. Cambridge, MA: Harvard University Press.

Middleton, D. and Edwards, D. (1990) *Collective Remembering*. London: Sage.

Pennebaker, J.W., Paez, D. and Rime, B. (Eds.) (1997) *Collective Memory of Political Events*. Mahwah, NJ: Erlbaum.

Sarbin, T.R. (1989) Emotions as narrative emplotments. In M.J. Packer and R.B. Addison (Eds.) *Entering the Circle: Hermeneutic Investigation in Psychology*. Albany, NY: State University of New York Press.

6

DIALOGIC POTENTIALS

Dialogue rejects the tyranny of a single system or dogma; it welcomes new ideas and guarantees them equality . . . it refuses to censor "dangerous" ideas; it cherishes and protects its capacity to learn and to grow; it guards as something precious its own access to joy and laughter.

Robert Grudin, *On Dialogue*

If we, as individuals, are born of relationship, as proposed in the last chapter, what follows? Is this simply a fancy metaphor – possibly inventive and even inspirational – but ultimately inconsequential outside academic walls? This is always a danger of intellectual work – trusting that what is printed actually makes a difference in the world. However, in the present case there is good reason to believe in an active relationship between words on the page and in the street. For the constructionist words are themselves a form of social practice and it is imperative that these practices not remain closeted in the house of privilege. This emphasis on practice will become increasingly central in the remaining chapters.

We begin here by confronting one of the most difficult problems of daily life – and indeed, within the scholarly world as well – namely how it is we understand each other. How do we come to share meaning (or not) within dialogue? By considering this problem from a relational standpoint we open new doors to action. This discussion will also set the stage for considering the potentials of dialogue in daily life. Previous chapters have made a case for dialogue as the origin of constructed worlds. We now confront the explosive challenge of dialogue and difference. That is, how can people who inhabit different and conflicting realities – worlds in which "the other" is discredited and demonized – sustain life together?

The Hermeneutic Question: From Mind to Relationship

"You just don't understand me . . ."
"You can't know what I feel . . ."
"I don't understand what you mean . . ."

These common refrains underscore the problem of understanding in everyday life. Without understanding, we are lost. (Think of traveling in a land where you could not understand anyone.) Without understanding, it seems, we cannot generate meaning together, cannot coordinate action, cannot co-exist. But how do we go about understanding each other, and why is misunderstanding so common?

The problem of how human understanding occurs has long been a challenge to scholars. Perhaps the most concentrated attention to the problem takes place in *hermeneutic* (hur-ma-noo-tic) study – or the study of interpretation. Just as Hermes, the messenger of the Greek gods, enabled humans to comprehend the words from Mount Olympus, so too hermeneutic inquiry is designed to reveal the roots of interpersonal understanding. Hermeneutic study owes its origins to the early religious concern with biblical texts. How are we, it was asked, to understand the "words of God" and early religious writings? What was meant by these words? On a more secular level we also confront this problem in interpreting early legal rulings. The way in which the Supreme Court of the United States interprets the meaning of the Bill of Rights – including matters of free speech and the right to bear arms – affects the lives of millions. In literary study we wish to know the meaning behind what we read – from Shakespeare's plays to the works of a T.S. Eliot. Hermeneutic scholarship is devoted to solving this difficult problem of understanding the other.

Beyond Truth Through Method

The guiding premise of traditional hermeneutics is dualistic: words and actions are outward or material expressions of an inward mind. On this account, to make a correct interpretation requires access to the mind of the author/actor. We wish to know what he or she *truly* means, intends or feels. In the present century many scholars sought to make interpretation more scientific. If there were standardized methods of interpretation, it was reasoned, then we could move beyond subjectivity or "mere opinion" and establish what is actually meant by a principle of law, poem, play, or gesture. As you can see, this romance with *truth through method* is not unlike that of the empirical scientist who employs standardized tests and procedures to assay everything from chemical composition to psychological depression. In the case of hermeneutics the attempt is nicely exemplified in the work of E.D. Hirsch, a professor of English literature. In his celebrated volume *Validity in Interpretation*, Hirsch proposed that "the meaning of a text is the author's meaning."[1] It is thus the task of readers to use careful observation and logical inference to determine, in so far as possible, the author's intent. Hirsch's model is drawn directly from the behavioral sciences. In effect, he proposes a process of hypothesis testing in which the reader compares various hypotheses about what the author means against the text. It is evidence from the text that, "indicates that one hypothesis makes functional more elements of the mute text than a rival hypothesis, and the hypothesis which makes functional the greater number of traits must, in relation to that limited evidence, be judged the more probable hypothesis."[2] Thus, for example, if you believed a complex poem was fundamentally written for purposes of seduction, you might look for sexual images or allusions. If you found many of them strewn throughout the poem, you might conclude that your hypothesis is probably correct.

Although it is very appealing to think that we might derive truth of interpretation through a systematic method, the preceding chapters certainly cast doubt on this idea. In hermeneutic study the chief enemy of such a view is the German scholar Hans Georg Gadamer. In his monumental work *Truth and Method*,[3] Gadamer argues that prior to the development of any method of interpretation, there is always a conception of truth – or a pre-understanding. It is this pre-understanding that gives our methods of interpretation their intelligibility, that makes interpretation possible in the first place. Or in effect, it is the pre-understanding of truth that produces methods, rather than methods that produce truth. No method can give us anything more than what it is we already assume. Thus, Hirsch's method already asks us to accept certain assumptions, for example, that the author has a singular or articulable intention, that there is a simple correspondence between intention and word, and that the intention will manifest itself in multiple expressions.

It is this view of method that also informs Gadamer's stance toward interpretation. As Gadamer proposes, we confront the text (or a person's actions) from a *horizon of understanding* – an array of prejudgments or prejudices – that inform the questions we put to the text along with what we accept as possible answers. We don't believe Shakespeare's *Hamlet* is an exploration of homosexual anxiety, or Mickey Mouse comics are secretly converting us to a pagan religion – not because this is impossible but because such interpretations are not constituents of our particular horizon of understanding. However, argues Gadamer, if we let this horizon of understanding completely dominate our interpretations, we end up in a solipsistic world – simply confirming our initial prejudices. If a committed Marxist interprets all news reporting as a capitalist plot to subjugate the people, then his horizon remains frozen and private.

One's horizon can only be expanded, proposes Gadamer, by joining with the text in a *dialogic relationship*. Through this dialogic relation a *fusion of horizons* is accomplished. Required in this dialogic effort is first a suspension of one's own forestructure of understanding; one must set the forestructure aside and let the text ask its own questions. As the text begins to present itself in its newness, one places its meaning "in relation with the whole of one's own meanings."[4] The dialogic relationship is one in which one's own meanings and the meanings of the text are engaged in a conversation. In the successful conversation they, "are thus bound to one another in a new community . . . [it is a] transformation into a communion, in which we do not remain what we were."[5] In effect, the fusion of horizons takes place in the interchange between reader and text. The result is not a correct or accurate reading, as in the case of Hirsch, but a new creation. The successful interpretation, then, brings forth new worlds.

Gadamer's work is helpful in avoiding the snares of truth through method; it is also quite optimistic in its hopes. However, in the end it raises as many problems as it solves. For example, how can we suspend our prejudices, step outside the interpretive stances for which culture has prepared us? And if this unusual demand could be met, how could we then apprehend the text (or another's action) on its own terms. What questions could it ask of us, other than those we are prepared to understand in terms of the initial horizon? As an analogy, if all I understood is French (my horizon of understanding), how can I suspend this forestructure of French in order to allow a text in Russian to speak to me, to ask me a question, to generate a dialogue? These questions about the plausibility of dialogue remain unanswered, and in the way the theory is constructed (Gadamer's own forestructure), possibly unanswerable.

Meaning in Relationship

At this point the problem of understanding others may seem rather hopeless. There seem to be little means by which we can locate the meaning behind people's words and actions, little means by which those who differ in perspective could ever learn to appreciate the other. However, as you may guess from the preceding chapter, our problem here largely stems from the way we have put the question – that is, in terms of an *individual mind* attempting to locate the meaning behind an action or text, to locate what is *within the mind* of the other. We are better positioned by heeding Wittgenstein's warning, "Try not to think of understanding as a 'mental process' at all. For *that* is the expression which confuses you. But ask yourself: in what sort of case, in what kind of circumstances, do we say, 'Now I know how to go on.' "[6] This is to suggest that we remove meaning from the heads of individuals, and locate it within the ways in which *we go on together*. In effect, this is to extend the focus of the previous chapter on relational being.

What is it to say that meaning resides within a relationship? Broadly, let me propose that meaning is an *emergent property of coordinated action*. To illustrate, if we approach each other on the street and I extend my hand, the action becomes a candidate for meaning. If you grasp my hand in yours, you grant it meaning as a greeting; if you push the hand aside and give me a big hug you have shown me that a mere greeting is insufficient for such a good friendship; if you glare at my extended hand and quickly stride away, you suggest that I have no right to call myself your friend. Or more formally, the way you coordinate yourself to my action functions as a *supplement* that begins to grant meaning to what my action lacks in itself.[7] Or to put it another way, in isolation I have no ability to mean anything; I gain my ability "to mean something" through the supplemental actions of others. The meaning of my words and actions is not fundamentally under my control. I need you in order to mean anything.

Let's explore this idea further: although my action may mean nothing until supplemented by you, you gain the capacity to supplement (make meaning) only through my action. Without my extending my hand you are not in a position to give it meaning as a greeting, an insufficiency, or a mis-calculation. Or more broadly, you gain the capacity "to mean something" through the actions I initiate. Meaning is not then located in either my actions or in yours, but within the action–supplement conjunction, or essen-tially, in the form of coordination we achieve. As social theorist John Shotter puts it, meaning results not from action or reaction, but from *joint-action*.[8]

Let us extend this further: as we pass in the street, we are not alone. We carry with us traces of myriad relationships extending into the past. In a sense, it is from this *history of relationship* that we draw our vocabulary of action and supplement. It is this immersion in a history of coordination that grants my initial handshake its right as a candidate for meaning. If we approach and I pat my leg, chances are it will go unnoticed or un-supple-mented. By virtue of previous relationships, such an action is not a candi-date for meaning. Thus we find that my possibilities for "meaning something" are not determined by you alone; they are prepared by a history of relationship. Similarly, this same history of relationship constrains your potential for supplementation. At the sight of my handshake you are not likely to fall on the street in a fetal position. Your vocabulary of coordination – your capacity to mean in relationship to me – derives as well from a history of relationship. We are granted possibilities for meaning together by virtue of the relationships of which we have been a part.

We can expand this account in one last direction, from the significance of preceding relationships to the *dependency on future unfolding*. You and I may marshal resources from the past to generate meaning together. However, our relationship is in motion, spontaneously moving toward an unfixed future. Two important aspects of this ongoing coordination must be noted. First, there is nothing about our past that strictly determines what we can mean together. We are not simply conditioned to repeat well-worn rituals. To be sure, there may be certain rituals – such as greetings – that are endlessly repeated. However, in normal conversation our lin-guistic and behavioral vocabularies provide enormous possibilities for novel juxtaposition – words and actions that have never been coordinated in just these ways. In this sense the meaning we make together is seldom fixed; it is subject to *continuous refashioning*. Another's sudden kiss may first invite definition as intrusive; with further coordination it may be seen as an indicator of hopeless dependency; and then again as a sign of deep passion: and still later as immature impetuosity; and then simply nothing at all – "hey, it just happened." It is also important to realize that this con-tinuous refashioning of meaning is not under any one person's control. Even within a dyad the voices of other relationships continuously intrude. And as we enter directly into dialogue with others, so can the emerging patterns of coordination change all that once seemed clear and apparent. As most children of divorce are painfully aware, their alienated parents are often very skilled in retrospectively destroying all that was once treated in adulation. Similarly, national histories are seldom stable. Each generation may redefine the heroes and the villains of the past.

Recalling the relational perspective developed in the preceding chapter, we thus find that social understanding is not a matter of penetrating the privacy of the other's subjectivity. If it were, we could never understand. Rather, understanding is a relational achievement; it depends on coordinating actions – and most frequently, coordination as specified within a tradition. To illustrate, return to the question of emotion, and how we can understand what another person is feeling. If emotions were private events, we could never understand each other's feelings. None of my facial expressions, for example, provides a window into my interior. That you believe my smiles to represent an *ex/pression* (a pressing outward) of happiness is not a result of your looking into my being and finding this to be so. How would this be achieved? Nor is it because I can somehow look inward and identify happiness flitting by like a butterfly (see Chapter 1 on identifying inner states). Rather you reach this conclusion by virtue of participating in a culture that holds "happiness" to be evidenced by smiles. You would scarcely infer that my smile indicated a state of *fago* (see Chapter 4 on the cultural construction of emotion). Further, in Western culture it is appropriate to respond to a smile with a smile, and possibly to comment on the other's feelings. This pattern goes virtually un-noticed; the participants seem fully "to understand each other." However, if I respond to your smile with a frown and say, "god you must feel lousy," you may well look at me dumbfoundedly. You might even say to yourself, "what a turkey; he doesn't understand me at all." My failure to understand in this case is not because I fail to grasp the inner workings of your mind; it is rather a breach in the common scenario of relationship. Mutual understanding, then, is akin to dancing smoothly together, coordinating actions in ways that emerge as acceptable.

Dialogue, Discourse, and Difference

> You see it your way . . .
> I see it my way
> We can work it out,
> We can work it out . . .
>
> The Beatles

There is a sense in which dialogue serves as the key organizing metaphor for social constructionist theory. If we mean by dialogue a conversation between two or more persons, then dialogue is centrally responsible for the generation of all that we take to be real and good. We have variously centered on the means by which persons together marshal discursive resources, perform, objectify, negotiate, position and so on to create comprehensible worlds. In a broad sense all these discussions are concerned with dialogue. Yet, there is a second meaning of dialogue that now demands attention. We often speak of dialogues not just as conversations in general, but as special kinds of relationships in which change, growth, and new understanding are fostered. About this sense of dialogue almost nothing has been said. Our discussions have broadly focussed on issues of creation, that is, how it is we create our realities together. However, once crystallized and institutionalized, how and why should we change? This is the challenge of dialogue as a *transformative* medium. We are not speaking here of a mere exchange of views, but of moving beyond alienated coexistence to a more promising way of going on together.

Alterity and the End of Meaning

Let's consider what is at stake in this concern with dialogical transformation. Most of us feel comfortable in certain groups but not others; indeed, there may be certain groups of people who seem just plain wrong-headed or evil – perhaps for you these could be neo-Nazis, the KKK, the Mafia, or terrorist groups. This sense of *alterity* – of difference from particular others – is virtually an inevitable outcome of social life. As outlined in Chapter 3, as we come to generate realities and moralities within specific groups – families, friendships, the workplace, the church or synagogue – so do our interlocutors become invaluable resources. With their support – either explicit or implicit – we gain the sense of who we are, what is real, and what is right. At the same time, however, all world constructing relations create a devalued exterior – a realm that is *not us*, not what we believe, not true, not good.

In important degree this devaluation derives from the structure of language out of which we construct our realities. Recall here the binary basis of language described in Chapter 2. Language is essentially a differentiating medium, with every word separating out that which *is* named or indicated from that which *is not* (absent, contrary). Thus, whenever we declare what is the case or what is good, we use words that privilege certain existents while thrusting the absent and the contrary to the margins. Recall here the way in which an emphasis on the material basis of reality suppresses or devalues the spiritual, or in which an emphasis on the world as observed subtly undermines beliefs in the unseen and intuitive. In effect, for every reality there is alterity.

The problem of difference is intensified by several ancillary tendencies. First, there is a *tendency to avoid* those who are different, and particularly when they seem antagonistic to one's way of life. We avoid meetings, conversations, and social gatherings. With less opportunity for interchange, there is secondly a tendency for *accounts of the other to become simplified*. There are few challenges to one's descriptions and explanations; fewer exceptions are made. Third, with the continuing tendency to explain others' actions in a negative way, there is a *movement toward extremity*. As we continue to locate "the evil" in the other's actions there is an accumulation; slowly the other takes on the shape of the inferior, the stupid or the villainous. Social psychologists often speak in this context of "negative stereotyping," that is, rigid and simplified conceptions of the other.[9] The present analysis shifts the focus from "prejudiced minds" to forms of discourse commonly circulated and supported within a group. In any case the result is social atomization, with the same processes that separate cliques and gangs in adolescence reflected at the societal level with conflicts between the political left and right, fundamentalists vs. liberals, gay activists vs. anti-gays, and pro-choice vs. pro-life. And more globally we find similar tendencies separating Jews and Palestinians, Irish Catholics vs. Protestants, Muslims vs. Christians, and so on.

As the present analysis suggests, tendencies toward division and conflict are normal outgrowths of social interchange. Prejudice is not, then, a mark of a flawed character – inner rigidity, decomposed cognition, emotional bias, and the like. Rather, so long as we continue the normal process of creating consensus around what is real and good, classes of the undesirable are under construction. Wherever there are tendencies toward unity, cohesion, brotherhood, commitment, solidarity, or community, so is alterity – or otherness – under production. And it is here that seeds of conflict are sewn. In the present condition, virtually none of us escapes from being undesirable to at least one (and probably many) other groups. The major challenge that confronts us, then, is not that of generating warm and cozy communities, conflict-free societies, or a harmonious world order. Rather, given strong tendencies toward conflict, how do we proceed in such a way that ever emerging conflict does not yield aggression, oppression, or genocide – in effect, the end of meaning altogether? This challenge is all the more daunting in a world where communication technology allows increasing numbers of groups to organize, mold common identities, set agendas and take action.[10] Perhaps the major challenge for the twenty-first century is how we shall manage to *live together* on the globe.

What resources are available to us in confronting this challenge? At least one important possibility is suggested by constructionist theory itself: if it is through dialogue that the grounds for conflict emerge, then dialogue may be our best option for treating contentious realities. In the remainder of this chapter, we shall consider three approaches to dialogue designed to ease conditions of conflict. The first is based on regulative rules of negotiation, the second on an ethics of discourse; both derive from rich but limited traditions. Finally we shall turn to transformative dialogue – an approach that emerges more directly from the relational perspective developed above.

From Argumentation to Mediation: Hopes and Hesitations

> Here's to you, and here's to me
> And if we two should disagree,
> To hell with you!
>
> Traditional toast

If we disagree on the state of things and wish to avoid mortal combat, an obvious option is "to discuss it." As we all know, however, such discussions are far from ideal: they are replete with misunderstandings, subterfuge, and subtle power tactics, and often lead to broken relations. One solution to these problems is formalization. That is, we may generate a series of rules or standards of argument designed to yield conclusions without warfare. Such rule-governed approaches have become increasingly popular in recent years, and demand our attention. What are the potential gains; where are they less than ideal? Broadly speaking, these orientations are lodged within the twin traditions of realism and rationalism. That is, on the rationalist side they tend to view persons as independent actors, ideally reasoning their way toward identifiable goals; on the side of realism, they tend to posit a single existing reality (or structure of rewards, punishments, payoffs). Ideally it should be possible, from these perspectives, to locate a single best logic (rational procedure) for resolving differences between competing parties. Most extreme in these respects is the *argumentation orientation*. Here, "the discussants must advance statements in which the standpoint under discussion is attacked and defended ... In an argumentative discussion the participants try to convince one another of the acceptability or unacceptability of the expressed opinion under discussion by means of argumentative statements. These are designed to justify or refute an expressed opinion to the listener's satisfaction."[11] Specific rules of argumentation are thus designed for broadest (and potentially universal) application. Perhaps the clearest exemplar of argumentation orientation at work is the judicial process. Each side amasses reason and evidence to defeat the other.

Under less formalized circumstances, but sharing much with argumentation theory, we find the *bargaining orientation*. Here each party in the conflict determines the costs and benefits of various outcomes, and attempts to negotiate trades to achieve the highest possible pay-off for self (maximization). As one bargaining impresario puts it, because of the common "clashing of preferences" among parties, "Bargaining is a search for advantage through accommodation."[12] In the bargaining domain, the emphasis on logic is manifest in discussions of optimal bargaining strategies (maximizing gain while minimizing loss). For example, potentials and consequences of using reward as opposed to punishment or threat strategies are deliberated. By exploiting the adversary's weaknesses, the hope is to achieve the greatest advantage while conceding as little as possible. Bargaining procedures are typically used when there are intense conflicts in business and political arenas.

Third, while sustaining the emphasis on independent adversaries, the *negotiation orientation* tends to shift focus from the mini–max strategies generally championed in bargaining, to a concern with maximum joint reward (*satisficing*.) In such bestsellers as *Getting to Yes* and *Getting Past No*, Roger Fisher and William Ury outline strategies by which each party to the negotiation may generate "options for mutual gain."[13] Each party is encouraged to identify their basic interests, what they want from the negotiation and how important it is for them. With these interests in view, participants are encouraged to search for those particular interests shared in common, or ways of dovetailing otherwise different interests, and then inventing solutions that both can find acceptable. Negotiation practices are most often found in business and government contexts where antagonism has not been long-standing.

Although overlapping substantially with negotiation, we may justifiably separate out the *mediation orientation* for its stronger emphasis on diminishing distance between the participants.[14] In mediation a major emphasis is typically placed on replacing the adversarial relationship with collaborative, integrative problem solving. Parties may be encouraged to listen to and understand each other's thoughts and feelings about the situation, to generate multiple options, and to work together to locate a mutually agreeable option. Mediation of this sort is often useful in cases of interpersonal conflict, such as divorce or child custody.

All of these practices – argumentation, bargaining, negotiation and mediation – have all been valuable resources in solving conflicts. From international conflict and labor-management disputes to community and family conflict, these practices have often proved efficacious. Yet, there is reason here to press further. Such practices are all lodged within a modernist worldview, where rationality and objective realities are presumed. From a social constructionist standpoint both the rational and the real are byproducts of communal relations. In the case of reason, constructionists see all rational arguments, strategic reasoning, or rules of rational deliberation as historically and culturally situated. While there are surely conventions of "good reason" about which many people in Western society agree, any fixed standard or requirement will always remove the privilege of meaningful participation from some person or group. Further, by solidifying such standards or requirements, we diminish the possibility of new alternatives (for example substituting some form of non-verbal interchange for "rational talk"). In the case of realism, constructionists hold all that we take to be real (for example "the problem," "my interests," "the optimal solution") as essentially moves in discourse, a discourse that is credible only for certain people at certain times, and which is both ambiguous and flexible. Thus, to fix "the problem," "my interests," and the like is to establish fixed limits within which the dialogue must proceed. If we agree that "this is the problem," then by common convention we shall move toward "solution talk." If we establish "your interests" as opposed to "mine," we discourage discourses of "rights," "duties," "justice," "the spirit," and so on. In these ways we diminish the possibilities for the mutual construction of the real.

This latter limitation is intensified by a further presumption shared by the existing traditions. As previous chapters have outlined, the construc- tionist sees the conception of independent individuals as a historical and cultural artifact. When we view dialogue as a relationship between sepa- rate, autonomous individuals, each with private interests, perceptions, and reasons we intensify the sense of conflict. We imply that in spite of temporary agreements the other will always be alien, unknown, and fundamentally untrustworthy. At the heart of the individualist view is a world of "all against all." In my view a relational view of persons offers more promise.

Habermas and Discourse Ethics

If rules of argument and negotiation are limited in these ways, what about encouraging a more general orientation to dialogue? That is, what if par- ticipants enter with agreements on the general values that will guide con- versation? It is this possibility that has sparked the work of German theorist Jürgen Habermas. Habermas' early work was of pivotal importance in placing limits on the scientist's claims to unbridled superiority over all competing forms of rationality (see Chapter 1).[15] Yet, while steadfastly opposing the oppressive tendencies of any dominant or monological auth- ority, Habermas also stubbornly resisted the opposing tendency, that is, toward *anything goes* anarchy. In particular, he is concerned with the enor- mous conflicts in contemporary society, particularly over issues of justice and morality. Consider, for example, the questions of whether we should have school prayer, a death penalty, programs of affirmative action, or save our forests at the expense of jobs. All are complicated questions of moral and ethical importance and much hangs on their outcome. For Habermas it would be a mistake to wheel out an ethical rule or prescription – a uni- versal dogma – and simply impose it on all the people. No religion, no government, no philosopher has any fundamental right to impose his/her will on the people. But, if we abandon all authority how are we to proceed? Is it simply to be an inchoate war of competing interests?

For Habermas the solution lies in *discourse ethics*, that is, ethical foun- dations for productive dialogue on how we should resolve our conflicts. In particular, Habermas has attempted to generate the rational grounds for peaceful, democratic, and just deliberation. Given a fair hearing of all reasons and an assaying of all relevant facts, Habermas believed, people will move toward consensus. Although Habermas' work on discourse ethics is complex and extensive, it is useful to summarize several of his major conclusions. In particular, Habermas champions the following:[16]

- Where there is conflict, a process of argumentation should be placed in motion. Argumentation should be directed toward consensus.
- Everyone should have equal rights to participate.
- Participants in the argument should be of equal power. There should be a level playing field in which no expression is suppressed or coerced.
- Everyone can introduce into the argument any assertion or expression of attitude or desire he/she wishes.
- Only those solutions will be valid that meet the approval of all participants. Everyone's interests must be satisfied.

While Habermas does not outline the details of how actual argumentation should proceed, on the face of it, these five stipulations seem very attractive. At the same time, there are problems. At the outset, there is no ultimate means of justifying this particular form of discourse ethics. Why should everyone accept these proposals, especially if they do not accept the modes of reasoning preferred by educated Westerners? Habermas' justification itself rests on his own moral commitment (to just this kind of democratic procedure); in effect, it is the product of a single authority (himself) as opposed to the very dialogic process he favors. In this way he shares the problem of argumentation theorists who treat rules of reason and evidence as unquestioned universals. Further, like argumentation theorists, Habermas believes that an ethics-governed exchange of opinion will lead to consensus. This hope seems unreasonably idealistic. If there are opposing parties, such as pro-life and pro-choice advocates in an abortion debate, is it likely that the opponents' reason and evidence will convince the other side of the debate that they are wrong – that they were simply operating under false assumptions? Scarcely. What is reasonable to one side is not often reasonable to the other, and the convincing evidence for one is hopelessly fallacious for the other. For example, many pro-life enthusiasts consider it a fact that the moment of conception is the beginning of a human life, while pro-choice advocates see this as a totally arbitrary conception. What additional evidence could prove either side correct?

Finally, as Habermas' critics point out, why should we necessarily seek consensus? Is there nothing to be said for recognizing and appreciating differences? Why not a multitude of religions, political values, cultural ideals, and ways of life? Even if we do not agree, and even if we think our way of life is superior, would the world not be enriched by "letting a thousand flowers bloom?" This criticism is especially supported by constructionist arguments. If there is no one "right answer" – no single logic, or body of evidence, or ethic, that transcends a given community – then why should we always anticipate or desire consensus? The existence of multiplicity and difference may, in fact, be our best strategy for sustaining the human project.

Yet, putting these problems aside, Habermas' particular stipulations for ethical discourse are appealing. That is, if we come together from antagonistic positions, would we not wish to be heard and without fear of punishment for our expressions? And would we not wish to have all resolutions carry with them our stamp of approval? While there may be no universal justification for such criteria, they do seem intuitively attractive as components of effective exchange. Can we move beyond models of antagonism and still retain these features?

Toward Transformative Dialogue

> If it is necessary to share meaning and share truth,
> then we have to do something different.
>
> David Bohm, *On Dialogue*

We can well appreciate the scholar's attempt to generate rules or ethics that would ease the anguish of colliding realities. However, we scholars live in a rarefied world where there are already deep traditions in place. Inevitably our theories will reflect these protected positions remote from the hurly-burly of everyday conflict. Inevitably they will favor the kinds of arguments that "people like us" are good at and they will fail to reflect the investments and traditions of those from other backgrounds or cultures. More broadly, it is difficult for any person or group of people to lay out rules or regulations for productive dialogue that are not biased in some way. As critics have shown, even the strict rules of argument and evidence that prevail in the courtroom – supposedly producing "justice for all" – favor the economically privileged.[17]

Does this mean abandoning the problem, simply giving up on the idea of what Habermas would call "ideal speech conditions?" I don't think so. There is another way of proceeding that may offer greater promise. Rather than working "top down" – with high level authorities laying out the rules or ethics for all – we might better proceed "bottom up." That is, we might move first to the world of action, to cases in which people are wrestling with problems of multiple and conflicting realities. By examining these cases we may locate conversational actions that often seem to help people in going on together. This is not to establish a set of rules for transformative dialogue, but rather a vocabulary of relevant action. On any given occasion we might then draw from this vocabulary as useful for the conditions at hand. This is not a vocabulary that can ever be set in stone for as meanings are transformed over time, and as further voices are added to the mix, the vocabulary itself will be altered and augmented. There are no universal rules for transformative dialogue, for dialogue itself will alter the character of what is useful.

To press forward, then, let us first consider a single successful case. We can then step back to examine some of its features and ponder their implications. In 1989, Laura and Richard Chasin, Sallyann Roth and their colleagues at the Public Conversations Project in Watertown, Massachusetts, began to apply skills developed in the context of family therapy to stalemated public controversies.[18] Their practice has evolved over the years and with impressive results. Consider their attempt to bring together committed activists on opposing sides of the abortion conflict. Here is a case in which debate has led nowhere, largely because the opponents construct reality and morality in entirely different ways. The stakes are high, there is enormous animosity, and the consequences are lethal. In the present case, activists who were willing to discuss the issues with their opponents were brought together in small groups. The Project guaranteed that they would not have to participate in any activity which they found uncomfortable. The meeting began with a buffet dinner, in which the participants were asked to share various aspects of their lives *other than* their stand on the abortion issue. After dinner the facilitator invited the participants into "a different kind of conversation." They were asked to speak as unique individuals – about their own experiences and ideas – rather than as representatives of a position – to share their thoughts and feelings, and to ask questions about which they were curious. As the session began, the participants were asked to respond – each in turn and without interruption – to three major questions:

1 How did you get involved with this issue? What's your personal relationship, or personal history with it?
2 Now we'd like to hear a little more about your particular beliefs and perspectives about the issues surrounding abortion. What is at the heart of the matter for you?
3 Many people we've talked to have told us that within their approach to this issue they find some gray areas, some dilemmas about their own beliefs or even some conflicts ... Do you experience any pockets of uncertainty or lesser certainty, any concerns, value conflicts, or mixed feelings that you may have and wish to share?

Answers to the first two questions typically yielded a variety of personal experiences, often stories of great pain, loss and suffering. Participants also revealed many doubts, and found themselves surprised to learn that people on the other side had any uncertainties at all.

After addressing the three questions, participants were given an opportunity to ask questions of each other. They were requested not to pose questions that "are challenges in disguise," but to ask questions "about which you are genuinely curious ... we'd like to learn about your own personal experiences and individual beliefs ..." After discussing a wide range of issues important to the participants, there was a final discussion of what the participants felt they had done to "make the conversation go as it has." Follow-up phone calls a few weeks after each session revealed lasting, positive effects. Participants felt they left with a more complex understanding of the struggle and a significantly rehumanized view of "the other." No, they did not change their fundamental views, but they no longer saw the issues in such black and white terms nor those who disagreed as demons.

The work of the Public Conversations Project is indeed impressive and has led to many additional ventures and variants. However, the question we must now confront is, what particular features of this kind of dialogue make it so effective? How can we conceptualize these components in such that they can be generalized to other contexts? We cannot use precisely these practices in all situations of conflict or difference, but if we can abstract from these practices we have a means of envisioning how we might proceed elsewhere. And too, we should be sensitive to absences within the practice; what might a constructionist standpoint suggest in terms of augmentation? Let us then focus on five prominent components of special relevance to transformative dialogue.

From Blame to Relational Responsibility

> "We have only one person to blame, and that's each other."
>
> Barry Beck, New York Ranger hockey player
> after a brawl at the championship playoffs

In the tradition of Western modernism we have a pervasive tendency to hold individuals morally accountable for their actions. We construct persons as originary sources of their own actions (moral agents), and thus responsible for their misdeeds. There is much about the tradition of individual responsibility that most of us greatly value. Because of a discourse of individual blame we are able to hold persons morally accountable for robbery, rape, murder and the like. By the same token we are able to praise individuals for singular achievements, humanitarian and heroic acts etc. Yet, this same discourse of individual blame is divisive. In finding fault with another, we begin to erect a wall between us. In blaming you, I position myself as all-knowing and all-righteous and you as a flawed being subject to my judgment. You are constructed as an object of scorn, subject to correction, while I remain praiseworthy and powerful. In this way I alienate and antagonize you. The problem is intensified in the case of opposing groups, for each may hold the other responsible – the poor will blame the wealthy for exploitation, while the wealthy will hold the poor responsible for their indolence; the religious conservative will blame the homosexual for corrupting the society, while the homosexual will blame the conservative for intolerance, and so on. Thus, each finds the guilty other not only denying guilt but unjustifiably attempting to reverse the blame. Antagonisms are further polarized, and the tradition of individual blame thus sabotages the possibility of transformative dialogue.

It is in this context that we may appreciate the potentials of *relational responsibility*.[19] If all that we take to be true and good has its origin in relationships, and specifically the process of jointly constructing meaning, then there is reason for us all to honor – to be responsible to – relationships of meaning making themselves. The quest, then, is for means of sustaining processes of communication in which meaning is never frozen or terminated, but remains in a continuous state of becoming. Obviously, mutual blame is an impediment to relational responsibility. How, then, can relational responsibility be achieved in practice? In the case of the Public Conversations Project, the tendency toward blame was simply defined out of bounds. The conversational tasks didn't permit blame talk, not even disguised as questions. Under normal circumstances, however, we scarcely have control over the rules of conversation. How can one shift from individual blame to a more relationally responsible language in daily life? Although there are no definitive answers to such a question, we can locate within existing cultural practices several means of shifting the conversation in directions other than individual blame. Consider:

Internal others: If I talk too much and too loud and you are drowned out of the conversation, you have good reason for blaming me. However, if you attack me directly our relationship may be cooled. One option is to locate within me another voice that is "speaking me" in the situation. If you say, for example, "The way you are talking, I seem to hear your father's dominating voice . . . ." or "You are really sounding very much like that teacher of yours . . ." In effect, you communicate your displeasure, but I am positioned to evaluate my actions as something other than "myself." What we take to be the "core self" is not placed on the defense – the "I" which must be defended at all costs – but rather, you construct me as one who carries many others in my repertoire. It is they who inhabit my present and problematic actions.

Conjoint relations: If in the heat of argument you insult me, I may justifiably blame you for your abuse and our relationship will suffer. However, I may also be able to locate ways in which it is not you alone who is to blame, but our particular pattern of relating. It is not you vs. me, but *we* who have created the action in question. Remarks such as, "Look what we are now doing to each other . . .," "How did we get ourselves into this situation . . ." or "We are killing ourselves going on like this; why don't we start from the beginning and have a different kind of conversation . . ." all have the effect of replacing guilty individuals with a sense of interdependent relationship.

Group realities: Alice finds Ted so irritating. He is messy, never picks up after himself, thinks only of his needs, seldom listens to her. Ted can scarcely tolerate Alice's pristine tidiness, her disinterest in his job, and her way of prattling on. They are seething with blame for each other. Yet, there is another vocabulary of possibility here, one that may shift the form and direction of conversation. Specifically, there is a way of seeing ourselves not as singular individuals but as representatives of groups, traditions, families and so on. We may avoid the habit of individual fault finding in the context of group differences. For example, if Ted and Alice could speak about gender differences, and trace their proclivities to an origin in different gender traditions, they might move into a space of more congenital conversation. If we move the discussion to focus on group differences, individual blame recedes in importance.

The systemic swim: When Timothy McVeigh was found guilty of blowing up the Oklahoma City municipal building and taking scores of lives, he was sentenced to death. There is a sense of collective relief; justice was done. Back to work. Yet, consider again the logic of the Militia Movement of which McVeigh was part. From their perspective the national government is destroying the American tradition, trampling on their rights, and forcing them off the land. Justice will be done when they revolt against this malevolent force. In effect, the same logic of blame underlies both McVeigh's crime and our reactions to it. Or to put it another way, there is an important sense in which McVeigh's crime was an extension of the very tradition that most of us support and sustain. This is not to forgive the crime. However, it is to say that the tradition of individual blame is insufficient. We may usefully broaden our vision to consider the ways in which we ourselves participate in creating the patterns we most devalue. It takes more than a village to create a rape, a hate crime, or a robbery; the entire system is implicated.

The Significance of Self-Expression

If we can successfully avoid blame, how can we move dialogue in the direction of change? The Public Conversations work suggests that the sense of self-expression may be vital. Participants in their conversations were each given opportunity to share views that were important to them. In part, the importance of self-expression can be traced to the Western tradition of individualism. As participants in this tradition we believe we possess inner thoughts and feelings and that these are essential to who we are; they virtually define us. Thus, if dialogue is to proceed successfully it is critical that the other understands who we are and what we stand for. Moreover, the other must not deny the intelligibility of what is said; the other must listen and comprehend. To paraphrase the logic, "If my position – what I think and feel – is not voiced, then there is no dialogue."

Yet, the self-expressions encouraged by the Public Conversations Project were of a very special kind. They asked the participants to speak personally as opposed to using abstract arguments, to tell stories of their own involvement in the issue of abortion. There are at least three reasons that *story telling* expressions are desirable for transformative dialogue. First, they are *easily comprehensible*: from our earliest years we are exposed to the story or narrative form, and we are more fully prepared to understand than in the case of abstract arguments. Further, stories can invite *fuller audience engagement* than abstract ideas. In hearing stories we generate images, thrive on the drama, suffer and celebrate with the speaker.

Finally, the personal story tends to *generate acceptance* as opposed to resistance. If it is "your story, your experience," then I can scarcely say "you are wrong." However, if you confront me with an abstract principle our common traditions of argumentation prepare me for resistance. By flogging me with a principle you set yourself up as a mini-god, issuing commandments from on high. My resentment will trigger a counter attack that you will find equally offensive. "Who are you to tell me that a fertilized egg, detected only microscopically, has a 'right to life?' ", "And who are you to tell me that a woman has a right to murder a child in the making?" Stalemate.

Affirming the Other

It is one thing to express one's feelings or relate life stories; however it is quite another to gain a sense of the other's affirmation. Because meaning is born in relationship an individual's expression doesn't acquire full significance until supplemented. If you fail to appreciate what I am saying, or I think you are distorting my story, then I have not truly expressed anything. For you to affirm means locating something within my expression which you can agree with or support. Such affirmation is important, in part because of the individualist tradition and the belief that thoughts and feelings are individual possessions. As we say, "It is my experience that . . ." or "These are *my* beliefs." If you challenge such expressions you *place my being into question*; in contrast, to affirm them is to grant worth, to honor the validity of my subjectivity. Second, as one's realities are discounted or discredited so are the relationships from which they derive. If you as reader dismiss social constructionism as absurd, and want me to "backslide into realism," so are you asking me to sever an enormous range of relationships. To embrace an idea is to embrace relationships, and to abandon one is to undermine one's community.

Of course, you may wonder how affirmation can be achieved when people live in oppositional realities. How can they affirm each other when they do not agree? The work of the Public Conversations Project is informative here. The conversations were effectively staged so as to promote forms of appreciation. Recall that curiosity was invited; to be curious is a signal of affirmation. Similarly, in listening intently to each other's stories participants' affirmation was expressed. To "be moved" by another's suffering is a high form of affirmation. The therapist Harlene Anderson speaks to the general importance of affirmation in listening. She proposes that therapy becomes transformative when, "the therapist enters with a genuine posture and manner characterized by an openness to another person's ideological base – his or her reality, beliefs, and experiences. This listening posture and manner involve showing respect for, having humility toward, and believing that what a client has to say is worth hearing."[20]

Coordinating Action: Invitation to Improvisation

In my view one of the most important contributions to the success of the Public Conversations Project derives from the fact that the meetings began with a shared meal. At the outset the participants exchanged greetings, smiles, handshakes. They began to converse in an unprogramed and spontaneous way about children, jobs, tastes, and so on. They developed rhythms of conversation, eye contact, speaking and listening. In my view transformative dialogue may thrive on just such efforts toward mutual coordination. This is primarily because meaning making is a form of co-ordinated action. Thus, if we are to generate meaning together we must develop smooth and reiterative patterns of interchange – a dance in which we move harmoniously together.

Perhaps the most important form of coordination may be termed, *co-constituting*. Here each person's moves in the conversation will reflect or resemble in some way the other's moves. One's actions or utterances will help to constitute the other's actions in their own terms. This does not mean duplicating or agreeing fully with what the other has done or said. Rather, one's actions will be a partial, provisional, and ambiguous reverberation of the other, reflecting the other in oneself. For example, co-constitution occurs when one's actions contain some fragment of the other's actions, a piece that represents the whole. If I express to you doubts about my parents' love for me, and you respond by asking, "What's the weather report for tomorrow?" you have failed to include my being in your reply. If your response includes the sense of what I have said, possibly concern over what I have said, then I find myself in you; I locate the "me" who has just spoken. At the same time, because it is you who has generated this expression, it is not quite mine. You move us closer, and in doing so I am invited to reply similarly to you. Transformative dialogue, then, may depend importantly on locating ourselves within each other. Let us consider two forms of co-constituting coordination:

Coordinating rhythm: Friends were vacationing in Jamaica and took their infant along with them to a brunch that featured a local band. They found themselves in dismay when, in the middle of a rousing performance, their baby began to wail loudly. With deep embarrassment they began searching for an available exit. However, the musicians had another idea. They began an intricate reshaping of their rhythms so that they were soon incorporating the rhythm of the child's cries. The music and the crying became one. The audience was ecstatic. This reshaping exemplifies co-constituting coordination; with deft and spontaneous movement the ill-fitting and disruptive becomes integrated into the process of making meaning.

Although the band's action represents a literal coordination of rhythm, it is useful to open the term "rhythm" to a broader usage. Let us include here any form of action that bears positive traces of what has preceded.

On the simplest level, to respond to a smile with a smile (as opposed to a blank stare), to carry the other's tone of voice, to express in one's clothing something of the formality or informality of the other's style, for example, would all be co-constituting coordination. Such moves can be contrasted with rhythms that are negating in effect. For example, in responding to warmth with coldness, to a calm voice with a shrill one, to an informal gesture with a formality, one's actions don't so much resonate with the preceding as negate them. The point of improvisation here is to secure a mutuality of rhythm by means of which conversational participants may move closer, to share a space from which a new building forth may proceed.

Coordinating discourse: If we construct the world in entirely different terms co-creation is impossible. However, there are means of moving toward mutuality in language, including the use of similar phrasings, cadences, or tone of voice. One of the most interesting routes toward mutuality is through *linguistic shading*, that is the substitution of a word (or phrase) with a near equivalent. For example, we shade "love" by calling it "attraction," and we shade "anger" when we call it "irritation." The potentials of shading are enormous, for every substitution of terms also brings with it an array of different associations, new ranges of meaning, and fresh conversational openings. In the midst of conflict to say that there is "tension between us," (as opposed to "hatred") is to reduce the degree of implied hostility and to suggest that harmony can be achieved. There are virtually no limits, other than practical, to the possibilities of shading. At the extreme, any term may possess infinite possibilities for meaning – even to the point of signifying its opposite. For example, "love" can be shaded as "intense attraction," "intense attraction" as an "obsession," and an "obsession" as "a sickness" – with the other now serving as "the source of my illness." Of course, the source of one's illness is "undesirable," and something that is "undesirable" is "not liked;" what is "not liked" is "hated." Thus, when its implications are fully extended, to love is to hate.

In this light consider again the challenge of co-constituting coordination. If our statements of belief contain words that are not fixed in their meaning, then they are open to linguistic shadings that can transform them into something else. Opposing beliefs need not necessarily remain in this condition. Everything that is said could be otherwise, and with appropriate shading could be brought into a state more resembling what is otherwise opposed. On a more practical level, with appropriate shading the most antagonistic arguments can be remolded in such a way as to allow an exploration of mutual interests. You may oppose someone who favors the death penalty for cold-blooded killers. However, if "favoring the death penalty" can also mean, for example, a "radical measure against heinous crime," chances are you could agree that "radical measures" are sometimes necessary. In such agreement you may locate common ground.

Self-Reflexivity: the Promise of Polyvocality

If one's grounding realities are heard and affirmed, and the conversation becomes increasingly coordinated, the stage is set for another significant move toward transformative dialogue: self-reflexivity. One unfortunate aspect of the modernist tradition is that we are typically positioned in conversations as *unified egos*. That is, we are constructed as singular, coherent selves. Logical incoherence is subject to ridicule, moral incoherence to scorn. Thus, as we encounter people whose positions differ from ours we tend to represent ourselves one-dimensionally, ensuring that our comments form a unified, seamless web. Under these conditions when we enter a relationship defined in terms of my position vs. yours, commitment to unity will maintain our distance. And if the integrity or validity of one's coherent front is threatened by the other, we may move toward polarizing combat. How many times have you ever heard someone locked in an argument turn and say, "Gosh, my reasoning was wrong; you win the argument."?

The transformative challenge here is to shift the conversation in the direction of self-reflexivity – toward questioning one's own position. In reflecting on our stand, we must necessarily adopt a different voice. We cannot question our statement that "X is true" or "Y is good," by saying the same thing. Thus, in self-questioning, we relinquish the "stand fast and firm" posture of conflict, and open possibilities for other conversations to take place. Such self-reflection is made possible by the fact that we are polyvocal. We participate in multiple relationships – in the community, on the job, at leisure, vicariously with television figures – and we carry with us myriad traces of these relationships. In effect we can speak with many voices. For example, with effort we can typically locate reason to doubt virtually any proposition we otherwise hold as true, and see limitations in any value we think central to our life. Suppressed at the moment I "speak my mind," or "say what I believe" is the chorus of internal nay-sayers. If these suppressed voices can be located and brought forth within the conversation of differences, we move toward transformation.

In the case of the Public Conversations Project self-reflexivity was built in as a conversational requirement. After the opportunity to tell their stories participants were asked about possible "gray areas" in their beliefs, pockets of uncertainty, or mixed feelings. As participants spoke of their doubts, animosities seemed to soften. Such reflections on the part of one participant seemed to encourage a similar response in others. Possibilities were opened for other conversations to take place than defending differences. Extending this line of reasoning, conflict specialists, Pearce and Littlejohn often employ "third person listening," in which one member of an antagonistic group may be asked to step out of the conversation and to observe the interchange.[21] By moving from the first person position, in which one is representing a position, to a third person stance, one can

observe the conflict with other criteria at hand (for example, is this a productive form of interaction, what improvements might be made?). In other
conflict work, participants have found it useful to introduce opinions or
beliefs of groups that differ from both the antagonists. Thus, for example,
a conflict between two religious groups (for example, Christians vs.
Muslims) takes on entirely different character when many alternative religions are made salient (for example, Judaism, Hinduism, Buddhism).

The Co-Creation of New Worlds

Each of the conversational moves outlined above may reduce animosities
and open the way to more mutually appreciative interchange. However,
none of them actively promotes the development of new realities. None
of them creates a new conjoint construction of the real or the good. Needed
are what might be called *imaginary moments* in the dialogue in which participants join in visions of a reality not yet realized by either. These imaginary moments not only sow the seeds for mutual building, but also shift
the orientation of the participants from combat to cooperation. They move
toward common purpose, and in doing so redefine the other as "us."
Perhaps the simplest way of moving toward a conjoint reality is through
locating a common cause. That is, antagonists temporarily suspend their
differences to join in an effort they both support. For example, battling
spouses may join together against an intruding do-gooder, or feminist
radicals and conservative traditionalists may join in a crusade against
pornography. More broadly, there is nothing so unifying for a country than
to be threatened by invasion. Social psychologists have long spoken of
these commonalities in terms of *superordinate goals*.

Yet, while finding common cause is often useful, it doesn't necessarily
create a new and lasting amalgam. Some of the most interesting work of
this kind has been carried out by Harvard psychologist Herbert Kelman.
Kelman's concern is with the Israeli–Palestinian dispute,[22] the origins of
which go back to the birth of Political Zionism at the end of the nineteenth
century. Violence first erupted in the 1920s, and conditions have been
unstable ever since. In the worst case, both sides deny the other's right to
identity and to property, and bloodshed results. It was not until 1991 that
a concerted peace initiative began, and while sometimes successful, animosities are often resumed.

Beginning in the 1970s, Kelman began a series of workshops that have
continued over the years to bring together influential leaders from both
sides. The "problem solving workshops," as they are called, are voluntary,
private, and unrecorded. Similar to the Public Conversations Project, there
is an attempt to curb tendencies for mutual blame and polemic critique.
Likewise, there is an emphasis on "here-and-now experiences" – as
opposed to abstract principles – as a basis for appreciating the position of
the other. Influenced by the negotiation model discussed earlier, participants are challenged to find a win–win solution to the conflict. Most

important for present purposes, the participants are encouraged to "work toward a shared vision of a desirable future."[23] Conversation about "who is in the wrong" is thus replaced by joint deliberation on what kind of world they might build together. As Kelman finds, "the process of producing these ideas contributes to building a new relationship between the parties, initially between the negotiators and ultimately between the two societies as wholes."[24] We shall say more about practices for building common realities in the following chapter.

Reflection

The unfolding conception of transformative dialogue has been very important to me both professionally and personally. In a world in which the globalizing process brings opposing realities into increasingly sharp conflict, new resources for communication seem essential. I have also found these practices very useful in my daily life. Conflict is always immanent in the classroom, and it is virtually endemic to family life, and indeed to any close relationship. Here I have found it especially useful to seek ways of affirming the other, and locate other "selves" that are not so antagonistic to the other. At the same time, I don't want to be too optimistic about realizing the potentials of transformative dialogue. I find too many cases where a transformative move is possible and desirable, but I simply can't bring it off. For example, I am all too skilled in blaming others if something goes wrong; in this sense I am not relationally responsible. I fail to use an option that would avoid driving a wedge between me and the other. This suggests significant limits to the kinds of academic treatments represented in this book. Analysis is helpful in giving intelligibility to new lines of action, but it is not sufficient. It is one thing to have new resources and another to put them into action. We need to experiment and practice together to become skilled in conversation.

Notes

1 Hirsch, E.D. (1967) *Validity in Interpretation*. New Haven, CT: Yale University Press. p. 25.
2 Ibid., p. 190.
3 Gadamer, H.G. (1975) *Truth and Method*. New York: Seabury.
4 Ibid., p. 238.
5 Ibid., p. 341.
6 Wittgenstein, L. (1953) *Philosophical Investigations*. Oxford: Blackwell.
7 For a more extended account see Gergen, K.J. (1994) *Realities and Relationships*. Cambridge, MA: Harvard University Press.
8 Shotter, J. (1993) *Cultural Politics of Everyday Life*. Toronto: University of Toronto Press.

9 See for example Brown, R. (1995) *Prejudice, Its Social Psychology*. Oxford: Blackwell.

10 See for example Hunter, J.D. (1991) *Culture Wars: The Struggle to Define America*. New York: Basic Books.

11 van Eemeren, F. and Grootendorst, R. (1983) *Speech Acts in Argumentative Discussions*. Dordrecht: Forris. p. 2.

12 Lebow, R.N. (1996) *The Art of Bargaining*. Baltimore, MD: Johns Hopkins University Press. p. 1.

13 Fisher, R. and Ury, W. (1981) *Getting to Yes*. Boston, MA: Houghton Mifflin; Ury, W. (1993) *Getting Past No*. New York: Bantam.

14 See for example Bush, R.A. and Folger, J.P. (1994) *The Promise of Mediation*. San Francisco: Jossey-Bass; Susskind, L. and Cruikshank, J. (1987) *Breaking the Impasse: Consensual Approaches to Resolving Public Disputes*. New York: Basic Books.

15 See especially Habermas, J. (1971) *Knowledge and Human Interests*, Boston, MA: Beacon Press; and Habermas, J. (1973) *Legitimation Crisis*. Boston, MA: Beacon Press.

16 Distilled from Habermas, J. (1993) *Moral Consciousness and Communicative Action* (Trans. C. Lenhardt and S. Nicholsen). Cambridge, MA: MIT Press.

17 See for example Hunt, A. (1993) *Explorations in Law and Society*. New York: Routledge; Griggin, S.M. and Moffat, R.C. (Eds.) (1997) *Radical Critiques of the Law*. Lawrence, KA: University of Kansas Press.

18 See for example Chasin, R. and Herzig, M. (1992) Creating systemic interventions for the sociopolitical arena. In B. Berger-Could and D.H. DeMuth (Eds.) *The Global Family Therapist: Integrating the Personal, Professional, and Political*. Needham, MA: Allyn & Bacon.

19 McNamee, S. and Gergen, K.J. (1999) *Relational Responsibility*. Thousand Oaks, CA: Sage.

20 Anderson, H. (1997) *Conversation, Language, and Possibilities*. New York: Basic Books. p. 153.

21 Pearce, W.B. and Littlejohn, S.W. (1997) *Moral Conflict: When Social Worlds Collide*. Thousand Oaks, CA: Sage.

22 See for example Kelman, J.C. (1997) Group processes in the resolution of international conflicts. *American Psychologist*, 52, 212–30.

23 Ibid., p. 214.

24 Ibid., p. 218.

Further Resources

The Hermeneutic Challenge

Bleicher, J. (1980) *Contemporary Hermeneutics*. London: Routledge & Kegan Paul.

Messer, S.B., Sass, L.A., Woolfolk, R.L. (Eds.) (1988) *Hermeneutics and Psychological Theory*. New Brunswick: Rutgers University Press.

Taylor, T.J. (1992) *Mutual Misunderstanding*. Durham, NC: Duke University Press.

Argumentation, Negotiation, Mediation, and Discourse Ethics

Arrow, K.J., Mnookin, R.H., Ross, L., Tversky, A. and Wilson, R.B. (Eds.) (1995) *Barriers to Conflict Resolution*. New York: W.W. Norton.

Bercovitch, J. and Rubin, J.Z. (Eds.) (1992) *Mediation in International Relations: Multiple Approaches to Conflict Management.* New York: St Martin's Press.

Billig, M. (1996) *Arguing and Thinking* (2nd ed.) Cambridge: Cambridge University Press.

Bush, R.A. and Folger, J.P. (1994) *The Promise of Mediation.* San Francisco: Jossey-Bass.

Habermas, J. (1993) *Justification and Application: Remarks on Discourse Ethics.* Cambridge, MA: MIT Press.

Lebow, R.N. (1996) *The Art of Bargaining.* Baltimore, MD: Johns Hopkins University Press.

Shailor, J.G. (1994) *Empowerment in Dispute Mediation.* New York: Praeger.

Transformative Dialogue

Baxter, L.A. and Montgomery, B.M. (1996) *Relating, Dialogues, and Dialectics.* New York: Guilford.

Folger, J.P. and Jones, T.S. (Eds.) (1999) *New Directions in Mediation.* Thousand Oaks: Sage.

Grimshaw, A.D. (Ed.) (1990) *Conflict Talk.* New York: Cambridge University Press.

Markova, I., Graumann, C.F. and Foppa, K. (Eds.) (1995) *Mutualities in Dialogue.* Cambridge: Cambridge University Press.

Pearce, W.B. and Littlejohn, S.W. (1997) *Moral Conflict: When Social Worlds Collide.* Thousand Oaks, CA: Sage.

Sandole, D.J.D. and van der Merwe, H. (1993) *Conflict Resolution Theory and Practice: Integration and Application.* Manchester: Manchester University Press.

7

A PROFUSION OF PRACTICES

Language enters life through concrete utterances, and life enters language through concrete utterances as well.

Mikhail Bakhtin, *The Dialogic Imagination*

"Walk the talk" is a common phrase in many professional training circles. Typically it directs trainees to take the abstract concepts they have learned and put them into practice. For the constructionist the phrase means something different. "Talk," for the constructionist, *is* a form of practice. One doesn't learn abstract concepts and then figure out how to apply them; to use a form of language is itself to engage in a practice, and this usage can have widespread impact. However, that talk is a form of practice raises serious questions for the constructionist regarding traditional scholarly work. We inherit a modernist view of science in which the task is to "map the world," to become experts on "the way things are." This view has contributed to the unfortunate development of two cultures – the supposed "knowers" within the scientific and scholarly spheres, and the "otherwise ignorant" outside the walls. The role of the knowers is traditionally to generate knowledge (in the form of abstract formulations of the truth); the ignorant are to learn the truth, and apply it in action. In effect we have the worlds of "pure research" and "application."

If we take a constructionist view, however, the formulations developed within scientific and scholarly circles are themselves practices. This perspective not only throws the existing tradition into question, but points in new and interesting directions. At the outset the hierarchy of theory over practice is replaced by a level field: we are all practitioners in the creation of cultural life. Further, because we are "all in it together" we are invited to share, to place practices of theory and action into collaborative, catalytic and creative relationship. We must consider ways of making abstract theory accessible and "actionable" within the society, and of linking concrete actions to communicable conceptions. The present chapter explores important developments in practice emerging from this collaboration. In particular, I will touch on constructionist practices in four significant areas: therapy, organizational change, education, and scholarly expression. I select these primarily because the developments are fascinating, and in some cases dramatic. With regret, page limitations prevent me from describing other adventures. However, at the end of the chapter I have included a bibliography earmarking some of these developments.

Therapy as Social Construction

> [We must] appreciate the power of redescribing, the power of language to make new and different things possible and important – an appreciation which becomes possible only when one's aim becomes an expanding repertoire of alternative descriptions rather than The One Right Description.
>
> Richard Rorty, *Contingency, Irony, and Solidarity*

Kibby frequently visited my yard when I was a child; he seemed anxious to play with my brothers and me; with broad smiles he joined in our games whenever he could. However, we couldn't understand the strange language he seemed to speak, so we couldn't communicate. And besides, Kibby was a grown man. My mother encouraged us not to play with him. As everyone said, "Kibby is a bit off." The Gaelic have a word for people like Kibby, which translates into English as "with God." The modern mental health industry has scuttled all these gentle appellations, and replaced them with a battery of almost 400 terms for "disorder" (see Chapter 2). Enormous research projects attempt to locate the causes of these "diseases" of the mind, and enormous hours are devoted to testing the efficacy of various therapies in curing the mentally ill. Increasingly the mental health professions turn to pharmaceuticals as a means for cure.

For the social constructionist these mammoth "scientizing" efforts are not only misguided, but the results are often damaging. Whatever is the case with Kibby and others like him, "illness" is only one of many possible constructions. To presume that he is ill is also to invite practices of "cure." If he was not defined as ill, practices other than curing might be set in motion. This *medical model* for treating unusual people also pervades most traditional forms of therapy and counseling. People report a problem – depression, violence, fear, incapacity and the like – and the therapist's job is typically to locate its roots or causes and to remove them, thus bringing relief (cure). In psychoanalysis the causes may be located in the deep recesses of the mind ("repression"); for the Rogerian they may reside in the person's lack of self-regard; the cognitive therapist will trace them to defective modes of thought. In all cases, it is the patient or client who possesses the problem, and the therapist who serves as the expert. The therapist is said to be "value neutral," simply doing his or her job of finding the source of the problem and working toward a solution.

Social constructionism challenges these approaches to therapy, along with the medical model on which they are based. Why, we ask, must we construct the client as "having a problem;" are there useful alternatives; on what grounds can the therapist claim superiority in understanding; and is any form of therapy really value neutral? Thirty years ago therapeutic experts claimed homosexuality to be a form of mental illness, and developed myriad means of cure. For example, electric shock was used to desensitize men to the nude images of other men. Is this cure or a form of political intolerance? And today, isn't the very attempt to rid the society of depression based on a vision of an ideal society in which everyone is happy? As it is said in Poland, "If you aren't depressed you must be stupid." The therapeutic and the political are inevitably linked.[1]

Informed by these constructionist concerns, a new range of therapeutic approaches emerges. Constructionist-based therapies generally share the following characteristics.

Focus on meaning: Traditional therapy is focussed on cause and effect realities – getting to the root of depression, locating the cause of marital violence, and so on. In contrast, for the constructionist therapist there are no pre-fixed facts – such as depression and violence – and the assumption of causes-producing-effects is viewed as but one narrative among many. Nothing must be taken for granted. Rather, the "facts of the case" are inevitably constructed, ways of making the world intelligible by persons in relationship. This does not make "the facts" any less significant. However, it is not essential to "get clear" on what is really happening. Rather, the emphasis is placed on the constructed meanings by which we make our way through life. For example, the psychiatrist will be very curious about a patient's feelings toward her parents; the Rogerian will explore a client's feelings about himself. In contrast, for the constructionist therapist "feelings" are not facts in the world that we can interrogate; they are conversational objects. And the therapist's questions invite the individual into one form of construction as opposed to another. Thus, rather than trying to probe the individual's "mental condition," the constructionist therapist will be more concerned with the individual's particular way of constructing him/herself. Typically the individual is given great latitude to speak, thus revealing possibly preferred constructions. The challenge is then to work with these constructions toward change.

Therapy as co-construction: The traditional therapist adopts the stance of expert on such matters as depression and marital conflict. It is this presumption of expert knowledge that allows the therapist to dictate the direction of therapy – often acting as a sleuth who will solve the problem and then guide the patient toward insight. The constructionist realizes, however, that his/her theories of depression, conflict and so on, are the byproduct of a particular professional community. Not only do these constructions lose their privilege over all others, but we must ask whether they are useful for all people. For example, most professionals view the discourse of romantic love as suspicious, and the discourse of the holy spirit as misleading mythology. Yet, for the vast share of the culture these are living and significant ways of constructing the world. As it is said, the constructionist therapist must enter the consultation with a stance of *not knowing*,[2] that is of relinquishing the grasp of professional realities, and remaining curious and open to the client's vocabularies of meaning. In this case it is not the therapist's task to "lead the way to knowledge" but to collaborate with the individual (or family) in generative conversations. The therapeutic relationship is thus one of conjoint meaning making.

Focus on relationship: Most therapies are preeminently concerned with the mental state of the individual – with emotions, thoughts, motives, the unconscious, and so on. For the constructionist therapist the reality of the mind recedes, and is replaced instead with a concern for relationships. It is from relationships that meaning is generated and patterns of action become reasonable or desirable. Thus, the focus on the interior of the mind is often replaced with an exploration of the networks of relations in which the individual participates. With whom is meaning made, and what are the outcomes? Who are the chief interlocutors – either present or past, actual or fictitional, present or virtual? In family therapy the troubled person is often said to the *designated patient*, in this way pointing to the possibilities that the family has selected a scapegoat for problems that are built into the family relationships.

Value sensitivity: Unlike the traditional therapists, the constructionist realizes that there is no value neutrality in the therapeutic relationship. Every intervention will favor some form of life, while undermining others. The therapist who favors heterosexuality closes the door on homosexual options; in favoring the client's industrious productivity the joys of hedonism remain unrealized; "empower" the male and the female loses options. Given this situation, there is an active movement toward standpoint therapy, that is, therapy that is avowedly political in its aims. Feminist, gay, and lesbian therapists are particularly noteworthy. However, most therapists are less singularly committed, and will simply make their values known to their clients when matters become sensitive.

Given these orienting attitudes, there is great latitude for practice. Let us consider three of the most popular forms of constructionist therapy.

Solution Focussed Therapy: the Power of the Brief Encounter

What if there were no problems; what if all the anguish and hopelessness that bring people into therapy had no basis? There is a sense in which constructionist thought prompts just this kind of question. It is not that we don't confront difficult problems in our lives, problems that are very real and often very painful. However, the constructionist reminds us, these realities are constructed; problems are not "out there" as realities independent of us, but come to be what they are by virtue of the way we negotiate reality. This insight has prompted many therapists to give up traditional practices of exploring and solving therapeutic problems. In fact, it is argued, when clients are encouraged to talk at length about their problems, to explore them in detail, to express all their feelings about what is taking place, the results may be detrimental to the person. All the talk – the exploration, the feelings, and so on – function to make "the problem" increasingly real, increasingly objective. Why go on endlessly exploring the ravages of early childhood, for example, when this reality is made increasingly salient, vivid, and depressing as a result of its very exploration? Are there other visions of reality, therapists ask, with more promising outcomes?

With these issues salient, many therapists seek ways of refocussing the therapeutic conversation. One widely shared practice is called *solution focussed*. One of its central exponents, Steve deShazer, proposes that clients feel it is often more helpful to talk about solutions to their problems than the problems themselves.[3] Solution talk is often full of hope and promise. Thus, for example, rather than exploring the depths of a client's depression, it is more helpful to talk about ways the client might "return to school," or "get some day-care help for the children." Further, deShazer proposes, clients are helped when the conversation shifts to their goals and their potential resources for achieving these goals. Talk about depression, for example, objectifies depression; to speak of one's aspirations and competencies brings forth a more promising domain of possibilities.

One significant means of prompting solution-oriented talk is called *the miracle question*. Here the therapist asks the client, "If a miracle happened tonight and you woke up tomorrow with the problem solved, what would you be doing differently?" The question is intended to provoke deliberation on positive courses of action, bringing attention to bear on what might be changed here and now to create a more positive future. The client is invited by the question to suspend problem language to focus on "life beyond the problem."[4] Through their questions and comments therapists may also help their clients to move away from an *either/or* mentality – in which they frame the world in terms of "either this" action or way of life or "that" – for example, heterosexuality or homosexuality, career or marriage, being firm or being compliant. In its place they encourage a *both/and orientation*, where clients are helped to envision multiple and even contradictory ways of living life.[5] Other therapists make use of a language of *on-track*,[6] in which clients generate a set of goals, and a conception of the steps needed to achieve them. This conceptualizing of life in terms of "a track into the future" can also be facilitated through *scaling questions*, that is queries into "how, on a scale of 1 to 10, do you feel you are doing?" Here clients are encouraged to stand outside their condition and to consider their actions comparatively.[7]

In contrast to traditional therapies, the emphasis on solutions and positive action often reduces the amount of time clients spend in therapy – so much so that the phrase "solution focussed therapy" is often used interchangeably with *brief therapy*. Solution focussed (or brief) therapy dramatically and refreshingly contrasts with the problem-centered preoccupation of most traditional therapies. The fact that it reduces the number of client hours also makes it a therapy of choice for many managed health care providers. However, it is not without its limitations. For many, it remains too closely cemented to an individualist model in which it is the individual who can simply decide on goals and work to achieve them. The relationships in which the person is embedded seem to play too little role. Others resist the strong emphasis on goals, arguing that the view of life as a "set of tasks," or accomplishments – complete with measures of progress – does not leave enough room for spontaneous, joyous, and sensual play. Perhaps the most pervasive doubt is in the efficacy of brief therapies with severe problems. A solution focus may be satisfactory for the kinds of day-to-day problems common to life, but what about severe, long-term disturbances?[8]

Narrative Therapy

For many constructionist therapists the concept narrative plays a pivotal role. Recall from Chapter 2 that narrative or story telling is a major means by which we make ourselves intelligible to each other. We live and die through narrative. If indeed narratives do have this centrality in our lives, giving us a sense of order and direction, holding our relations in place, then a client's suffering is not independent of his/her narratives. The anguish of marital break-up is primarily derived from a couple's narrative in which marital happiness was their principal goal; anger becomes intelligible when one sees oneself thwarted in living out a successful narrative. In this sense, effective therapy enables clients to *re-story* their lives, to conceptualize their life trajectories in new and more livable ways.

How is such change accomplished? In their groundbreaking work *Narrative Means to Therapeutic Ends*, Michael White and David Epston describe various means by which they help clients to re-story their lives. One of the most interesting innovations is what they call *problem externalization*.[9] As suggested earlier, it is traditional to view problems as inhering within people, for example, "my depression," "my impotence," "my hostility." For White and Epston, a major step toward re-storying is taken when the person – along with family members and friends – can separate the problem from the self. "If family members separate themselves and their relationships from the problem, externalization opens up possibilities for them to describe themselves, each other, and their relationships from a new, nonproblem-saturated perspective; it enables the development of an alternative story of family life."[10]

To illustrate externalization, a six-year-old boy, Nick, was brought to therapy by his parents. Nick's problem was essentially one of impulsive defecation (enopresis). Not only was Nick prone to unpredictable "accidents," but he would streak his "poo" on walls, smear it in drawers, roll it into balls and plaster it around the house. The habit seemed uncontrollable and the parents were beside themselves. Externalization was facilitated by separating Nick from the "poo problem." A name, Sneaky Poo, was developed to personify the problem, and which term allowed discussion to center on how Sneaky Poo would try to trick Nick into becoming his playmate, how Sneaky Poo was preventing Nick from having friends, and how the parents could join Nick in resisting Sneaky Poo's trickery. The externalization of the problem, in turn, began to reveal *unique outcomes*, that is events or aspects of the case not included in the story of "Nick's problem" with which they entered therapy. The family began to recall times in which Sneaky Poo had not gotten the best of them, cases in which they had worked together against Poo's advances. These unique outcomes, in turn, became the basis for creating a new story, one in which they were banding together to resist an outside threat. This new narrative proved successful in solving the problem.

White and Epston are also deeply concerned with the politics of therapy. As they reason, many of the problematic narratives people bring into therapy are essentially the result of power relations in society more generally. Recall the discussion of Foucault's theory of the way in which dominant discourses function to subjugate people (Chapter 2). For example, if I believe I am depressed, and I must find a cure for my depression, I am essentially reflecting a story created by the mental health professions; I have swallowed the medical model in which I am the one who requires cure for my deficiency. For White and Epston, a major therapeutic emphasis is placed on helping people escape the subjugating grasp of the dominant discourses of the culture, to create "an insurrection of the subjugated knowledges."[11] For example, in one of Michael White's many letters to his clients, he wrote,

Dear Sue,
   Bulimia has required a great deal of you. Its survival has been expensive to you. It has required you to operate upon yourself. It has required you to reject yourself. It has required you to subject yourself to a constant evaluation of your body and your person. It has required docility . . .

In this letter, White is essentially trying to help Sue challenge the dominant discourse of the psychiatric profession that looks at bulimia as a disease, equates the disease with the patient, and looks at the patient as needing a therapist for cure. He is challenging her to throw off the reins of the societal discourse, and to generate an alternative conception of self and future that are more uniquely hers, tailored to her particular circumstances.

The focus on narratives has been enormously useful for many therapists. It brings into sharp focus issues of meaning, opens a rich space of exchange between the therapeutic and academic communities, and lends itself to fostering political consciousness. However, many also see opportunities for further development. There is first the frequent presumption that the client's story is defective, and that it must ultimately be dissolved or deconstructed and then replaced. Although far from the intent of the narrative therapist, one can locate here a subtle discrediting of the client story. It is ultimately the client's account of the world that is "re-storied." If I believe I have special abilities to communicate with the dead, for example, why is it my story that is defective? Why should we not work with those around me so that their stories of the real are not expanded to include mine? There is also a question of whether people do indeed live within the structure of single narratives – a life story? Do we carry with us only a single story of our lives, of who we were and where we are now going? Or is it not more likely that we harbor multiple narratives, employed on different occasions for different audiences? And what is it to say that we live by or within our narratives? It is perhaps more useful to see narratives not as determinants of action but as forms of action themselves. Or, recalling the Chapter 3 discussion of narrative, we use narratives to carry out relations with people. If this is so then we must ask whether narratives developed in therapy have use-value in outside relationships.

Polyvocal Collaborations: the Virtues of Multiple Meanings

A third focus of constructionist therapy is captured by the term *polyvocality*. Here the major emphasis is on expanding the number of voices bearing on the problematic situation. The aim is not to locate "the solution," or "the new story" but to generate a range of new options. With many voices at hand the deep puzzlements which the client brings into therapy are replaced by a plethora of possible actions. For some therapists there is also a secondary hope: when one is exposed to many "views of the matter," the grounds are laid for developing a consciousness of construction. One finds that "*the* truth of the matter," is but "*a truth*." This kind of consciousness may have the liberating implications described in the previous chapters.

At the simplest level, therapists may encourage polyvocality within the individual. For example, when individuals begin to talk about their problems, the therapist might ask them if they can locate another voice within, a voice that would construct the world in a different light or with different possibilities. For example, if a client suffered from feelings of hatred toward his father, is there a voice that is "not being heard" and might have other feelings toward him. In a variation on this theme, Karl Tomm accesses the voices of *internalized others*.[12] We possess many feelings and attitudes acquired from our relationships with others. What we say on any occasion – even when we are convinced that it is "my belief" – is often reflecting a voice we have appropriated from another. Thus, with a little effort, we can often locate alternatives that we find plausible; we thus become more flexible and can see alternative ways to go on.

In an interesting variation on individual polyvocality, Peggy Penn and Marilyn Frankfurt have clients write letters to others – living or dead.[13] As they reason, in addressing another – in writing to them so you can be heard – you also address yourself through their anticipated reaction. Or, in

Bakhtin's terms, when one looks inside himself, "he looks with the eyes of another."[14] In writing letters one can thus set in motion new *internal dialogues* that can lead in new life directions. One client, Mary, was furious with her ex-husband; she felt she had been victimized by him and there was nothing good she could say about him. The therapists asked if he had any good qualities at all, and Mary finally admitted that he was a good father to their son. Thus Mary was encouraged to write a letter to him – which might or might not be sent – telling him of her opinion of him as a father. The result of the writing was not only a shift in the way she talked about him, but as well the capacity to see herself in other ways than a victim.

Polyvocality can also be achieved by adding contributors to the conversation. One of the most popular practices, *the reflecting team*, was introduced by Norwegian family therapist Tom Andersen.[15] Families often develop shared constructions of themselves, their members, their problems and so on. Andersen wished to avoid any radical challenge to these realities; in his view change is most effectively brought about through a process of comfortable conversation. Thus, while a family talks with an interviewer about its problems, a team of therapists (often three in number) observe the interview (often from behind a one-way mirror). While the interview takes place each team member carries on "a private dialogue" about what is taking place. Later in the session, the team leaves its remote position and joins the family to discuss together their views of what took place. To avoid authoritative closings of conversation, reflecting team members speak with uncertainty, "I am not sure . . . maybe . . . one could think of . . ." etc. Instead of attempting to rule out competing views, a both/and orientation prevails: "You can see it this way . . . and another possibility is . . ." Then, the family members are asked to comment on the discussion of the reflecting team. They are asked, for example, "Is there anything from what you have heard you would like to comment on, talk more about . . .?" As therapists find, the reflecting team loosens the grip of professional authority, and invites a dialogic, open-ended search for useful meanings. "Therapy becomes both client and therapist focussed, with an emphasis on what fits . . . at any particular moment in the conversational life of the treatment system."[16]

Making Meaning in Organizations

> Both organizations and sensemaking processes are cut from the same cloth.
> To organize is to impose order, counteract deviations, simplify, and
> connect, and the same holds true when people try to make sense.
>
> Karl Weick, *Sensemaking in Organizations*

As this quote from Karl Weick suggests, the process of generating realities is as central to organizations as it is to personal or family well-being. Weick also reflects the investments of numerous other organizational theorists who believe the fate of any organization depends on capacities to navigate within the multiple and ever-changing sea of realities – both within the organization and without. Exemplary contributions to this dialogue are included in the list of resources at the end of the chapter. Yet, it is one thing to theorize organizations in social constructionist terms, and another to generate effective practices. Perhaps the first significant move in the direction of practice was developed in Gareth Morgan's revolutionary work *Images of Organization*.[17] Here Morgan made it clear that all our major ways of understanding organizations – and thus our ways of living within them – are metaphoric. They are lived fictions in a world where there is no living beyond fiction. For example, if the *machine* is our metaphor for the ideal organization, we are likely to divide the organization into specialty units, in which each person has a specific function (like the parts of an automobile). In contrast, if we view the organization as a living organism we may be centrally concerned with its health and the way the participants function in teams, and coordinate actions in times of stress. And if the brain is our central metaphor, we may be drawn to ways in which the organization collects and stores information, learns, and deliberates. For Morgan, a manager's success depends on his/her becoming "skilled in the art of seeing and understanding situations in different ways" and thus "to be able to move forward on the insights this generates."[18] In his view the effective manager must be able to imagine multiple realities and put them into use as he or she negotiates the world with others.[19]

Yet, for many constructionists it is not enough to improve the capacities of organizational managers. Much needed are ways of increasing full and productive participation in the meaning making process. One of the most exciting developments in constructionist practice moves in precisely this direction.

Appreciative Inquiry: From Conflict to Community

Life in organizations is dynamic. Everywhere within the organization – from the mail room to the board room – participants are continuously generating their local sense of the real and the good – who is doing what to whom, and is it good or bad. Realities and moralities will necessarily conflict, and with such conflicts often come suspicion, animosity, loss of morale, and more. These are the daily challenges of organizational life, and when the problems prove intractable, they become the challenges for a host of organizational consultants. Traditionally, both managers and consultants have approached these problems as realists. That is, the problems are treated as "things," – the equivalent, let's say, of an organizational illness. Further, because they are problems they demand solutions – cures for the illness. Certain people are fired, pay is raised or lowered, new positions are created, new training procedures are put in place: all are common treatments for the problems ailing the organization.

Yet, recall that for a constructionist problems exist primarily because of the way reality is negotiated. There are problems if we agree there are problems, and any situation may be defined as problematic or not. Informed by this logic, organizational specialist David Cooperrider and his colleagues at Case Western Reserve University have developed an eye-opening approach to conflict called *appreciative inquiry*.[20] The emphasis on appreciation sprang from the conception of "the appreciative eye" in art, where it is said that within every piece of art one may locate beauty. Is it possible, Cooperrider asked, that within every organization – no matter how embroiled in conflict – one can also find beauty? And if beauty can be found, can organizational members use it as a basis for envisioning a new future?

The specific means of fostering appreciation draws from the constructionist emphasis on narrative. People carry with them many stories and within this repertoire they can typically locate stories of value, wonderment, and joy. Within an organization these stories are valuable resources, almost like money in the bank. To draw them out and place them in motion, proposed Cooperrider, is to invest in new visions for the future. In sharing these stories confidence is stimulated that indeed the vision can be realized. In effect, appreciative narratives unleash the powers of creative change.

A single example will convey the potential. Acme Farm Equipment, as we shall call it, suffered from gender conflict. Women in the company felt poorly treated by the men, seldom acknowledged, sometimes harassed, underpaid and overworked. At the same time, their male counterparts felt unfairly blamed, and accused the women employees for being unnecessarily touchy and hostile. Distrust was rampant; there was talk of litigation and the company began to falter.

The Acme executives then asked Cooperrider and his associates for help. In particular, the executives felt, there should be a code of good conduct, a set of rules specifying appropriate conduct for all parties, along with penalties for misconduct. Yet, for Cooperrider this orientation simply objectified "the problem," and such a "solution" would still leave a strong residue of distrust. An appreciative inquiry was thus carried out in which small groups of men and women employees met together; their specific challenge was to recall some of the good experiences shared within the company. Were there cases where men and women worked very well together, had been effective and mutually regarding; were there times when men and women had especially benefited from each other's contributions; what were these experiences like and what did they mean to them as employees? The employees responded enthusiastically to the challenge and numerous stories were recalled about past successes. The groups then shared and compared their stories. As they did so a discernible change began to take place: the animosities began to melt; there was laughter, praise, and mutual regard. In this positive climate, Cooperrider then challenged the employees to begin to envision the future of the company. How could they create together the kind of organization in which the experiences they most valued would be central? How could they make the organization the kind of place that could bring them this kind of joy? As the participants entered this discussion of the future they also began to think of new practices – policies, committees, social planning, and the like. Optimism and a high sense of morale prevailed. "The problem" drifted into obscurity as positive plans were set in motion.

Future Search and Community Building

> We are caught in an inescapable network of mutuality, tied in a single garment of destiny. Whatever affects one directly, affects all indirectly.
>
> Martin Luther King

Although appreciative inquiry is deeply conjoined with constructionist theory, there are related practices that – while not specifically constructionist – are highly congenial with its outlook. These deserve special attention, because they extend the implications of appreciative inquiry beyond the specific organization. Of special interest, they lay a strong emphasis on collaboration across boundaries – between the organization and the surrounding community, or among otherwise alienated subcultures within a community. To illustrate, the practice of *future search* is dedicated to locating and building a common ground among people. Future search specializes in large group planning, bringing together representatives from a "whole system" together to work on a task-force agenda. Open dialogues are set in motion, and all participants share in the leadership. Typically, participants in a future search program meet for several days of intense discussion. The attempt is not to reduce complexity, to resolve disagreements, or to solve long-standing problems, but to generate a vision of a viable future together.

To illustrate, a future search was generated in the community of Santa Cruz, California, to explore the problem of housing.[21] Invited to participate in the three-day event were: educators, farm workers, students, retirees, people from churches, business, and government. One participant commented upon arrival, "If nothing else comes out of this, this is the most diverse party anybody's ever given." After extensive introductions, the group began exploring the past, and particularly the various problems emerging in the preceding decades: drugs, AIDS, gang violence, and the like. As one participant commented, "The sense of community was destroyed so long ago that a lot of us have forgotten what it's like to know the person next door." The group then turned to an appreciation of the present – the resources, the latent desires, the shared values. A community activist commented, for example, "We're proud of our ethnic and religious diversity." From this discussion the group developed a series of "ideal scenarios" for the future. Envisioned, for example, were a cultural center for agriculture and a regional market. This discussion led to a search for common ground – key themes that might unite the group in planning. Finally, from these key themes a set of action programs was developed. A plan to help low income residents become homeowners, and to increase the employment and education opportunities for the Latino community were among the outcomes.

Programs combining appreciative inquiry and future search methods are now used in numerous communities and cities in the United States to generate participatory future building. In programs such as "Imagine Chicago" and "Imagine Atlanta" broad participation is sought, from high-ranking city officials to residents of low-income housing projects. Within mixed enclaves, and across the generations participants tell their stories of positive experiences in the city. They also speak of what they value most in their communities and within the city as a whole. As these stories are shared and collected, participants work toward planning a future in which the ideals embedded within these stories can be realized. The attempt, then, is to replace the alienated sense of helplessness so common to urban life with a meaningful sense of connection from which a new future can spring. Let us turn now to constructionist practice in another domain of organized life, namely schools.

Education: Collaboration and Community

> I conceive of schools and preschools as serving a renewed function within our changing societies. This entails building school cultures that operate as mutual communities of learners, involved jointly in solving problems with all contributing to the process of educating one another.
>
> Jerome Bruner, *The Culture of Education*

We frequently speak of "the rewards of a good education." Yet for many people the actual experience of "schooling" is (or was) harrowing. It is replete with fear of failure, anxiety over competition, and excessive boredom. These common experiences are largely owing to two premises that pervade most educational systems: first, it is commonly held that the chief purpose of education is to move students from a condition of ignorance to one of knowledge – replacing mere opinion, mistaken thought, and blind faith with solid fact and logical reasoning. On these grounds experts determine what is true and valid, and thus the curriculum that students must master. The second major premise is that education is aimed at improving the minds of individual students. Thus, to ensure that each individual mind properly masters what is true – that each student "possesses knowledge" – frequent assessment is essential. The individual must ultimately "measure up" or be punished. Students are thus confronted with curricula which have little intrinsic interest, and are subjected to frequent examinations of their capacity to repeat the truths as determined by the experts.

This orientation toward education has scarcely gone without criticism. One of the most vociferous critics, Paulo Freire, calls the traditional model *nutritionist*.[22] Knowledge is essentially treated as "healthy food," educators are the dispensers of the nutrients, and students are defined as needy (in spite of their remonstrations). Ultimate authority in this case lies with those engaged in knowledge-production itself – for example, scientists and scholars. These experts "dispense the truth" that students will ultimately be "fed." Next within the hierarchy are educational experts such as curriculum designers, who package the knowledge into educational units. Following are administrators and bureaucrats who select among these units. Teachers enter only at the end, as instruments to dispense the educational nutrients to the students. Students are expected merely to consume the knowledge. As critics point out, there is a progressive disempowerment in this arrangement, from origin to consummation. And when teachers are required to teach a standardized curriculum, they lose their capacity to reflect on larger educational issues and to create educational experiences tailored to their particular situation. They are *deskilled*.[23] Students, on this model, are often treated as empty vessels, passive beings expected merely to absorb information. Creativity and innovation are stifled.[24]

Social constructionism lends support to Friere's arguments. As previous chapters have put forward, what we take to be true or rational (knowledge) is an outgrowth of communal relations. There is no truth beyond community. Further, the concept of the individual mind is deeply problematic, both intellectually and politically. If both truth and mind are placed in doubt, then so is the hierarchical structure of education – with certain classes determining what is true and rational for all others, and individual students the unwitting victims. Rather than extending the critique at this point, let's briefly glimpse three pedagogical alternatives favored by constructionism. Given a troublesome educational tradition, what kinds of activities does constructionism nurture?

Reflexive Deliberation

In the nutritionist tradition, knowledge is "cooked up" within the various disciplines – biology, economics, history etc. – and fed to the needy student. As the constructionist points out these "bodies of knowledge" are essentially the vocabularies (and associated activities) of particular professional groups. In this sense the student is invited (or forced) by the curriculum into an alien territory. He or she must master its ways, while the aliens sit in judgment. Yet, this process seldom encourages the student to ask questions about the territory from the outside – from other vantage points or value positions. The student *learns history* without being encouraged to ask, for example, "whose history is this," "why are we talking about kings and wars and wealth, and not music or art or love," and "why is this important to me now?" Further, the student is seldom encouraged to "see it another way," to generate alternative histories or alternative views of "what really happened." For the constructionist, then, a premium is placed on means for increasing reflexive deliberation. How can students be encouraged to challenge the authoritative discourses from alternative standpoints, to discuss assets and liabilities, and to create alternative interpretations? Toward these ends students may be encouraged to help in planning the curriculum, to bring their own experiences to bear on the classroom material, and to collect materials that might help them to reach their own conclusions.

For many educators, the first important steps toward reflexive pedagogy were taken by critics of the *hidden curriculum*, a phrase referring to beliefs and values that lie implicit but unarticulated in the subject matter. These hidden beliefs and values often reflect the interests of particular classes or ethnic groups, namely those responsible for the curricula. Critics proposed, for example, that mainstream curricula systematically prevent members of subordinate groups from achieving academic success, and reinforce and justify the values of dominant groups.[25] Working class students, in particular, are encouraged to be obedient, passive, and un-original.[26]

Resonating with these concerns, educators have developed *pedagogies of liberation*, educational practices that encourage students to engage in active critique, empowering them to join in determining their futures as opposed to simply swallowing the truth as given. One active exponent of emancipatory pedagogy, Henry Giroux, points to ways in which teachers can demystify the official curriculum by revealing the evaluative choices implicit in them – the gender, class and racial biases for example – and then encourage students to explore alternatives to these mainstream beliefs.[27] As Aronowitz and Giroux advocate, we must "make a firm commitment to cultural difference as central to the meaning of schooling and citizenship," and we must, "educate students for the maintenance and defense of the principles and traditions necessary for a democratic society."[28]

Although these are indeed important steps toward reflexive pedagogy, further development is needed. First, as even the liberation educators acknowledge, there is a danger that the teacher will now simply impose another ideology on the students. As Patti Lather points out, "Too often, tied to their version of truth and interpreting resistance as 'false conscious-ness,' liberatory pedagogies fail to probe the degree to which 'empower-ment' becomes something done 'by' liberated pedagogues 'to' or 'for' the as-yet-unliberated."[29] For example, how does the liberationist give voice to those who do not believe in full equality or democratic de-cision making – for example, Orthodox Hindus or Muslims? In effect, a liberation curricu-lum may run the same risks of hierarchy and suppression as those insti-tutions under attack. The second challenge for liberationist pedagogy is that of going beyond critique. Most liberation curricula emphasize critique of the dominant traditions, but do little to help students appreciate positive aspects of existing traditions. Further, there is insufficient emphasis on building from deliberation (pro and con) to more positive futures. Here the constructionist will emphasize practices of creative interchange, ways in which students, teachers, and others can together move in more adequate directions. A second line of practice amplifies this theme.

Collaborative Classrooms

On the nutritionist view, the teacher possesses the knowledge that must be communicated to students. Thus, teachers tend to favor monologue (for example, lecture, demonstration) over dialogue. For the constructionist, however, the advantages of monologue are highly circumscribed. To be sure there are times when informative lectures are valuable. However, a reliance on monologue not only fails to take advantage of the multiple skills that students bring to class, but there is little opportunity for the students to appropriate the subject matter in their own terms. There is little opportunity for them to take what is useful from the material in ways that can enrich their particular circumstances; more colloquially, they fail "to own the material."

Educator Kenneth Brufee is a leader in developing pedagogical practices designed to reduce the monologic voice of authority in the classroom and its emphasis on the univocal or "one right answer."[30] For example, his classes in English literature are often built around *consensus groups*, which groups are challenged with answering in their own terms questions posed by various texts – questions that also invite students to challenge the received opinions of authorities in the field. However, the group must reach a consensus which they are willing to share with other groups. This means that the group must learn how to deal with disagreements – sometimes extreme – in generating an opinion. They must learn how to live in a world of multiple realities. As Brufee also feels, "Being required to arrive at a position that the whole group can 'live with' can hurl students headlong into the knottiest and most sophisticated issues of almost any discipline."[31]

Extending these efforts further, educators also seek ways to extend dialogue beyond the classroom. The specific hope is to link the classroom to the world in such a way that education becomes more relevant to societal life. At times this may mean that students gain credit from working within the community, working for example in a tutoring program for underprivileged kids or apprenticing with a voluntary agency or community service. In other cases, internet communication is established between classrooms around the world; students in far-flung locales talk over problems of global significance.[32] Internet communication is only one means of working across borders. In some schools students are encouraged to develop their own "real world" projects. For example, students in the Foxfire program work with each other, with their teachers, and with professionals from outside the school to publish magazines and books, and produce radio and TV programs. For such projects, the classroom materials serve largely as resources to be placed in the service of relations outside the classroom.[33]

Polyvocal Pedagogy

Consider what it is to "write well." From the early grades to graduate school, one is typically taught to identify the topic, define the key concepts, maintain clarity, link sentences and paragraphs logically, illustrate key points with evidence, and so on. In certain respects, these demands stem from the belief that processes of sound reasoning are universal, and that good writing should not only reflect these processes, but help bring them to fruition. As we find in the Foreword of the *Harper Handbook of College Composition*, "Learning to think clearly and learning to write correctly, clearly, effectively, appropriately are worthwhile intellectual processes valuable not only in composition classes but in all other outreachings of the mind."[34] Yet, as previous chapters demonstrate (especially Chapters 1 and 2), the idea of universal reason – an inward process manifest in our spoken and written words – is deeply flawed. Moreover, from a political standpoint, there is a certain colonialist attitude inhering in the presumption that all intelligent writing should conform to certain standards – namely the standards popular among the educationally elite. And finally, on a pragmatic level, we must ask, for whom is this form of educated writing most effective? Given the vast heterogeneity of world peoples, and the increasing tendencies toward globalization, when, where and for whom is the "standard" form of writing ideal. Further, the critical theorist might add, the standard style prepares one for a subservient role in society, for reporting clearly, economically, and instrumentally to one's superiors. This is not the style of an inspiring leader or the agent of social change, but a writer of reports.

It is in the context of such questioning that constructionist educators search for means of facilitating polyvocality, that is, ways in which students can develop multiple voices, forms of expression, or ways of putting things. One fascinating innovation has been developed by Patti Lather.[35] Typically college teachers ask students to write about a subject – to describe, explain, and analyze, for example, psychopathology, social movements, the French revolution, etc. However, as Lather reasons, this kind of writing is essentially *realist*; that is, it presumes the existence of the subject matter. The "objects of study" are typically uncontested. Because of her investments in liberation pedagogy, Lather asks students to add another form of writing to their standard report. This time they are asked to write in a *critical* frame, approaching the topic from a politically invested standpoint. They may ask, for example, what part does authority, suppression and marginalization play in the production of psychopathology? Who benefits from traditional practices of therapy, who is dismissed? However, because of the problems of oppression within critique itself (see above), Lather then asks for a third writing on the topic, this time *deconstructive*. Here students might explore the multiple interpretations that can be made of the subject matter, the many vantage points from which it might be seen. Further, students might question their own categories of understanding; why these and not others? Finally, Lather asks for a writing that is more personal or *self-reflexive*. Students are asked in this case to write in more innovative, non-linear, expressive ways about the subject and their engagement in it. In the end, Lather believes, by engaging in these different writing forms, students are not only freed from the demands of a realist mode of representation, but they are enabled to generate multiple perspectives and to speak effectively to multiple audiences.

Other teachers achieve polyvocality by having students write to different audiences. A paper on environmental protection, for example, could be written first for student peers, then for an environmental protection agency, and finally for an opposing group. With each new writing new voicings are developed, and one learns new ways of seeing the issues. Many argue that the written word itself is waning in its efficacy; print technologies are giving way to visual media – film, video, computer graphics, photography and the like. In this case, educators emphasize expanding voice through training in visual media.[36]

These educational developments – in reflexivity, collaboration, and polyvocality – are only a few of those favored by constructionist dialogues. However, to appreciate more fully the impact of constructionism in education, it is useful to consider finally how scholarship itself is being transformed.

Scholarly Representation: New Ways of Worldmaking

> To be able to dance with one's feet, with concepts, with words: need I still add that one must be able to do it with the pen too?
>
> Friedrich Nietzsche, *The Gay Science*

It is one thing to draw inspiration from constructionism in teaching others; but what about setting one's own house in order? Don't the implications of constructionist dialogues impact on academic work itself? Of course, this question is partly answered by all the work treated in the preceding chapters. These are all new departures in analysis and inquiry. Yet, the present chapter on societal practices shifts the focus from content to action. Our concern is not so much with what is being communicated, but the very practice of scholarly communication itself. Consider: for the traditional realist, communication is simply a matter of reporting accurately on what is the case. For the constructionist, "accuracy" is a problematic concept; the scholarly report is essentially an invitation to a relationship between writer and reader. To secure the point, consider your reactions as you read the following examples of sound academic writing:

> If P's only want in C at t is to achieve G, and if P believes that trying to do A in C at t is the alternative with the highest likelihood of leading to G, if P believes that he or she can perform A in C at t, and if the alternative acts that P believes he or she can perform are believed by P not to involve less exertion than A, then P will try to do A in C at t.[37]

> It is also predicted that when silence (in communication) occurs, it will be differentially assigned, on the basis of the rules as either (i) a gap before subsequent application of Rules 1(b) or 1(c), or (ii) a lapse on the non-application of Rules 1(a), (b) and (c), or (iii) a selected next speaker's significant (or attributable) silence after the application of Rule 1(a).[38]

By traditional standards these are examples of first class scholarship. Nevertheless, there is a good chance that you felt discomforted. First, the style of writing tends to create a sense of distance between you and the writer. The writing is formal, it doesn't allow you to glimpse the human behind the formalisms. The writing is flat and emotionless; it is difficult to feel a resonating passion with the author. The style also positions the author as the knower – rational and insightful – and the reader as ignorant. The writing is flawless, thus thrusting the reader into doubt regarding all his/her own failings. One feels embarrassed to hazard a response. Finally, such writing is elitist. It speaks only to that minority who are educated to take their place in elite society. As black feminist scholar bell hooks responds, "To make the liberated voice, one must confront the issue of audience – we must know to whom we speak."[39]

Of course, you might say "so what?". If this form of writing is the most efficient and effective way to communicate about the subject matter then stylistics should make little difference. One shouldn't judge a gift by its wrapping. However, for the constructionist there is good reason to be concerned with the form of writing. As proposed in Chapter 2, our accounts of the world are not maps of the world, but operate performatively, to do things with others. If this is so, our attention is drawn to what various forms of expression do for or within a community. What forms of relationship are welcomed by a given way of putting things, what is discouraged or rendered invisible? Or more broadly, what kind of world do we build together through our forms of inscription?

Informed by this line of reasoning, many scholars are inspired to experiment with new modes of expression. The results are fascinating:

Personalization: Embodied Writing

Among the most popular forms of experiment are those attempting to abandon the god's-eye view of traditional scholarship, and to reveal within the work a warm-blooded author, complete with passion, biases and shortcomings. The author may lace his/her writings with "street talk," for example, ethnic idioms or dirty words. Here is a more graceful illustration from cultural studies scholar Rosanne Arquette Stone, writing about her relationship with technology:

> The first time love struck was in 1950. I was hunkered down in the dark late at night, on my bed . . . helping a friend scratch around the surface of a galena crystal that was part of a primitive radio. We were looking for one of the hot spots, places where the crystal had active sites . . . and could detect radio waves. There was nothing but silence for a long, long time, and then suddenly the earphones burst into life, and a whole new universe was raging in our heads . . . I was hooked. Hooked on technology.[40]

One senses here the presence of the author in the text, even if the author as presented is a construction of the text.

Self-reflection and the Polyvocal Author: Who am I?

Traditional scholarship defines the author as a unified subjectivity, one who employs the highest standards of rationality to achieve the last and only word. Personalization does bring the reader into a more intimate relationship with the author but the style still carries traces of the author as a singular self. Challenging the presumption of monologic mind, other scholars search for means of inserting multiple voices into the text, voices that may even comment critically on what is being put forward. These additions not only create the sense of a polyvocal author, but invite the audience to have an opinion (or many opinions).

Michael Mulkay's sociological treatise *The Word and the World* is a classic in self-reflexive writing. For example, after introducing the volume in a traditional scholarly voice, Mulkay introduces two additional voices, the "reader" and the "private author" behind the scholarly presentation.

The "reader" says, *"Well, Author, that's very interesting, but I'm not sure that I properly understood all that the Book has to say. Is it possible for me to ask (the author) some questions?"*

The private author responds, *"I'm afraid not. That's the trouble with books, research reports and so on; once they've made their statement, that's it. . . . There's a built-in rigidity in such texts."*[41]

After the private author chastises himself for his rigid control of the text, the reader again interrupts, *"Surely that's your fault, not his! You're the author. The Book will say anything that you want him to."*

Where is Mulkay *himself* in all this? Everywhere of course.

Invocation: Stirring Voices

As we saw, traditional scholarly writing often seems dead, without passion or inspiration. To breathe life into the writing, and thus to move the reader to a richer and more engaged experience, some scholars invoke the voices of non-scholarly traditions of writing – from genres of the novel, poetry, spiritual writing, mysticism and more. Not only are readers likely to be more stirred by the writing, but employing these genres eradicates the misleading distinction between "straight talk" – objective and rational – and "rhetoric." The reader is continuously reminded of the constructed character of the writing.

To illustrate, consider first a fragment from *The Unspeakable*, a work by iconoclastic anthropologist Stephen Tyler, in which he places the idea of rational systems under attack:

> In the end, the idea of system is only nostalgia for the wholeness analysis has killed and thinks to resuscitate by reinfecting the corpse with the germ that killed it. "System" is another name for the great spider goddess.[42]

Tyler's metaphors are colorful and strong. Adding to such metaphors the cadence of the black ministerial tradition, Professor of Afro-American Studies Cornell West writes powerfully on contemporary race relations:

> The accumulated effect of the black wounds and scars suffering in a white-dominated society is a deep-seated anger, a boiling sense of rage, and a passionate pessimism regarding America's will to justice.[43]

Then arguing against a nihilistic response to such anger,

> Nihilism is not overcome by arguments or analyses; it is tamed by love and care. Any disease of the soul must be conquered by a turning of one's soul.[44]

As West's writing suggests, writers can invoke more than one tradition in their work, employing several different genres that may speak in different ways to different audiences. An excellent example of this kind of pastiche is found in *Death at the Parasite Cafe*, by the innovative sociologist Steven Pfohl. Throughout the text Pfohl adopts several different personae, including that of the traditional scholar, an editor, a translator, himself as autobiographer, RadaRada, Jack O. Lantern, and Black Madonna Durkheim. Here is Black Madonna responding to Pfohl as a young sociologist seeking help for field research in the southern United States:

> Listen Yankee! . . . No more closed-circuited white male revolutionaries! No more saviors! No more pimps! We've enough of those already. But some other form of parasite? Perhaps? Maybe in time you'll discover and re-mask yourself in a form that's more power-reflexive. But that's an expensive proposition and (k)not one that will make you feel complete . But . . . pack up your belongings and let's dance.[45]

Toward the Performative

Experiments in representation are scarcely limited to the domain of writing. If "what there is" makes no demands on how it is represented, there is no strong reason for privileging words above other forms of expression. In important degree the privilege given to words in the academic world derives from the traditional belief that reason (logical thinking) resides in the head of the individual, and that words are its chief expression. The flaws inherent in this view have been made amply clear. More importantly, much is gained by opening the door to the full range of human expression – to art, drama, music, dance, comedy, film, multi-media, and more. In doing so there is a vital expansion in the range of those who can be reached. For example, because of the high degree of visual literacy in the culture, film potentially invites a larger audience into relationship than traditional academic writing. The charge of elitism is also softened. Second, many of these expressive forms invite a fuller form of audience participation. If you are given a crossword puzzle, your participation is reduced to verbal manipulation; if the puzzle is also humorous, you may also react with laughter; if the letters were also in the form of bricks, you might have to carry them to their location. In effect, the degree of participation is expanded as the task is changed. The challenge, then, is to communicate in ways that invite a full range of participation – visual, emotional, musical, bodily, and so on.

There are significant moves in the performative direction. There are longstanding movements of visual anthropology and sociology emphasizing the power of film. The field of communication places special emphasis on performance as both a medium and means to education. The American Psychological Association has featured annual symposia on *performative psychology*, which have featured dance, poetry, drama, stand-up comedy and multi-media – all expanding the range of professional expression in significant ways. Such work also begins to blur the boundaries between scholarship and performance art, independent filmmaking, multi-media dance, and other forms of cultural performance.[46] To share the flavor of such work as it has emerged within the academic sphere, I close the chapter with a single exemplar of *relational art*. The work is from a series of text/graphics developed by a Zurich artist, Regine Walter, and myself, and designed specifically to resonate with the kind of relational thinking and practice outlined in the last two chapters. Regine's work emphasizes complex human connection – the entwinement of being. My writing speaks to relatedness in a verbal dimension. Here we work together, with the two explorations of relatedness now combining in their own relationship.[47] They now seek a relationship with you as reader:

You are my delight,
And your laughter celebrates my being.
My pleasure inhabits your heart,
And my smiles are those of adoration
Joy resides in the resonance.

Reflection

Although trained as a traditional social scientist – thus to stand outside, observe and report – I have come to see through constructionist dialogues the narrowness of such activities. If my scholarly observations are not so much truth telling as actions in the world, then I have had to ask for whom are they significant actions, to what effect, and should my actions be limited only to academic words? Such questions have opened new vistas for me outside the academic setting – working with therapists, in organizations, with religious groups, and negotiators. One result of this sea-change for me has been the creation of the Taos Institute, a community of scholars and practitioners exploring the intersection between social constructionist theory and a range of societal practices.[48] However, even my day-to-day practices of teaching have been dramatically altered as a result of constructionist dialogues. For example, some of my most exciting moments as a teacher in recent years have resulted from giving my advanced students the option of replacing the typical "term paper" with a creative expression of their choosing. The result has been a cornucopia of video projects (made with camcorders and/or splicing movie and television fare), paintings and collage, audio recordings, web sites, enacted dramas, poetry, and dance among them. Does this mean that I can no longer evaluate students according to a single standard? Sure it does. I count this as one of the advantages. Do I ever have doubt that these and other practices represent "improvements" in our condition? Sure I do. To count them as improvements is, after all, a construction. However, given the options of seeing life as a progressive narrative as opposed to a road to hell, on most days I'll go for the former.

Notes

1   See for example Unger, R. and Crawford, M. (1992) *Women and Gender: A Feminist Psychology*. Toronto: McGraw-Hill; Szasz, T. (1984) *The Therapeutic State*. Buffalo, NY: Prometheus.
2   Anderson, H. and Goolishian, H. (1992) The client is the expert: a not-knowing approach to therapy. In S. McNamee and K. Gergen (Eds.) *Therapy as Social Construction*. London: Sage.
3   See for example deShazer, S. (1994) *Words Were Originally Magic*. New York: Norton.
4   Freedman, J. and Combs, G. (1993) Invitation to new stories: using questions to suggest alternative possibilities. In S. Gilligan and R. Price (Eds.) *Therapeutic Conversations*. New York: Norton.
5   Lipchik, E. (1993) Both/and solutions. In S. Friedman (Ed.) *The New Language of Change: Constructive Collaboration in Psychotherapy*. New York: Guilford.
6   Walter, J. and Peller, J. (1992) *Becoming Solution-Focused in Brief Therapy*. New York: Brunner/Mazel.
7   Berg, I.K. and deShazer, S. (1993) Making numbers talk: language in therapy. In S. Friedman (Ed.) *The New Language of Change*. New York: Guilford.

8 For a counter-argument see Duncan, B.L., Hubble, M.A. and Miller, S. (1997) *Psychotherapy with "Impossible " Cases*. New York: Norton.

9 White, M. and Epston, D. (1990) *Narrative Means to Therapeutic Ends*. New York: Norton.

10 Ibid., p. 38.

11 Ibid., p. 32.

12 Tomm, K. (1998) Co-constructing responsibility. In S. McNamee and K.J. Gergen (Eds.) *Relational Responsibility*. Thousand Oaks, CA: Sage.

13 Penn, P. and Frankfurt, M. (1994) Creating a participant text: writing, multiple voices, narrative multiplicity. *Family Process*, 33, 217–31.

14 Bakhtin, M. (1986) *Speech Genres and Other Essays* (Eds. M. Holquist and C. Emerson) Austin, TX: University of Texas Press. p. 287.

15 Andersen, T. (Ed.) (1991) *The Reflecting Team*. New York: Norton.

16 Lax, W. (1991) The reflecting team and the initial consultation. In T. Andersen (Ed.) *The Reflecting Team*. New York: Norton. p. 142.

17 See now the third printing: Morgan, G. (1998) *Images of the Organization*. Thousand Oaks, CA: Sage.

18 Ibid., p. 11.

19 Morgan, G. (1997) *Imaginazation, New Mindsets for Seeing, Organizing, and Managing*. Thousand Oaks, CA: Sage.

20 Cooperrider, D.L. (1996) Resources for getting appreciative inquiry started. *OD Practitioner*, 28, 23–34.

21 Also see Weisbord, M.R. and Janoff, S. (1995) *Future Search*. San Francisco: Barrett–Koehler.

22 Friere, P. (1985) *The Politics of Education*. South Hadley, MA: Bergin and Garvey.

23 See for example Wise, A. (1979) *Legislated Learning*. Berkeley, CA: University of California Press; Apple, M. (1982) *Education and Power*. Boston, MA: Routledge & Kegan Paul.

24 See for example Mehan, H. (1979) *Learning Lessons, Social Organization in the Classroom*. Cambridge, MA: Harvard University Press.

25 See for example Aronowitz, S. and Giroux, H.A. (1993) *Postmodern Education: Politics, Culture and Social Criticism*. Minneapolis, MN: University of Minnesota Press.

26 Bowles, S. and Gintis, J. (1976) *Schools in Capitalist America*. New York: Basic Books.

27 Giroux, H. (1992) *Border Crossings*. New York: Routledge.

28 Aronowitz and Giroux, *Postmodern Education*. pp. 12 and 34.

29 Lather, P. (1994) *Getting Smart*. New York: Routledge. p. 105.

30 Brufee, K. (1992) *Collaborative Learning*. Baltimore, MD: Johns Hopkins University Press.

31 Ibid., p. 41.

32 See for example Taylor, M.C. and Saaranen, E. (1994) *Imagologies: Media Philosophy*. London: Routledge.

33 For more on the Foxfire program see Boyte, H.C. and Evans, S.M. (1986) *Free Spaces, The Sources of Democracy in America*. New York: Harper & Row.

34 Wykoff, G.S. (1969) *Harper Handbook of College Composition*. New York: Harper & Row.

35 Lather, P. (1991) op. cit..

36 See, for example, Ulmer, G. (1989) *Applied Grammatology, Post-Pedagogy from Jacques Derrida to Joseph Beuys*. Baltimore, MD: Johns Hopkins University Press.

37   Smedslund, J. (1988) *Psycho-logic*. New York: Springer-Verlag. p. 63.
38   Levinson, S.C. (1983) *Pragmatics*. New York: Cambridge University Press. p. 222.
39   hooks, b. (1989) *Talking Back*. Boston, MA: South End Press.
40   Stone, A.R. (1996) *The War of Desire and Technology at the Close of the Mechanical Age*. Cambridge: MIT Press. p. 3.
41   Mulkay, M. (1985) *The Word and the World*. London: George Allen & Unwin. p. 8.
42   Tyler, S. (1987) *The Unspeakable*. Madison, WI: University of Wisconsin Press p. 54.
43   West, C. (1994) *Race Matters*. New York: Vintage. p. 28.
44   Ibid., p. 29.
45   Pfohl, S. (1992) *Death at the Parasite Cafe*. New York: St Martins. p. 47.
46   See, for example, Carr, C. (1993) *On Edge, Performance at the End of the Twentieth Century*. Hanover, NH: University Press of New England.
47   See also Gergen, K.J. and Walter, R. (1998) Real/izing the Relational. *Journal of Social and Personal Relationships*, 15, 110–26.
48   For additional information see http://www.serve.com/taos

Further Resources

On Therapy as Social Construction

Anderson, H. (1997) *Conversation, Language, and Possibilities*. New York: Basic Books.
Friedman, S. (1993) *The New Language of Change: Constructive Collaboration in Psychotherapy*. New York: Guilford.
McNamee, S. and Gergen, K.J. (Eds.) (1993) *Therapy as Social Construction*. London: Sage.
Monk, G., Winslade, J., Crockett, K. and Epston, D. (Eds.) (1997) *Narrative Therapy in Practice*. San Francisco: Jossey-Bass.
O'Hanlon, W.H. and Weiner-Davis, M. (1989) *In Search of Solutions: A New Direction in Psychotherapy*. New York: Norton.
Riikonen, E. and Smith, G.M. (1997) *Re-Imagining Therapy*. London: Sage.
Rosen, H. and Kuehlwein, K.T. (Eds.) *Constructing Realities, Meaning-Making Perspectives for Psychotherapists*. San Francisco: Jossey-Bass.

On Organizational Process

Boje, D.M., Gephart, R.P. and Thatchenkery, T.J. (Eds.) (1996) *Postmodern Management and Organization Theory*. Thousand Oaks, CA: Sage.
Czarniawska-Joerges, B. (1996) *Narrating the Organization: Dramas of Institutional Identity*. Chicago: University of Chicago Press.
Gergen, K.J. and Thatchenkery, T.J. (1997) Organizational science in a postmodern context. *Journal of Applied Behavioral Science*, 32, 356–77.
Grant, D. and Oswick, C. (Eds.) (1996) *Metaphor and Organizations*. London: Sage.
Hassard, J.H. and Parker, M. (Eds.) (1993) *Postmodernism and Organizations*. London: Sage.
Hosking, D., Dachler, H.P. and Gergen, K.J. (1995) *Management and Organization: Relational Alternatives to Individualism*. Aldershot: Avebury.
Weick, K. (1995) *Sensemaking in Organizations*. Thousand Oaks, CA: Sage.

On Education

Freire, P. (1978) *The Pedagogy of the Oppressed*. Harmondsworth: Penguin Books.

Jennings, T.E. (Ed.) (1997) *Restructuring for Integrative Education*. Westport, CT: Greenwood.

Petraglia, J. (1998) *Reality by Design, the Rhetoric and Technology of Authenticity in Education*. Mahwah, NJ: Erlbaum.

Usher, R. and Edwards, R. (1994) *Postmodernism and Education*. London: Routledge.

Walkerdine, V. (1990) *Schoolgirl Fictions*. London: Verso.

On Scholarship as Performance

Carlson, M. (1996) *Performance, A Critical Introduction*. London: Routledge.

Clifford, J. and Marcus, G.E. (Eds.) (1986) *Writing Culture:The Poetics and Politics of Ethnography*. Berkeley, CA: University of California Press.

Game, A. and Metcalfe, A. (1996) *Passionate Sociology*. London: Sage.

Gergen, K.J. (1997) Who speaks and who responds in the human sciences? *History of the Human Sciences*, 10, 151–73.

Other Practices in a Constructionist Frame

Best, J. (Ed.) (1995) *Images of Issues: Typifying Contemporary Social Problems*. New York: Aldine de Gruyter.

Fox, C.J. and Miller, H.T. (1995) *Postmodern Public Administration*. Thousand Oaks, CA: Sage.

Frank, A.W. (1995) *The Wounded Storyteller, Body, Illness and Ethics*. Chicago: University of Chicago Press.

Guba, E.G. and Lincoln, Y.S. (1989) *Fourth Generation Evaluation*. Newbury Park, CA: Sage.

Klineman, A. (1988) *The Illness Narratives*. New York: Basic Books.

Newman, F. (1996) *Performance of a Lifetime*. New York: Castillo International.

Young, K. (1997) *Presence in the Flesh: The Body in Medicine*. Cambridge, MA: Harvard University Press.

8

POSTMODERN CULTURE:
ADVENTURES IN ANALYSIS

> We move away from romanticism and modernism, not calmly and
> with reflection, but desperately and under siege.
>
> Robert Jay Lifton, personal communication

Let's say that you are curious about the emergence of new cultures on the
internet, and you wish to study them. You hope your observations will help
to understand the importance (or possible triviality) of these cultures. You
are willing to accept the constructionist warnings, that the categories you
use for sorting and describing internet culture are not mirrors of nature but
are culturally dependent and value laden. You only wish to say something
to members of your culture about what is taking place in terms they can
appreciate. You decide to focus your analysis on a particular use.net group
devoted to discussions of *Star Trek*. For three months you monitor the postings of the group, and now armed with an enormous volume of verbatim
data, you find that six months are needed for the analysis. In another three
months you have a manuscript ready in which you describe a large but
close-knit, mutually engaged, and supportive sub-culture who seem very
appreciative of each other's humor, clever insights, and imaginative
musings. Your manuscript stimulates one of your friends to check in to the
Trekkie newsgroup. He calls the next day to ask how on earth you could
ever have drawn such conclusions. He felt the postings on the net were few,
nasty, and alienating. You check it out, and you see his point. The culture
you described has now disappeared. And if you began now to study the
new culture, it might also vanish before you could report on it.

This kind of problem is becoming increasing prevalent in the human
sciences. Most methods of study are designed to study some behavior or
social pattern of current interest. However, because of the rapid rate of
social change the phenomena of interest are transformed before the study
is complete. In effect, our research seems forever looking backward to
something that was. Or, as government policy makers chide, "social

research is history in slow motion; by the time we receive the reports they are outdated." It is precisely here that social constructionism offers a significant alternative to traditional research paradigms. If our world is in a state of often rapid flux, then what we need is not so much the arduous counting of past events, but sensitive and continuous social analysis. Required are the kinds of analysis that enable us to understand what is taking place from multiple standpoints, that will help us to engage in dialogue with others from varied walks of life, and that will sensitize us to a range of possible futures. Most important, social analysis should help to generate vocabularies of understanding that can help us to create our future together. For the constructionist, the point of social analysis is not, then, to "get it right" about what is happening to us. Rather, such analysis should enable us to reflect and to create.

In the present chapter I want to share some of the most interesting and engaging work of this kind. Some of this work is fanciful, even bizarre. However, the point of such inquiry is to shatter our comfortable assumptions and to play with meaning so that we can "see again." In this sense the work is not to be taken as dead serious – as if these are authoritative pronouncements on what is – but seriously in the sense that the character of our future hangs on the outcomes of our constructions.

More specifically, the chapter is devoted to explorations into contemporary cultural life. Like many of the sweeping changes taking place in the scholarly world (see Chapter 1), our present condition is often described as *postmodern*. Because the term "postmodernism" is used in many different ways, perhaps it is best to view it as pointing to a range of inter-related dialogues on our current condition – and as many would say, a condition particularly characterizing post-industrial, information-based, globalized economies. Why *post*? Most generally this term suggests that many feel their lives are in rapid transition. To coin an early Marxist phrase, "all that was solid melts into air." It is this giddy sense of spiraling and chaotic change that sparks the contemporary dialogues. Such dialogues are often concerned with a creeping sense of fragmentation. Commentators point to a pervasive sense of erosion in a firm sense of self, the falling away of traditional values, and the loss of confidence in the *grand narratives* of the past – a trust that governments, economic planners, or scientists, for example, can lead us toward a better future.[2] Such transformations are also reflected in the academic world; indeed social constructionism is itself seen by many as a postmodern project, as set against the modernist faith in the individual mind, rationality, objectivity, and truth. The present chapter will focus on postmodernism as a cultural condition. Obviously I must be selective. However, because of their fascination and the way the topics bear on social constructionism, I have chosen three areas of special interest: the profusion of mediated messages, images, and opinions; changing configurations of power; and the impact of technology on cultural life.

The Swirl of Signification

> Everything that was lived has moved away into a representation.
>
> Guy Debord, *The Society of the Spectacle*

I recently escaped to the shore for a weekend – to renew my sense of "natural rootedness," in sun, water, fresh air, and simplicity. While gazing into the blue I was suddenly distracted by the sound of an aircraft. Overhead a small plane was trailing a banner advertising a brand of rum. A few minutes later another plane passed, this time advising bathers of a nearby restaurant. Suddenly I began to feel invaded; this was the world I had endeavored with difficulty to escape and now it was returning via an air raid. In a moment of reflection a more unsettling image emerged. Isn't this advertising but one form of language or symbol commonly used to invite others into a reality, a way of life, or a politics? Perhaps the circus barking has become a way of cultural life, and we can nevermore escape. Scanning the beach confirmed my suspicion. People scarcely came to the shore to *escape* the symbolic: books and magazines were everywhere, as were signboard t-shirts and designer labels. This was not a secluded world of nature; I was engulfed by a swirl of signification.

For some analysts, the manufacture of meaning on multiple sites throughout the culture – radio, television, film, books, magazines, newspapers, the World Wide Web, and more – is one of the chief hallmarks of the twentieth century. In the seventeenth century the West moved from a primary basis in oral communication to greater dependency on print. In the twentieth century the vast proportion of communication is technologically mediated. How should we evaluate this transformation; how are we to understand the implications for our lives; and given dramatic new developments in technology, how should we now proceed? These are profound and complicated questions, and in no way can I do justice to them in the present offering. However, to appreciate the role of constructionism in cultural analysis, it is useful to consider three major positions emerging in recent years. Each furnishes a different and significant lens for understanding our condition of immersion.

Media and Manipulation

> The average person is exposed to 3,600 commercial impressions every day, making advertising the most pervasive message system in the consumer culture.
>
> Sut Jhally, *Advertising and the End of the World*

Consider my first reaction to the intrusion of the advertising air squads: irritation and resentment. In my search for nature pure and simple I had become a victim of sales hype. This image of the audience *as victim* underlies perhaps the most significant corpus of contemporary analysis. In one form or another, it is proposed, we are the unwilling victims of a barrage of communication – largely associated with the mass media. And this communication constructs a world for us – of glamour, excitement, knowledge, fulfillment, and so on. It attempts to appropriate us, to transform our thoughts and desires and ultimately our buying habits, political preferences, and more general ways of life. We are the victims of mass manipulation. This orientation has early roots in one of the burning questions of the 1940s: how could the German people give way to the Nazi ideology? At least one compelling answer was propaganda. The people had been victims of the powerful and systematic attempts of Goebbels' propaganda ministry. This theme was also vivified in George Orwell's (then) futuristic novel *1984*, depicting a completely totalitarian state in which the Ministry of Truth taught the people to believe that "War is Peace, Freedom is Slavery, and Ignorance is Strength."[3] In 1957, Vance Packard's *The Hidden Persuaders* informed the public about the ways in which commercial advertising used subtle, psychological devices to subvert the audience.[4] This alarm at the debilitating consequences of mass-mediated materials – aggressive, pornographic, lurid – continues to the present.

With the emergence of social constructionist ideas, concern with media influence has become dramatically intensified. If we live in a constructed world, then it is essential to understand the sources of construction. Because they saturate our everyday existence, the media are obvious candidates of critical inquiry. In particular, analysts direct their attention to the way in which the media subtly seep into our everyday lives to stimulate our desires, generate our ideals, create our values, and ultimately create our sense of personal identity.[5] Feminist scholars have long been critical of the way in which advertising defines standards of beauty (what it is to be desirable and acceptable), and lends such importance to the frivolous and artificial.[6] In his book *All Consuming Images*, Stuart Ewen describes a more sweeping shift in Western culture from persons defined by substance to the contemporary centrality of style.[7] In Ewen's view, the tradition of conceptualizing ourselves in terms of what we actually do – what we accomplish in the world – is slowly being replaced by a concept of self-as-appearance. Our sense of self is increasingly dependent on the image we give off to others – in what we own, or wear, or the places we are seen. "The *dream of identity*, the *dream of wholeness*, is intimately woven together with the desire to be known: to be visible; to be documented for all to see."[8] This shift, as Ewen sees it, is brought about largely through the combination of a massive growth in media (television, radio, magazines, etc.), advertising agencies, and big business. For Ewen, when we live in a world of *commercial truth* we cease to think or be ourselves.

Analyses such as these play an important role in societal life. Already, for example, they play a part in restrictions placed on film viewing, advertising curbs (consider the warnings now placed on cigarette packages), the demand for equal air-time for all political parties, and controls placed on sex and violence in film and television. Such commentaries also spark movements to reduce television advertising for children, remove racist and homophobic material from television content, and remove porno-graphic material from the news stands.

However, issues of free speech not withstanding, there are significant limits to the metaphor of the manipulated audience. First, there is too little attention paid to the ways in which the mass media, in particular, are not so much movers of the public as they are themselves victims of public desire. For example, television producers are scarcely free to generate whatever shows or news agendas they wish. They must be acutely sensi-tive to audience ratings, and the latter often function as cruel dictators. As a second shortcoming, the manipulated victim metaphor is lodged in a model of psychological being. The media, it is said, "change attitudes," "create prejudices," "kindle desires," and so on. Yet, as we have seen throughout this volume, this view of "minds" – independent of relation-ships – is highly problematic. We may all be capable of the most racist statements, but live our entire lives in relationships in which they would never be appropriate. In this sense, while the media may prepare us for participating in relationships of robbery, rape, and racism, the media themselves demand nothing, cause nothing. There is another important limitation of this tradition, revealed most fully in a second important approach.

From Victim to Avenger: the Active Audience

> Each of us is encased in an armor whose task it is to ward off signs.
>
> Martin Buber, *Between Man and Man*

Return again to the scene on the beach. To be sure, I was confronted by a swelter of advertising, but what was my response? I didn't rush out to buy a bottle of rum or search for the nearby restaurant. Instead I was moved to critical consideration of the situation. It is this failure of the audience to succumb to the swirl of signification that constitutes the second major wave of analysis. In this case the audience is not portrayed as passive victims, but as active, thoughtful, searching, and critical. Even more boldly, audience participants are sometimes portrayed as avengers who use the communication to undermine the unwitting establishment. They appropriate and reconstruct.

The metaphor of the active audience has been a useful antidote to the mechanistic model of cause and effect central to the manipulated victim approach. It has also lent itself to dignifying various groups who would otherwise be portrayed as so many unthinking sheep. For example early British cultural studies emphasized the way in which adolescent groups appropriated from the mainstream its various images, music, and styles but reassembled them in such a way as to separate themselves from the mainstream.[9] In his classic work *Subculture: The Meaning of Style*, Dick Hebdidge showed how punk culture used common cultural symbols – such as swastikas and safety pins – to generate an oppositional sub-culture.[10]

In a similar vein, feminist scholars take issue with analysts who portray women as poor, unwitting creatures whose dress, manners, eating habits, and life investments simply dance to the tune of the media moguls. Rather, they argue, women appropriate the media for their own purposes, which frequently includes rebellion against the oppressive thrall of the dominant discourse. In one early attempt to "rescue the reader," Janet Radway explored women's responses to the romance novel,[11] a genre that seems to support patriarchal dominance and the submission of women. Yet, as Radway shows, women often read the novels in a different way, deriving pleasure from the ways in which otherwise independent men finally give up and commit themselves to their one true love. There is a second and more subtle way in which women's readings resists the influence of the dominant culture. Specifically, in their choosing a private space for reading such novels, a space in which they can exercise their own fantasies without interruption, women defy the demands of husband and family for being the responsible wife and mother.

In more recent work, Mary Ellen Brown[12] has explored women's responses to soap operas. Again, "the soaps" appear only to depict women in traditional gender roles, and thus reinforce the status quo. Yet, as Brown reasons, resistance to the media depends importantly on communication, or more specifically, relationships in which participants can together step outside the received reality and reflect on it. As Brown proposes, it is precisely this kind of interchange that the soap opera invites. The soaps generate topics for lively discussion among women, discussions enabling them to remove themselves from a state of suspended disbelief, and to see the soaps from alternative standpoints. For example, in Brown's study women proved highly sensitive to television production problems, flaws in the stories, and the absurdities of the characters. As one viewer said, "I don't like *Days of Our Lives*. There are too many characters and they're not following through on them."[13] Or another viewer comments on the plight of the television producers themselves, "They have brought in a whole series of new families and characters which they might run for a couple of months; and it doesn't work terribly well, so they get rid of them, and [the producers] are just at the stage where they are beginning to panic a bit."[14]

Over and above the content of these conversations, Brown proposes, the soaps also change the nature of relations among women. Specifically, they enable women to join together in pleasureful activity, to construct the world in their own terms. The soaps treat issues of female power, morality, and strategies for living. In effect, they generate a common consciousness and stimulation to dialogue. "Such networks tap into female friendship networks that exist outside dominant hierarchic arrangements . . . These groups can be socially invisible, intentionally and subversively."[15] It is this process of informal bonding, Brown contends, that forms the basis for active resistance to oppressive conditions.

Arguments for an active audience are a refreshing and necessary alternative to the traditional emphasis on media manipulation. At the same time, the standpoint is not without limits. As analysts are quick to point out, avenging audiences do not always remain so. On the one hand, if a rebellious subculture does successfully emerge, the advertisers and mediapreneurs are soon likely to cash in. For example, young people succumbed to advertisements for jeans, but demonstrated resistance by wearing them to shreds or sewing on patches. As such defiance became widespread, so were new jean designs manufactured in which these anti-commercial markings were simulated. The dominant culture essentially co-opted the sub-culture so that the latter became a vehicle for increasing profits of the former. Nor is the commodification of resistance always limited to members of the dominant culture. Counter-culture participants themselves may reap great profit from selling their trappings of resistance as style. Motorcycle gear, body piercing, and porno-chic are only a few cases. Such matters suggest more complex interdependencies among centers of signification.

Swimming in Simulacra

> I woke up this morning and was shocked to find everything
> in my room had been replaced by an exact replica.
>
> Stephen Wright, comedian

Consider a third significant approach to the swirl of signification. Again let us revisit the shore. Recall the way I looked over the beach to find people everywhere engaged in reading magazines or wearing self-advertisements on their t-shirts and bathing suits. The vulturous aircraft seemed but a small part of a vast circulation of signification in which we all take a willing part. It is this metaphor of a large, uncontrollable torrent of signification that informs a third analytic posture. There is no single person or institution "out there" feeding us a diet of signs, on this account, nor are we appropriating the media for our own integral purposes. Rather, from this perspective we all participate together in the massive circulation of words, images, sounds, and so on: we are both the producers and the victims and there is no exit to a world outside the swirl.

This metaphor of a larger system in which we are enmeshed, finds its roots in early semiotic thinking. Recall the Chapter 1 discussion of language as based on a system of pre-existing rules from which we cannot escape if we are to communicate at all. This image of language as a shared social system acquires a particularly sharp bite if you begin to think of language as representing the real. That is, the system that creates what we take to be true and good operates without significant dependence on what is the case. Or to put it another way, as the range of images, opinions, reports, and the like expands exponentially, are we not spending increasing amounts of time engaged in a world of representations as opposed to reality itself? This form of critique gained its first significant voice in the work of French Marxist critic Guy Debord. In his major work *The Society of the Spectacle*, Debord lamented at what he saw as a cultural drift toward a pseudo-world of images.[16] "The spectacle is the main production of present-day society"[17] and the spectacle creates our sense of the real. For Debord we live together increasingly in a world of appearances, experiencing not life itself – not genuine relationship – but a "negation of life." "The concrete life of everyone has been degraded into a speculative universe . . . The spectacle is the guardian of sleep."[18] With Marxist theory in hand, Debord then traces the production of images to the ruling class, and sees this production as but one more attempt to alienate workers from their material condition and each other. It is in this flourish, however, that Debord returns to the manipulation metaphor described above. In effect, behind the spectacle there resides a wicked wizard.

This image of an enemy class is entirely eliminated in the later works of Jean Baudrillard. Although attracted to Communism in his early work, after the failure of the revolutionary outcry of 1968, Baudrillard became disenchanted with the possibilities of major societal transformation. It might be said that in the barricades, the clash with police, the student passions, the mass demonstrations, and the like, Baudrillard saw intimations of Debord's spectacle. This was not true revolution, but simulation – a display of postures, rhetoric, signs, conventional actions – possibly borrowing its glamour from the French Revolution. Moreover, in the oppressive actions of the police, the massive arrests, and strong words of government officials, there was no defense of a sacred tradition. These too were simulations, mere moves in a game that required the actions of the revolutionaries to realize their function. Or, more bluntly, there was no real political conflict, nothing was truly at stake, all was sham politics. As Baudrillard sees it, we are moving to a condition in which true political conflict is coming to an end. We are fully immersed in a simulated world.

To elaborate further, Baudrillard imagines an historical drift composed of several stages – from primitive culture to mass society. In the more primitive or preindustrialized epoch, reasons Baudrillard, there was little function for images, representations, or abstractions. People lived in close, face to face relationships, where objects, actions and words were closely interwoven. However, as industrialization advanced and society became increasingly organized, there was greater dependency on sign systems, for example, words and images that could create and sustain forms of organization across large numbers of people spread over great distances. A good illustration is the standard organizational chart used by business and government to instruct workers about their particular function and its place in the hierarchy. In effect, the chart functions as an image, or what Baudrillard calls a *simulacra* of the organization.[19] The

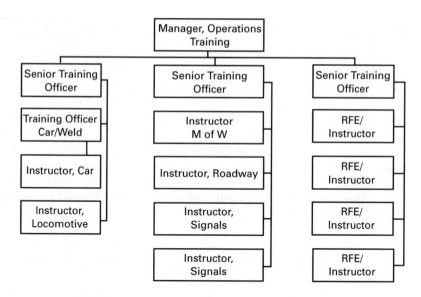

Figure 8.1   *Organization as Structure*

simulacra is not a map of the real, but creates an image that informs and
organizes the activities of the participants. It tells people what they are
responsible for and to whom. However, because this is a simulacrum, and
not the ongoing activity itself, problems begin to develop. Representations can *mask* or pervert that which they are supposed to represent. The
organization, for example, could actually be controlled by outside forces
of government or Mafia. The representations can also be used to mask the
absence of a basic reality. As Daniel Boorstin has described, the government and other powerful institutions manipulate words and images to
create "pseudo-events" – occurrences that are chiefly located within the
media and nowhere else.[20]

Finally, argues Baudrillard, in mass societies of the information epoch,
radio, television, film, magazines, and the like serve as giant factories for
the production of simulacra. We are now dominated by the circulation of
signs, and there is no means of returning to the real. Where signs could
once "reflect a profound reality" in the present era the sign "has no relation to any reality whatsoever; it is its own pure simulacrum."[21] For Baudrillard we now dwell not in a real world, but in the realm of the *hyperreal*.
As an example of the coming world of the hyperreal, Baudrillard points
to Disneyland:

> Disneyland is a perfect model of all the entangled forms of simulation . . . a play
> of illusions and phantasms . . . the objective profile of America . . . may be traced
> throughout Disneyland, even down to the morphology of individuals and the
> crows . . . Disneyland is there to conceal the fact that it is the "real" country, all
> of "real" America . . .[22]

These are indeed challenging, even unsettling views, and have been the subject of broad controversy. They invite us into a reality that seems resonant with so much of contemporary life, but simultaneously leave us in a wasteland. Here the world seems to be imploding, collapsing in upon itself, rotting, putrefying. Baudrillard goes further than "critical theory" (Chapter 3) – which functions to emancipate – to generate a nihilistic kind of *fatal theory*. Must we remain in this dismal space? Scarcely. It is important to realize that in the end Baudrillard's thesis fails to escape its own conclusions. For indeed, the analysis is itself a form of signification, circulating as a simulacra. In particular, it is an extension of a long-standing genre of apocalyptic writings dating back at least as far as the biblical book of Revelations. And if this is not a map of the way things are, why should we necessarily accept this kind of story as opposed to one of more uplifting dimension?

Further, what kind of story is this from an intellectual standpoint? Is Baudrillard not engaging in a bit of nostalgia for a non-existent past when words or images did not somehow float free of their everyday moorings, when they were tied in a close and trustworthy manner to the real? Constructionist theory suggests there never was such a time; representations have always had a slippery relationship to their supposed referents. Even people's names, suggesting as they do a stable referent, seem quite disjunctive with the protean plasticity of the living being. And finally, must we be so gloomy about living in a world of representation? Do we not require abstract signifiers – work, play, family, justice, the economy and so on – for carrying out most of our daily deliberations? Could there be political or economic debates without forms of construction we might otherwise call the hyperreal? And what of the joys of life – the grand pleasures, enthusiasms, and desires? Would they exist without the drama and vitality lent to them by the hyperreal? Without vast repositories of culturally shared stories – on film, in novels, and on television – a kiss might simply be skin friction. The zest of life is not derived from what there is, devoid of construction, but is dependent upon just these processes of creation.

Patterns of Power

> The desire . . . for the power necessary to render persons and their
> properties subservient to our pleasures is a grand governing
> law of human nature.
>
> James Mill, *An Essay on Government*

While Baudrillard's work leads us to imagine a world spiraling out of control, we are probably more aware of ways in which we are being controlled. We often sense that we are not free, that our actions are in so many ways observed, evaluated, limited, channeled, and suppressed. Often these controls seem to issue from institutions: schools, the police, government offices and the like. More formally, scholars speak of these experiences in terms of *structural power* – the control exerted by organized institutions within a society. Traditional Marxists view structural power in terms of economic classes and the suppression of the "have nots" by the "haves." Feminists are inclined to view structural power in terms of men's control over the dominant institutions, and particularly the ways in which women's opportunities are constricted.

Although we are accustomed to understanding the world in terms of structural power, we can no longer rest easy in this view. New formulations now break upon the scene, formulations that somehow speak to our current condition in more compelling ways. To appreciate the significance of these new perspectives it is important to trace a subtle but important shift in twentieth century theories of structural power. At the turn of the century it was easy enough to account for structural power simply in terms of differences in material control, for example, armies, weapons, property, or money. Over time, however, analysts turned their attention from such material differences to the shared reasoning that renders these material differences reasonable and right. In effect institutional control rests on sets of beliefs – shared ideas, values, and sentiments often called *ideology*. Thus, it is argued, through a sharing of capitalist ideology class differences are comfortably maintained; the ability of males to dominate our institutions derives from a broadly attractive sexist ideology. Without the requisite ideas, values, and sentiments, the structures would give way; we would be free to generate other and perhaps more equitable arrangements. As theorists variously propose, ideologies are also marked by *hegemony*, that is, by a capacity to gain and sustain control through the unification of multiple institutions (for example, government, education, military).[23] In this sense the common practices of hiring and firing in business, grading in schools, and placing individuals on trial, all support a single ideology of individualism (Chapter 5). When ideology is hegemonic, it is not open to dialogue or critique; its furtherance is primarily served through dissemination of ideas, images, symbols, and it is fortified through the silencing of alternatives.

As the neo-Marxist theorist Louis Althusser has proposed, hegemonic interests are realized in particular by a process of *interpellation* – literally being called into account.[24] More metaphorically, we are asked "to explain ourselves" in the terms of the dominant ideology. As we answer – attempting to make sense of ourselves in its terms – so is our state of consciousness absorbed by the ideology; gradually we come to reproduce the dominant order in our words and deeds. To illustrate, in the simple act of yielding to the teacher's questions in class we are interpellated (called into account) by the ideology of the existing educational hierarchy. ("The teacher knows: I am ignorant.") Further, since the educational system is linked to the government, the economic system, and the military, when we answer as willing students we reproduce the dominant hierarchies of society. As it is also argued, when we accept the terms of the dominant ideology we lose our ability to evaluate our condition, our wants and needs, and our ability to see how the power structure prevents their fulfillment. When we come to think like the system, so are our desires molded by the system. As Steven Lukes proposes, "men's wants may themselves be a product of a system which works against their interests."[25] In effect, we come to exist in a state of *false consciousness*, where we willingly give up our freedom to the existing order.

These are significant ideas with a broad following; they alert us to the ways in which even our most trivial actions – buying a hamburger, filling a car with gas, or reading a newspaper – feed powerful institutions whose resources are used to bind us further to their purposes. Moreover, the structural concept of power has important ramifications for social action. To appreciate its importance consider three close associations. First, there is a close connection between the concept of structural power and suffering or anguish. It is primarily when we believe others are responsible for our pain (or suppress our actions), and there is no obvious means of deterring them, that we are likely to speak of power. If our government acts as we wish, the issue of power seldom arises. It is when the government takes actions at odds with our sense of the good, and we can do nothing about it, that we begin to speak of power. Second, structural power is closely associated with the sense of injustice (a denial of rights, possessions, life chances, etc.) It is not simply that we suffer at the hands of others; they have no right to their actions. Thus, we do not speak of power when we suffer at the dentist's drill; although the dentist is in control of our future we ultimately approve of the filling. Finally, there is the close connection between the idea of structural power and the concept of freedom. It is when we feel our options and potentials reduced or controlled by others that we speak in terms of others having power over us.

With these close associations to pain, injustice, and oppression in place, we find that the discourse of structural power has enormous value as an incitement to action. For those feeling they suffer unjustly or have been robbed of freedom, the term functions as a rallying cry for uniting forces for social change. Structural power, in this sense, is equated with evil, and to fight against those in power is to restore the good. This logic of the "good fight" has sparked the movements of French revolutionaries, as it has Marxists, civil rights activists, feminists, and myriad minority groups today. It also serves as a chief catalyst for ideological critique as discussed in Chapter 2. Yet while the discourse of structural power is a rich resource for mobilizing resistance and fighting against anguish, injustice, and oppression, it is not a resource without problems. As we found in the earlier treatment of critique (Chapter 3), and again in our discussion of argumentation (Chapter 6), the impulse to attack those we view as "in the wrong" typically produces resistance and counter-attack. People are divided into warring camps, distrust mounts, communication deteriorates, rationalities of "the evil other" are formulated, complex issues are reduced to the simple binary of us vs. them, other voices and issues are ignored, and there is a slow move to mutual annihilation. These problems are often intensified because those blamed for the abuse often feel unjustifiably attacked. Often they object to the idea that they have power to misuse. Does commercial television have power over people's tastes and buying habits? Perhaps, but one can also see viewers as controlling television content; unpopular materials quickly die. Does the President of the United States have structural power? Perhaps, but the President is under continuous surveillance – by the press, staff members, Congress, and even the Secret Service. Did the Marxist government of the Soviet Union have structural power? Surely in a sense, but their ability to command was simply exhausted by a people who lost faith in them. Power is a highly plastic term; all of us are subject to critique for the power we are said to wield, and all have reason to rebel against others.

Given these problems, there is good reason to open the concept of power to alternative conceptions; as new constructions develop, so do new lines of action present themselves. Consider, then, the emergence of alternative visions from the dialogues on postmodernism.

Discipline, Discourse and Distribution: Post-Structural Power

For many observers of contemporary life, the metaphor of structural power seems inadequate. While relevant in a world of kings, dictators, and warlords, it is more difficult to locate such hierarchies in the turmoil of the democratic process, the multiplicity of organized institutions, the proliferation of multinational organizations, and the uncontrollable expansion of internet communication. A pivotal figure in theorizing power in a post-structural key is Michel Foucault. Foucault's work was introduced in the earlier treatment of ideological critique (Chapter 2). However, here you may be able to appreciate the significance of the work in new ways. As Foucault argued, the shift away from hierarchical structures of power can be traced to Enlightenment thought of the seventeenth and eighteenth centuries.[26] With growing emphasis on individual powers of reasoning and the equality of all people, there was a shift away from top-down physical control of the populace. Because, as it was believed, individuals are capable of reason – and thus growing through knowledge – the challenge for the society is to mold good citizens. Thus, the tradition of structural power was slowly replaced by programs of education and facilities of correction. One outcome of this trend was the development of the modern prison system. Rather than simply locking away undesirables in dungeons, the modern system attempted to improve the imperfect person. Emblematic of this movement, for Foucault, was Jeremy Bentham's eighteenth century plan for a Panopticon, that is, a form of prison in which the actions of all prisoners could be observed from a single, elevated watch-tower. This tower was ringed by an array of single cells, each illuminated from behind. The observer could thus

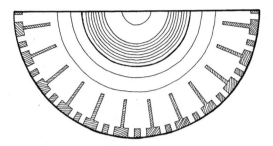

Figure 8.2 *Adapted from J. Bentham. Plan of the Panopticon (*The Works of Jeremy Bentham, *ed. Bowring, vol. IV. 1843. 172–3). Cf. p. 201.*

see all actions, and very importantly, without being seen. By this arrangement the prisoner could never know when he was being observed; in effect he could do nothing that was not subject to inspection. For Foucault, such an arrangement carries with it several significant implications for conceptualizing power.

Power has no exact location: Unlike the structural view, there is no one set of persons or distribution of material in which power resides. For Foucault, "Power has its principle not so much in a person as in a certain concerted distribution of bodies, surfaces, lights, gazes; in an arrangement whose internal mechanisms produce the relation in which individuals are caught up."[27] More generally, we may say that power resides not in a structure or a person but in a set of relationships. *Power relations* may not only include various physical artifacts, but may also be extended outward to the more general conditions of the culture. For example, the Panopticon can only function within a supportive socio/political context, from which issue its rationality, funding, support systems, and so on.

Power relations are manifest in bodily dispositions: Whereas the structuralist will direct attention to the actions of "those in power," for Foucault it is more important to focus on the actions of we who are caught up in power relations. Our very actions reveal or carry the stamp of these relations. In the Panopticon, the prisoner acts first to avoid being penalized by the observer. However, because there is never a moment without the possibility of observation, over time these proper actions become simply a way of life – even when no one is looking. For Foucault, then, power relations operate on what he calls *docile bodies*, bodies that give themselves up to the existing forms of relationship. Or, in different terms, we see here the operation of *bio-power*, power relations that incorporate the biological existence of the person. We illustrate bio-power when we brush our teeth at night. Here we yield up our bodies to a complex set of relations that include the discipline of dentistry, tooth brush manufacturers, common aesthetic standards, wash basin design, and more.

Power is neither malevolent nor mystifying, but productive: Unlike the structural view of power, which invites suspicion of those at the top of the hierarchy (the "big whigs," "power mongers," "military–industrial complex" etc.), for Foucault power is more pedestrian. Power relations are constituted by normal people simply carrying out everyday activities – from sweeping floors and ordering office supplies, to prescribing an anti-depressant or buying stock. It is not a privileged few, sitting at large desks or larger banquets, who are responsible for power relations, but people engaging in large numbers of inter-related activities spread across the culture. Such a view also complicates the traditional relationship between power and injustice. We are not speaking here of a few privileged people who grind others down or get something for nothing. Rather, for the most part people are simply carrying out small-scale activities that to them seem morally acceptable. In this sense, power for Foucault is productive; power relations invite us in, give us things to do, and provide a sense of satisfaction. We participate productively in power relations when we read approvingly a newspaper account of new prison facilities – safer, more sanitary, and electronically operated. The very representation – common-place and congratulatory – invites us into a productive relationship with existing power relations.

As you can see, these ideas all function as preludes to Foucault's concept of *disciplinary power*, discussed in Chapter 2. Recall Foucault's concern with the ways in which various regimes of knowledge – schools, academic disciplines, professions of medicine and psychiatry, religions – function so as to generate discourse and practices that invite us into their realities. And as we unwittingly accept these invitations to Reality or Truth, so are we subjugated.

This concept of power as dispersed throughout the culture – as opposed to the traditional view of a single, monolithic hierarchy – is extended in an important work, *Hegemony and Socialist Strategy*, by Ernesto Laclau and Chantal Mouffe.[28] As they reason, the traditional idea of hegemony, as the unified and interdependent efforts of multiple institutions to form a mono-lithic whole, is no longer applicable in Western democratic societies. Rather, they propose that we see power in terms of a multiplicity of *nodal points*, or confluences of shared discourse and practice, each growing from particu-lar traditions, local conditions, and so on. Nodal points in contemporary society might include, for example, the computer industry, the Christian right, the liberal press, managed health care systems, and the movie indus-try. Each brings thousands of people together in shared discourses, insti-tutions, agendas, and the dissemination of images and information.

As is also clear, these nodal points are not fixed – as in the conception of structural power – but are continuously in motion. As the discourses of the cultural continue to circulate and societal conditions remain in motion, so do nodal points develop and erode. Managed health care is a relatively recent arrival on the cultural scene; the movie industry is splitting between the major studios and the independents. Thus, we find multiple and shift-ing points of conflict in society, instances in which various peoples are vari-ously marginalized, suppressed, or exploited. Participation in the complex societies of the present century virtually guarantees a field of ever-shifting power differences.

These postmodern moves toward discourse and distributed disciplines still retain the urgent call to activism so congenial to the structural view of power. We are still urged toward action. However, there are several significant differences in the kinds of resistance they invite. First, rather than focussing resistance against a single target (for example, the government, the capitalists, the educational system) typically located at a distance, the postmodern revisions invite us to look locally, to the day-to-day activities in which we are engaged. Begin with small matters – for example, choice of purchases, of media, of diet, of entertainment – for power relations are part of all we do. The refusal to own a credit card is not merely an economic issue; it is a small step toward a different future. Second, from the postmodern standpoint, a strong emphasis is placed on movements in meaning. In certain respects this is to accentuate the structuralists' concern with ideological domination. However, in the post-structuralist case, the way in which people construct their world together is pivotal. Rather than guns, molotov cocktails, and bombs, the race is for media coverage, radio programing, demonstrations, or bumper stickers. Even the manner of one's clothing or hair styling can function as an agent of resistance.

Finally, from a postmodern standpoint, there is less emphasis on a successor project – a new economic system, a new organization of government, or any other utopian vision to replace the present. In part this is because the postmodernist rejects the concept of ideology as *false* consciousness. There is no false view of society from which people must be emancipated, no underlying truth of power to be revealed; all positions are discursive constructions, including the grounds for resistance. Further, born of the recognition of power as within relations as opposed to within malevolent individuals, there is a pervasive tendency toward dialogue as opposed to attack. As Laclau and Mouffe propose, we require a form of radical democracy that "consists of the recognition of the multiplicity of social logics along with the necessity of their articulation. But this articulation should be constantly recreated and renegotiated, and there is no final point at which a balance will be definitively achieved."[29]

Technology and Society

> One has only to image the absence of technological efficacy today to foresee the speedy disruption and eventual collapse of our entire society.
>
> Lewis Mumford, *Technics and Civilization*

What do the following have in common: automobiles, telephones, movies, radios, televisions, jet planes, the internet, camcorders, and faxes? Yes they are all technologies but specifically of the twentieth century; further they are all deeply entwined with our patterns of relationship. These technologies are available to the great percentage of the population; their use is widely distributed. In the United States over 99 percent of households have television, which exceeds the percentage of those with indoor plumbing. The average worker in a thriving business today receives over eighty technologically mediated messages a day. Typically we ask about the costs and relative advantages of new technologies. However, for the cultural analyst these are trivial issues. The major question is how these technologies transform our lives, our relationships, and our institutions. What is silently being destroyed, what kind of future are we creating? Can it be otherwise?

These are questions of profound importance, and there is no way to do justice to the emerging discussion in these pages. However, it may be illuminating to consider several ways in which constructionist ideas inform these explorations. We turn, then, to life on the internet and techno-being.

The Internet: Communities or Charades?

Consider the following bit of conversation:

> I met a bear in a bar once, and followed him home. That led to an S&M scene where he was dominant . . . He bit me and threatened me with his teeth and claws.[30]

Such a tid-bit could scarcely be dropped into a conversation of the preceding century; in fact, it is difficult to imagine its occurrence even ten years ago. However, with the development of the computer and internet technology – linking over 10 million people throughout the globe on a continuous and instantaneous basis – the vistas of intelligibility are radically expanded. In terms of what can be said – what is reasonable and what is right – we enter a world of *anything goes*. The above quote is from an inhabitant of the cyber-land of sexual make-believe. Participants from around the globe adopt fictitious identities and enter into fabricated sexual relations limited only by their conjoint imaginations.

These new vistas of communication hold special interest for the social constructionist. If our sense of the real and the good – that which gives us direction and desire, curiosity and control – derives from relationship, then new forms of relationship may bring forth new worlds. As proposed in earlier chapters, we owe to communal relations whatever we have in the way of moral standards. But consider: if by community we mean a group of people relating face-to-face across time in a geographically circumscribed habitat, we might well suspect an erosion in moral standards. As I attempted to outline in *The Saturated Self*,[31] twentieth century technologies of social connection are everywhere eroding the traditional face-to-face community as a generative grounds for moral action. Mass transportation systems have separated home from workplace and neighborhoods from commercial and entertainment centers; families are frequently scattered across continents; and largely owing to career demands the average American now moves households more than eleven times during the life course. Even when neighbors' families are within physical proximity, face-to-face interaction has dramatically diminished. Forms of technologically mediated exchange – telephone, television, radio, CD players, computers and the like – carry us into worlds away. As Peter Druker has put it, "The old communities – family, village, parish, and so on – have all but disappeared in the knowledge society."[32]

Yet, while technological developments are reducing the significance of face-to-face communities within the culture, we also find a striking increase in the number and importance of *techno-based communities*. These are communities whose participants rely largely on communication technologies for sustaining their realities, values, and agendas. Television evangelism is an obvious case in point. Several million Americans are linked primarily through mediated communication to a set of beliefs that affect decisions from local school systems across the country to the posture of national political parties.[33] Less obvious is the organization of over 20,000 nongovernmental organizations (NGOs) operating internationally – to combat starvation, overpopulation, AIDS, environmental erosion, and other threats to human well-being – and over a million such private organizations advancing human welfare within the United States. Such organizations are vitally dependent on existing communication technology for continuing sustenance.

Less pointed in their moral agenda are also the countless number of computer-mediated or *virtual* communities emerging over the past decade. The sense of community often created within such groups is illustrated in Howard Rheingold's *The Virtual Community*:

> Finding the WELL (a computer mediated community) was like discovering a cozy little world . . . hidden within the walls of my house; an entire cast of characters welcomed me to the troupe with great merriment as soon as I found the secret door . . . A full-scale subculture was growing on the other side of my telephone jack, and they invited me to help create something new. The virtual village of a few hundred people I stumbled upon in 1985 grew to eight thousand by 1993.[34]

The WELL is only one of many thousand computer-mediated networks currently in operation. Such networks vary enormously in such features as size, subject matter, exclusivity, and form of communication (for example, real-time interchange, bulletin boards, etc.). Can such networks replace the face-to-face community in their capacity to supply nurturance and care, and as generative sources for moral action? While generalities are scarcely permitted, hundreds of thousands of users will attest to the importance of such connections in their lives. In one significant inquiry, participants on a suicide network were interviewed on-line.[35] This network was established to enable people contemplating suicide to communicate with each other. Most of the participants come to the network in anguish, seeking support, guidance, and possible ways out of their misery. When queried on the importance of this communication in their lives participants commented in these ways:

> It's always helpful when you know there are others like you out in the world, regardless of the situation. My parents always treated me like I was abnormal, so I get a lot of reassurance knowing that I'm "not the only one" with this problem or that one.

> To pretty much sum up my own experience with this medium, I feel that it is absolutely invaluable. The last year . . . has been, to put it mildly, the low point in my (and my family's) life . . . I no longer sleep a full night . . . This message board has been my rock, as it is always available to me, and people are checking in on a daily basis. It is enough to know that you are never alone in the battle and there is always another person (or twelve!) there to help you through the rough times.

> I am very thankful for these on-line support groups, and miss them when I am away! Now that I have a laptop I can take them with me.

The emergence of techno-communities is now facilitated by the World Wide Web, on which virtually any organization can mount a colorful invitation to participate. At the present time there are, for example, highly active web sites inviting membership into every major religion, a host of resuscitated traditions (including the Druids and Pantheists), and a range of newly emerging groups – for example, worshippers of Lilith and Kali, and followers of Yan Xin Qigong.

Although optimism regarding the burgeoning of techno-communalism is widespread, many also doubt its significance. Many of these are not "real" communities, it is said, but pallid simulations. They create an artificial sense of "we-feeling," in which people are egoistically self-absorbed. Rather than encountering others in the flesh – for who they really are – people project onto others their own desires. They imagine the others according to personal wishes. People are actually isolated from community, it is argued, falsely believing they are participants, "when the other is not really other, but is actually a moment in my own self-becoming."[36] The problem of knowing the other and the self through network relations is exacerbated by the frequent tendency of people to experiment with alternative identities on the net. As Sherry Turkle describes in *Life on the Screen*,[37] thousands of people spend up to eighty hours a week participating in various forms of simulated reality. On many of the networks, participants are required to adopt fictitious identities – mythical names, make-believe creatures; in communities devoted to cyber-sexual relations participants are also expected to use disguised names. However, even in communities where authentic communication might be anticipated, many participants seize the opportunity to experiment with alternative identities. The anonymity of the situation makes it possible to explore otherwise suppressed aspects of identity. As one young man, who used a variety of on-line female personalities reported,

> For me, my female characters are interesting because I can say and do the sorts of things that I mentally want to do, but if I did them as a man, they would be obnoxious.[38]

The result of such identity-switching for those users seeking "genuine relationships" has often been profound disillusionment. Because of this lack of "real contact," critics point out, people do not really develop a sense of caring or mutual responsibility. In one relevant case, the city of Santa Monica, California, established a Public Electronic Network to help the people of the area solidify a sense of community. Here was to be a new kind of public meeting ground in which all voices could be equal and anyone could speak at any time. In addition to individual access, over twenty public terminals were placed in libraries, elderly housing, and city buildings. After two years of operation only two percent of Santa Monicans were using the system![39]

These analyses hardly lead us to a singular conclusion, but this is scarcely unsatisfying in a world of such quixotic developments that stability is equivalent to going backwards. It does appear from these analyses that computer technology can – under specialized circumstances – be used to generate and sustain strong and abiding relationships. In this respect we may find within the technosphere new repositories for the growth of morality, new means to galvanize belief, and generate pockets of optimistic action. Yet, to the extent that this is so, there remains a lingering concern: most techno-communities remain isolated and insulated. The participants talk only among themselves, celebrating the reality they construct while derogating those outside. One need only to consult the Web pages of the Neo-Nazis and White Power movements to appreciate the point. Required in the future are means of generating *contact zones*, or electronic domains in which dialogue among traditions can occur.

Let us consider a second line of postmodern exploration.

Cyborg Being: My Machine and I are One

> Current runs through bodies
> and then it doesn't.
> On again.
> Off again. Always two things
> switching.
> One thing instantly replaces another.
> It [is] the language
> of the Future.

> Laurie Anderson, *United States*

What is more obvious than the difference between human beings and machines? As commonly held, we are living, breathing beings possessed with thoughts, feelings, values, and desires, and not an assemblage of assembly-line objects. Not only does the distinction seem obvious, but for many it is also a difference that matters. Our value as human beings derives from precisely the fact that we are not simply inert matter. Human life is significant in a way that the life of machines is not. We mourn the loss of young people at war in a way that is different from the loss of tanks or planes. It is an insult to call a person a robot or a machine. At least, these are the sentiments of what we call the *humanist* tradition. It is also a tradition in decline.

The major opposition to the humanist position has traditionally issued from science. In the scientific tradition, "the cosmos is just one great machine," that is, composed of material elements linked in systematic, causal relationships. On this account, humans are not in any significant way different from the natural order. However, realize that the battle between humanism and scientism is fought on realist or essentialist grounds. Scientists tend to argue there are no principled differences between humans and machines, while humanists declare that there are. Social constructionism offers an alternative to both traditions. From this standpoint, both scientism and humanism are traditions of practice rationalized by differing discourses; truth is not at issue. We needn't decide between the two any more than we must decide whether opera is any more true than jazz. Let us applaud the contribution of both traditions, then, but not without simultaneously recognizing their limitations. Further, urges the constructionist, let us generate new conceptions that open new alternatives for action. The point is not to search for what is fundamentally true or real, in this case, but to add to the cultural resources for relating. The technological explosion of the twentieth century invites precisely this response. Consider, then, the newly emerging metaphor of the cyborg.

For the humanists, people are distinct from machines; for scientists, humans are a form of machine. Are these our only possibilities? Consider the possibility of abandoning the distinction altogether and conceptualizing an entity that is part human and part machine. This is the *cyborg*. The cyborg is also to be distinguished from the *android*, a machine that is indistinguishable from a human in appearance and action, and a *robot*, which is a machine that does not look like a human but carries out functions typically assigned to humans. "Fine," you may say, "the cyborg may be a fanciful concept but we are not cyborgs!" The constructionist responds, "well, then, what in reality are we?" More interestingly, are there not ways in which we are indeed cyborgs? When we place fillings in our teeth and use glasses to see, it becomes difficult to separate ourselves from our technology. Hearing aids, pacemakers, artificial limbs, and wheelchairs add to the ways in which we and our technology are one. And, with the technological revolution our existence as cyborgs becomes increasingly evident. The radio extends our ears to sounds from far distances. The television represents an extension of our eyes, carrying our visual field outward into the universe. The computer keys represent the global extension of our voice. And, for many of us, it becomes difficult to separate our memories from what is stored in our computers, including addresses, date books, letters, writings, and our memory for spelling. In significant degree, most of us live a cyborg existence.

To construct ourselves as cyborgs is all very well and good. But why do so? What new alternatives does this metaphor generate? In a classic essay, feminist biologist Donna Haraway proposes that, indeed, the image of the cyborg should serve as a guiding metaphor for political action.[40] Her particular concern is with the efficacy of the feminist movement in an age of technology. How is the cyborg metaphor political? Recall here the Chapter 1 discussion of linguistic binaries, and their divisive effects. Haraway shares this concern, arguing that our clear binary distinctions are deeply injurious. The distinction between humans and animals, for example, contributes to practices that have extinguished many living species; by distinguishing science from nature, we rationalize practices of environmental rape; clear distinctions between the genders disguise forms of interconnection and invite a logic of victimization. When we attempt to make firm distinctions, we crystallize the arbitrary and we create totalizing worlds. It is not that Haraway is against political action. On the contrary. What she is against, however, are political stands that treat their realities as the "one true world." As she proposes, our political stands should be partial and contingent, active but open and on the move. When we can see ourselves as cyborgs, this view gains intelligibility.

There are additional advantages to the cyborg metaphor. As Haraway sees it, the technological revolution is changing the patterns of world politics, domination, and exploitation. Communication networks, data bases, interfaces, simulations, robotics – all functioning on a global level – require a form of techno-political activism that can "go with the flow." One must not be alienated from the technological processes – seeing them as different from and less than human. Rather, the political warrior must be able to join and use technology for good purposes. The current technological movements are defining women out of the power elite and relegating them to menial and peripheral positions. The woman can no longer take refuge in an old-fashioned view of the feminine, argues Haraway. Rather, she champions the "feminist speaking in tongues to strike fear into the circuits . . . building and destroying machines, identities, categories, relationships, spaces, stories . . . I would rather be a cyborg than a goddess."[41]

Haraway's use of the cyborg metaphor to strengthen the feminist movement has stimulated widespread dialogue. As many now see, the metaphor has an enormous range of application, indeed providing a conceptual fulcrum for building the postmodern future. For example, in the field of medicine analysts see the cyborg metaphor as marking a divide between modern and postmodern practices. Under modernism the central attempt was to gain control of the body and its functions through universal technologies. As we move into postmodernism, we find the body and technology merging. The body and technology unite in various ways to generate new potentials. Our memories are now partially housed in computers (addresses, letters, spelling); our vision in eyeglasses; and our hearing in amplifiers. In the case of reproduction, women can now select a range of technologies with whom "to couple," including artificial insemination, in vitro fertilization, intra-fallopian transfer, and an array of hormonal fertility treatments.[42] We and our technologies become one.

Let's move to the global level. Here analysts also believe the cyborg metaphor stimulates dialogue on the future of global politics. Whereas the nation state has long served as the basic political unit, in a wired world this unit becomes increasingly meaningless. Technological linkages transcend geographic boundaries, and increasingly the centers of making meaning are technologically based. Thus, like the cyborg's challenge to the common binary of machine/human, the postmodern "states" mix "human, eco-systems, machines, and various complex softwares . . . in one vast cybernetic organism, linked itself in many ways to the rest of the polities and other forms of life of the Earth."[43]

Reflection

I find these explorations of contemporary culture both fascinating and important; not only is the direction of academic attention turned outward to what's happening now and in the future of our world, but the results of such study have immediate implications for the way we live – what we buy, what we ingest from the mass media, and how we relate. I am particularly struck by the enormous importance of technology in our lives, and the ways it is affecting out relationships and our sense of self. This is largely the reason for my writing an earlier and somewhat autobiographical book, *The Saturated Self*. One theme, underdeveloped in that book, has grown increasingly strong as I have worked on the present one. It has to do with the way the computer world – e-mail and the World Wide Web – enter into a changing sense of my identity. Consider this: in earlier decades the computer served as a central metaphor for human functioning. The mind was likened to the functioning of the computer. The cognitive revolution in psychology, along with the artificial intelligence movement and cognitive science, were all sparked by this equation of person and computer. However, with the dramatic expansion of the internet, and our deep immersion in electronic mail and Web-surfing, the computer is gradually replaced by the network as the source of fascination. The internet brings instantaneous relationship to an exponentially increasing population throughout the globe. It is a domain so vast and so powerful that it can scarcely be controlled by any nation state. It can be legislated by no institution; it functions virtually outside the law. The internet seems a gateway into a domain without obvious end. The metaphor of the person as computer now seems limited and parochial. We can now more easily see ourselves as participants in a process of relationship that stretches toward infinity. Internet experience is like a wired womb, a constant reminder of how I am realized within a systemic swim, a process that eclipses me but which is also constituted by my participation.

Notes

1 See the list of Further Resources for relevant works on postmodernism.
2 See especially Lyotard, J.F. (1991) *The Postmodern Condition: A Report on Know-ledge*. Minneapolis, MN: University of Minnesota Press.
3 Orwell, G. (1949) *1984*. New York: Harcourt Brace.
4 Packard, V. (1957) *The Hidden Persuaders*. New York: David McKay.
5 See for example http://www.adbusters.org
6 See for example Faludi, S. (1991) *Backlash: The Undeclared War Against Ameri-can Women*. New York: Crown.
7 Ewen, S. (1988) *All Consuming Images*. New York: Basic Books.
8 Ibid., p. 94.
9 Groundbreaking was Hall, S. and Jefferson, T. (Eds.) (1976) *Resistance through Rituals*. London: Hutchinson. For more recent contributions see Fiske, J. (1989) *Understanding Popular Culture*. Boston, MA: Unwin Hyman; Jenkins, H. (1992) *Textual Poachers*. New York: Routledge.
10 Hebdidge, D. (1987) *Subculture: The Meaning of Style*. London: Methuen.
11 Radway, J. (1984) *Reading the Romance: Women, Patriarchy and Popular Litera-ture*. Chapel Hill, NC: University of North Carolina Press.
12 Brown, M.E. (1994) *Soap Opera and Women's Talk*. Thousand Oaks, CA: Sage.
13 Ibid., p. 119.
14 Ibid., p. 124.
15 Ibid., p. 173.
16 Debord, G. (1983) *The Society of the Spectacle* (Originally published in 1967.) Detroit: Black and Red.
17 Ibid., section 15.
18 Ibid., section 21.
19 Baudrillard, J. (1994) *Simulacra and Simulation* (Originally published in 1981.) Ann Arbor, MI: University of Michigan Press.
20 Boorstin, D. (1964) *The Image: A Guide to Pseudo-Events in America*. New York: Harper.
21 Ibid., p. 000.
22 Baudrillard, J. (1988) *The Ecstasy of Communication*. New York: Semiotext(e). p. 12.
23 For a classic elaboration of hegemony and power see Gramsci, A. (1971) *Selec-tions from the Prison Notebooks*. London: Lawrence & Wishart.
24 Althusser, L. (1971) *Lenin and Philosophy and Other Essays*. London: New Left Books.
25 Lukes, S. (1974) *Power: A Radical View*. London: Macmillan. p. 34.
26 See especially Foucault, M. (1979) *Discipline and Punish*. New York: Vintage.
27 Ibid., p. 202.
28 Laclau, E. and Mouffe, C. (1988) *Hegemony and Socialist Strategy*. London: Verso.

29   Ibid., p. 108.
30   From McRae, S. (1997) Flesh made word: sex, text and the virtual body. In D. Porter (Ed.) *Internet Culture*. New York: Routledge. p. 78.
31   Gergen, K.J. (1991) *The Saturated Self*. New York: Basic Books.
32   Druker, P. (1994) The age of social transformation. *Atlantic Monthly*, Nov. (274), 53–6.
33   See for example Hoover, S.M. (1988) *Mass Media Religion*. Thousand Oaks, CA: Sage.
34   Rheingold, H. (1995) *The Virtual Community*. London: Minerva. p. 7.
35   Miller, J.K. and Gergen, K.J. (1998) Life on the line: therapeutic potentials of computer mediated conversation. *Journal of Marriage and Family Therapy*, 24, 189–202.
36   Taylor, M. (1971) Parlactics. In R. Scharlemann (Ed.) *On the Other*. Baltimore, MD: University Press of America. For more on the superficiality of electronic communities see Foster, D. (1997) Community and identity in the electronic village. In D. Porter (Ed.) *Internet Culture*. New York: Routledge.
37   Turkle, S. (1995) *Life on the Screen*. New York: Simon & Schuster.
38   Ibid., p. 219.
39   For further discussion see D. Healey (1997) Cyberspace and place. In D. Porter (Ed.) *Internet Culture*. New York: Routledge.
40   Harraway, D. (1991) A cyborg manifesto: science, technology and socialist feminism in the late twentieth century. In *Simians, Cyborgs and Women: The Reinvention of Nature*. New York: Routledge, Chapman and Hall.
41   Ibid., p. 170.
42   For further discussion see Clarke, A. (1995) Modernity, postmodernity and reproductive processes ca. 1890–1990. In C.H. Gray (Ed.) *The Cyborg Handbook*. New York: Routledge.
43   Gray, C.H. and Mentor, S. (1995) The cyborg body politic. In Gray (Ed.) *The Cyborg Handbook*. p. 454.

Further Resources

Cultural Studies

Barthes, R. (1973) *Mythologies*. London: Paladin.
Grossberg, L., Nelson, C., and Treichler, P. (Eds.) (1992) *Cultural Studies*. New York: Routledge.
Strinati, D. (1995) *An Introduction to Theories of Popular Culture*. London: Routledge.

On Postmodernism

Borgmann, A. (1992) *Crossing the Postmodern Divide*. Chicago: University of Chicago Press.
Connor, S. (1989) *Postmodernist Culture*. Oxford: Blackwell.
Harvey, D. (1989) *The Condition of Postmodernity*. Oxford: Blackwell.

The Swirl of Signification

Fiske, J. (1989) *Understanding Popular Culture*. London: Methuen.
Gane, M. (1991) *Baudrillard: Critical and Fatal Theory*. London: Routledge.

Gergen, K.J. (1991) *The Saturated Self.* New York: Basic Books.

Hebdige, D. (1988) *Hiding in the Light: On Images and Things.* London: Routledge.

Mellencamp, P. (Ed.) (1990) *Logics of Television.* Bloomington, IN: University of Indiana Press.

Conceptions of Power

Clegg, S.R. (1989) *Frameworks of Power.* London: Sage.

Huspek, M. and Radford, C.P. (Eds.) (1997) *Transgressing Discourses.* Albany, NY: State University of New York Press.

Radtke, H.L. and Stam, H.J. (Eds.) (1994) *Power/Gender.* London: Sage.

Techno-Culture

Gray, C.H. (Ed.) (1995) *The Cyborg Handbook.* New York: Routledge.

Grodin, D. and Lindlof, T.R. (Eds.) (1996) *Constructing the Self in a Mediated World.* Thousand Oaks, CA: Sage.

Kiesler, S. (Ed.) (1997) *Culture of the Internet.* Mahwah, NJ: Erlbaum.

Porter, D. (Ed.) (1997) *Internet Culture.* New York: Routledge.

Poster, M. (1990) *The Mode of Information.* Chicago: University of Chicago Press.

Rochlin, G.I. (1997) *Trapped in the Net.* Princeton, NJ: Princeton University Press.

Stone, A.R. (1995) *The War of Desire and Technology At the Close of the Mechanical Age.* Cambridge, MA: MIT Press.

Turkle, S. (1997) *Life on the Screen.* New York: Simon & Schuster.

CONSTRUCTIONISM IN QUESTION

Many scholars deplore this flight from reason and fear not only the hobbling of science but also the threat to democracy that is inevitable in a world filled with faith healers, religious fundamentalists, paranormal charlatans, and postmodernists.

Donald G. Ellis, Editor, *Communication Theory*

In his highly influential work *The Discourse on Method*, René Descartes voiced sentiments that reverberate across the centuries. His was the voice of supreme doubt. On what ground can the foundations of knowledge be established, he asked? On what solid base can we rest our beliefs? Authorities claim knowledge, proposed Descartes, but how can we trust authority? Nor is there compelling reason to trust our senses (they may be wrong), and certainly we should not place our trust in the fluctuating opinions of the crowds around us. How can we, then, make mature and rightful claims to knowledge? The painful question now posed, Descartes moved on to furnish a voice of resounding reassurance. We begin, says Descartes, with the recognition of doubt itself. Although our reason may lead us to doubt all that we survey, we cannot doubt that we are reasoning. It is this process of reasoning, then, that guarantees that we exist at all: *Cogito ergo sum*.

The celebration of the individual mind – its capacities to organize experience, reason logically, speculate intelligently – has continued until the present day. We prize the individual who doesn't "follow the crowd," but "makes up his own mind," demonstrates "sound decision making," and shows "integrity of moral choice." And we trust that individual scientists, endowed with powers of reason and attentive to the contours of the objective world, can improve our lives and help move society toward prosperity for all.

Yet, as the present volume has attempted to demonstrate, Descartes' doubts were not sufficiently extended. On what grounds did he equate the process of doubt with individual reason? Is doubting necessarily an activity of the private mind? Should this assumption not itself be doubted? And is it not more fully compelling that doubt is a process carried out in language? To raise questions concerning the trustworthiness of authorities, our senses, community opinion and the like is to enter a discursive process. It is to communicate with others about the nature of things; even when we doubt alone we borrow from the culture's ways of talking and writing. And if this much is granted, we also find that such discourse is not the possession of the single individual. The creation of meaningful language requires social coordination; there is nothing we call language that is born within the private mind. Until there is mutual agreement on the meaningful character of words or actions, they fail to constitute language. If this line of argument is carried to its conclusion, we find that it is not the mind of the single individual that provides the sense of certitude, but the process of communal relationship. If there were no relationships there would be no meaningful discourse; and without discourse there would be no intelligible "objects" or "actions" or means of rendering them doubtful. We may properly replace Descartes' dictum with, *Communicamus ergo sum* – We relate, therefore I am!

Yet, while social constructionism lodges our sense of the true and the good in communal relationships, this is no final resting place. What is "obviously true and good" for one community is often specious or morally repugnant for another. In this sense constructionism invites a continuous posture of self-reflection – even regarding itself. Each word, proposition, or proposal must be provisional, open to deconstruction and moral/political evaluation. With each move in discourse a myriad of possibilities are abandoned, meanings suppressed, and life forms threatened. We are compelled to make meaning together, but each movement in meaning is also a potential death to the alternatives. Some might even be moved to withdraw from all discursive commitments . . . only to find that withdrawal itself is but another form of commitment.

It is in this context that we must finally call into question the social constructionist orientation itself, and to open it to critique from many quarters. As we have seen, the kinds of formulations developed in the preceding chapters have opened new and exciting vistas of understanding and action. At the same time, many find these proposals fraught with problems, dangers, and even moral deficiency. For many, the response is even hostile. Invectives such as "nihilist," "anti-rational," "anti-scientific," "bourgeois mystification," and "morally bankrupt" are not uncommon. And, undergirding these epithets lie bodies of discourse that are themselves eminently reasonable in their own terms. Further, there are many who are not so much opposed to constructionist dialogues, as they are curious about the implications for related endeavors; are the repercussions likely to be helpful or destructive? This chapter reflects on these lines of critique and question.

Because these various queries emerge in differing contexts, it is difficult to generate a smooth and progressive narrative for the present chapter. Questions are voiced by certain philosophers, scientists, humanists, religious thinkers, practitioners and more. It would also be surprising if you, the reader, did not share in some of these doubts. I have thus selected seven of the most commonly voiced questions, and will proceed in each case to develop a constructionist rejoinder. In particular, I shall treat each of the following questions:

1   What status does the physical world and its very real problems have in constructionism?
2   Does constructionism deny the importance of personal experience and other mental states?
3   Is constructionism, as a form of skepticism, logically incoherent?
4   Does constructionism have a moral or political position, or does it advocate moral relativism?
5   If all that we take to be real and good is constructed, what is worth doing?
6   Are constructionist dialogues in danger of dogmatic insularity?
7   What account can constructionists give of the obvious gains made by the natural sciences?

Realism: "But There is a World Out There !"

> In the world without foundations, everyone is equal and the imposition of any system of meaning on others is violence and oppression.
>
> Gianni Vattimo, *The Transparent*

A frequent reaction to constructionist ideas is a frustrated sense of disbelief. "How can you question the existence of material reality? Are you trying to say that pollution is not real, or poverty, or death? Are you saying that there isn't a world out there, that we are just making it up? Absurd!" Although these common objections seem reasonable, they are unfortunately based on a misunderstanding of constructionist arguments. Constructionism makes no denials concerning pollution, poverty, or death, for example; nor does it make any affirmations. As noted in earlier chapters, constructionism doesn't try to rule on what is or is not fundamentally real. Whatever is, simply is. However, the moment we begin to articulate what there is – what is truly or objectively the case – we enter a world of discourse – and thus a tradition, a way of life, and a set of value preferences. Even to ask whether there is a real world "out there" is already to presume the Western metaphysics of dualism, with a subjective world "inside" the head and an "objective" world somewhere outside (see Chapter 1). As we speak so comfortably we often forget that we are functioning from within a particular tradition. Too often we treat the words as stand-ins or pictures of the world as it is. The results can be stupefying if not ethically reproachable. Consider the following.

Whenever we hold firm to a particular account of the real, we seal ourselves off from other possibilities. In this sense, what is most obvious to us – most fully compelling at any given time – is also most delimiting. If the earth *simply is flat*, a once obvious fact, there is no room for those who wish to explore the potentials of "round;" for those who believe the grass truly is green, there is little room for psychophysiological research on color as a psychological phenomenon resulting from light reflected on the retina; or for those who believe that stones are solid, there is no reason to suspect that they might also be composed of molecular particles, the position of a contemporary physicist. Each commitment to the real eliminates a rich sea of alternatives, and by quieting alternative discourses we limit possibilities of action.

These arguments also suggest that our robust claims to understand "more" and "better" than previous generations may be numbing in their effects. With every thrill of "breakthrough" – the sense of "now we truly know" – there is a simultaneous silencing, a loss or absence. For example, as the historian Mircea Eliade points out, in the Middle Ages people held that the quintessentially real lay *behind* the material events of everyday life. "The crude product of nature, the object fashioned by the industry of man, acquired their reality, their identity, only to the extent of their participation in a transcendent reality. The gesture acquired meaning, reality, solely to the extent to which it repeated a primordial act."[1] This deeper reality was revealed to the culture through myths and fantasy stories – in stories of saints, tales of heroes and magic. Of course, now we "know better;" the world as we know it, including human beings within it, are simply material – all composed of minute particles of matter. At the same time, as we become satisfied with the "really real" of the physical or material world, the early appreciation of the magic of day-to-day life is cast away. When committed to a language of materiality we lose a precious voice of enchantment. The same erasure takes place as the sciences tell us that love is merely hormonal arousal, desire a conditioned response, religion a neurosis, and a mother's care for her children a genetic disposition. As we convert all human actions to "mere material," they become flat and meaningless. Do we truly wish to give up the discourse of mystery and deep significance?

Putting the case somewhat differently, as we make declarations of the real – what is true, what really happened, what must be the case – we close off options for dialogue. Such declarations, in effect, operate as conversation stoppers; they establish the limits of what others can say, who can be heard. Consider, for example, the discourse of medicine. Who could doubt the reality of breast cancer, heart disease, or cystic fibrosis? Of course, these are all daily realities in society, and the point here is to eliminate neither the words nor the research and treatment practices in which they are embedded. However, as these terms of the medical profession expand into the culture, and become the "really real," so are competing voices eliminated from dialogue.

To illustrate, consider the reality of AIDS. There have been active attempts by many groups to bring this reality home to the public at large. One of them, an exhibition of Nicholas Nixon's photographs, called "Pictures of People," toured widely in the United States. The exhibition, depicting AIDS victims as they slowly wasted away toward death, was a powerful statement of the horrors of the disease. The Museum of Modern Art described its purpose as, "telling the story of AIDS: showing what this disease truly is, how it affects those who have it, their lovers, families and friends . . ."[2] Yet, in all their photographic clarity, are we informed about what the disease "truly is"? Not according to a group of AIDS activists who demonstrated against the exhibition. They handed out fliers which accused the exhibition of perpetuating misconceptions, and failing to "address the realities of those of us living every day with this crisis." As their flier proclaimed, "We demand the visibility of persons with AIDS who are vibrant, angry, loving, sexy, beautiful, acting up and fighting back."[3] Would this additional set of images finally depict the real? Not according to other analysts. Some point to the way in which such depictions reduce the full, complex individual to a disease; others argue that depictions of persons with AIDS are essentially acts of exploitation used to feed the public spectacle. And as still others point out, the focus on the victim circumscribes our concerns, blinds us to the context of the disease, to governmental neglect, funding deficiencies, and failures in health care. Are not all these voices – and still others – needed in deliberation about AIDS? And in this case should we not be wary of attempts to terminate discussion by appeals to "the true" and "the real?"

The Question of Experience and Other Mental States

> How did we ever come to use such an expression as "I believe . . .?" Did
> we at some time become aware of a phenomenon of belief?
>
> Ludwig Wittgenstein, *Philosophical Investigations*

Consider the many times each day we use such words as "think," "hope," "want," "need," and "remember." And consider the significance in our relationships of such words as "love," "sadness," and "joy." We use such terms as if they refer to states or events inside ourselves, in our minds or private experience. Yet, social constructionism seems to cast a gray shadow over their existence. In Chapter 1 an array of criticisms was lodged against the traditional view of knowledge as residing in the heads of single individuals. As it was argued, there seemed no viable means of explaining how ideas can be built up from observation, or how ideas can give rise to action. If this is so, isn't strong doubt cast, as well, on the existence of the remainder of the psychological vocabulary. If the mind doesn't serve as a mirror to the world, what sense does it make to talk of "knowing," "believing," "remembering," and the like? In Chapter 2 we explored the way in which mental health professionals construct the world of the mind, and the inimical consequences of deficit vocabularies for social life. Chapters 3 and 4 demonstrated how the world of the mind is constructed in language, and particularly metaphor, and how this language changes across time and culture. In Chapter 5 an argument was made against the individualist ideology favored by assuming the existence of mental states, and an alternative, relational view was elaborated. In all these cases, constructionists seem not only to destroy the foundations for belief in "the mind," but to challenge the entire vocabulary on political and moral grounds.

So, it may be asked, doesn't social constructionism argue for the abandonment of such terms? Aren't they misleading, based on a fallacious tradition of understanding? Shouldn't we eradicate such "folk talk" from our daily lives? And why not purge the various disciplines of knowledge of these terms as well? Mental explanations are not only the mainstay of psychology and psychiatry, but are also common fare in history, anthropology, economics, and political science. Shouldn't these disciplines be called into question? Are all those clinical practices where therapists try to understand the "interior life" or "lived experience" of their clients simply futile exercises? And what about personal agency? Where would we be without our belief that we have choices over our actions, that we are responsible for what we do. Is all this eradicated as well?

Such questions are of no small consequence; continuing dialogue is essential. To stimulate such interchange, however, realize that while constructionism does remove the foundations for the vocabulary of mental life, it does not in any way attempt to eradicate the use of mental terms – either in the personal, political or scientific spheres. From the constructionist perspective, the question is not whether these vocabularies of understanding – or indeed, any alternative forms of discourse – are objectively valid or not. As we have seen the entire array of inter-related concepts – "valid," "real," "objective," "accurate," and "true" – cannot be justified in their traditional usage. Whether mental concepts are true – whether experience or agency are real, for example – are simply questions that do not require answers. The more important question for the constructionist concerns the consequences in cultural life of placing such terms into motion.

When we ask about the practical implications of mental terms, we first realize that they are of inestimable importance. The language of the mind plays a pivotal role in Western cultural life. For example, without a language of the passions, of love, desire, needs and wants, it would be difficult to engage in the tradition of romantic love; the language is essentially constitutive of doing love, just as much as gazing, holding hands, or caressing. Similarly, without terms objectifying "reason," "memory," and "attention," educational institutions would falter; similarly if we lacked the words "intention," "conscious choice," "knowledge of right and wrong" our system of justice would deteriorate. Without prizing a language of "individual reason" and "free choice" the very idea of democracy makes little sense. Psychological discourse is an essential ingredient of Western cultural tradition. I can assure you that although I write extensively about constructionism, I will continue to use these words in most of my relationships.

But, you may respond, somehow there is something more than discursive practice at stake here. "I do have my experience," you might say, and "I feel something when I say I am in love, and this experience is different than when I say I am angry or hungry." How can this be denied? The constructionist does not wish to deny that "something is taking place" on these different occasions. However, recall that language is not a picture of the real. We may use the term "experience" to make ourselves intelligible, but this does not make the term true or accurate with respect to what there is. For example, on conventional grounds we might ask whether you could have an experience of anger, let's say, without your neurons. The answer is clearly negative, and therefore "experience" is not only "in mind" but "in physiology." The physiologist might then say that the term "experience" is a misnomer; all that you are talking about here is a physiological response; to say that it is "experience" is to add an overlay of folklore. However, it might then be asked, could neurons function without a blood supply, and is blood supply independent of oxygen? In this latter sense, "experience" is also constituted by the surrounding atmosphere, and it would be a mistake to locate it solely "in physiology." Of course, oxygen, in turn, is dependent on further environmental supports (for example, photosynthesis) and in this sense what you call your experience is part of nature as a whole – not your own, private possession. This is not to declare the truth of this latter position, but simply to point out that there are many ways of framing "what is happening" on those occasions we speak of "my experience." At least one of these would link experience to all of nature. The consequences of envisioning experience and nature as a unity (as opposed to separating experience from its object) are interesting to consider.

Given the emphasis on the practical use of mental language, it also follows that disciplines using mental explanations can make an important contribution to society. Disciplines such as psychology, anthropology, history, and the like carry the culture's traditions on their shoulders. They keep the language of the mind alive, and thus the forms of relationship in which these languages are embedded. The same argument holds for mental health professions such as psychiatry and clinical psychology. It is not that such professions succeed in "plumbing the depths of the psyche," as traditionally supposed. How is this sensible? Yet, such professions do work with a potent vocabulary of human change. People will change the course of their lives for what they index as their "unconscious desires," "hidden yearnings," and feelings of self-revelation and psychological growth.

Yet, in spite of all that may be said in support of mental discourse, you are also quite aware of its shortcomings. The ways in which the language of mind lends itself to an ideology of individualism – with all its invitations to alienation, narcissism, and exploitation. In Chapter 5, efforts were thus made to transform the language of individual minds, to reconstitute the discourse so that it points to our essence within relationships. As we find, then, constructionism does not attempt to eradicate psychological talk. In fact, we are invited to appreciate the tradition of mind, but at the same time to be sensitive to critical shortcomings, and to explore the possibilities of alternative constructions.

On the Incoherence of Skepticism

> The point is not a set of answers, but making possible a different practice.
>
> Susanne Kappeler, *The Pornography of Representation*

Over the centuries many philosophers have critically appraised the concepts of objectivity, truth, and empirical knowledge. Perhaps the most frequently resounding response to these various forms of skepticism was first posed in Plato's *Theatetus*. In brief, the relevant question emerging from this text is: "If there is not truth, objectivity, or empirical knowledge, as skeptics claim, then on what grounds should skepticism be accepted? By its own account, the skeptic's proposal cannot be true, objective, or empirically based. Skepticism is thus incoherent; it asks us to accept the truth of its position while simultaneously proclaiming that there is no truth." It would appear that constructionist arguments fall heir to this form of critical charge. If all intelligibilities are socially constructed, then how can constructionism be true?

Before considering constructionist replies to this critique, it is first important to realize that claims to truth are no more grounded than claims to skepticism. The skeptic cannot claim empirical evidence to justify the claim that there is no empirical truth. However, neither can those who claim to know what is real or true. There is no theory of knowledge – whether empiricist, realist, rationalist, phenomenological, or otherwise – that can coherently furnish the warrants for its own claims. It is common for scientists to say, for example, that a theory approximates truth when all available data are confirming and no evidence is falsifying. However, on what grounds can such a proposal be justified? It would scarcely be appropriate to go out and test the proposition by gathering data. The very attempt to prove the theory in this way is already committed to the theory. It would be circular to test the empirical view of truth empirically. And to use any other grounds, such as "we know this theory to be true by virtue of logic," would subtly undermine the proposal. If you proved empiricism true by reasoning alone, then it is reasoning that tells us what is true and not empirical data. In effect, there are no claims to truth that can justify themselves.

Let us consider three variants of the incoherance critique. First, there are critics who ask, "Isn't the social constructionist position itself a social construction? And if so, why should we believe it any more than its contenders?" To this question, the constructionist replies in the affirmative. The arguments for constructionism are, after all, tied together by metaphor and narrative, they are historically and culturally bounded, and they are used by persons in the process of relating. However, consider two matters of special note. First, by raising the question the critic has vindicated the constructionist position. That is, the attempt to undo constructionism in this case is based on the same premises that the critic strives to undo: he/she seeks to establish the constructed character of the constructionist position. As a result, the critic not only fails to put forward an alternative to constructionism, but in addition, embraces these very premises in order to move the dialogue forward. More important, for the constructionist the process of dismantling constructionist "rhetoric" is an end much to be valued. It is just such questioning that enables us to move reflexively (see Chapter 2), to step out of the discourse and entertain other possible realities. In this kind of critique we may begin to ask about the effects of constructionist discourse in various situations, its gains and its losses, its potentials and shortcomings. In effect, constructionism does not itself seek to be a *final word*, but a form of discourse that will help us to avoid building a world in which there is no end to dialogue.

As a second variation on the incoherence argument, there are critics who ask how constructionism can be true when it criticizes this very presumption. The constructionist replies that such critics fail to appreciate the limitations of their own question. The question relies on the very concept of "objective truth" that has been placed into question by the constructionist. To amplify, the traditional empiricist argues that (1) there are empirical grounds for establishing the truth of various propositions. It therefore follows that (2) empirical validity should serve as the appropriate grounds for accepting or rejecting a given theory, and (3) social constructionism is such a theory and should therefore be evaluated according to empirical standards of truth. Yet, as the preceding chapters have elaborated, the first of these premises is without justification or intelligibility. As a result, it is no longer tenable to use "objective validity" as the criterion by which constructionist arguments should be evaluated. "Truth" as a criterion is simply rendered irrelevant to the acceptance or rejection of constructionist propositions. Constructionism does not ask to be accepted because it is true. Rather, constructionism invites collaboration among people in giving sense and significance to the world, and pressing on toward more inclusive futures together. Alternative "truths" are not thereby abolished; they are invited as participants in the dialogue. In sum, constructionism is more like an invitation to a dance, a game, a conversation, or a form of life. The most pressing question is, what happens to us when we begin to employ constructionist ideas? How is our life changed, for better or worse?

The third major form of the incoherence critique attempts to rescue rationality from the clutches of constructionism. From early Enlightenment philosophy to its emanation in twentieth century modernism, a strong faith has been placed in the power of reason. As variously argued, it is the power of human reason that lifts us above other forms of animal life, that stands as a bulwark against religious and political totalitarianism, and from which we may ultimately be able to derive ethical foundations. Yet, as the previous chapters demonstrate, such faith itself has little basis. For the constructionist rationality is not an inner state of mind, but a form of public performance (in language, symbols, material arrangements). "Good reasons" derive their intelligibility and power from relationships. One person's "reasons" are another's "foolishness;" "sound logic" in one camp is "mere sophistry" in another. Thus, it is argued, reason itself does not constitute a firm foundation for any social, ethical or political position; it is always lodged within a particular culture, itself committed to particular values and ways of life.

Yet, the defender of rationality replies, is the case against reason not an exercise in reason itself, and thus in fact a tribute to the significance of universal logic in human affairs? Philosopher Thomas Nagel articulates the position:

> Whether one challenges the rational credentials of a particular judgment or of a whole realm of discourse, one has to rely at some level on judgments and methods of argument which one believes are not themselves subject to the same challenge: which exemplify, even when they err, something more fundamental and which can be corrected only by further procedures of the same kind.[4]

At this point you may be able to predict the constructionist reply. To be sure, constructionists use "methods of argument" against claims to foundations of reason. This book is a clear example. However, these arguments are subject to the same charge made against reason itself: they are communal constructions, historically and culturally situated. The very capacity of this book to make sense depends on this lodgment. So, contrary to Nagel, the constructionist does not hold to the belief that constructionist arguments are appeals to universal logic, or that "correction" or "improvement" must take the form of what we (educated people) consider rational argument. The whole of the constructionist picture can be destroyed with the single epithet, "The words of Western imperialism!" And when this reaction occurs, we must – if we are to go on together – locate other means to make meaning.

The Ravages of Relativism

[Deconstruction] . . . is mischievously radical in respect to everyone else's opinions, able to unmask the most solemn declarations as mere disheveled

plays of signs, while utterly conservative in every other way. Since it
commits you to affirming nothing, it is as injurious as blank ammunition.

Terry Eagleton, *The Illusions of Postmodernism*

The saints are gathering at the real places, trying tough skin on
sharp conscience . . . you can hear them yelping.

A.R. Ammons, *The Confirmers*

Perhaps the most heated attack against constructionist views is directed
against its moral and political posture. As it is said, constructionism has
no values; it seems to tolerate everything and stand for nothing. Worse, it
discourages commitment to any set of values or ideals; all are "just constructions." Constructionism fails to offer any social criticism or directions
for change. What could constructionists say against the Holocaust. How
can complete "tolerance" ever be acceptable?

How can a constructionist respond to such charges? First, it is important to realize that constructionism has served as a powerful friend to dialogues on good and evil. During the first half of the twentieth century, the
discourse of ethics and morals grew into disrepute. The source of this
erosion can largely be traced to the hegemony of the scientific world-view.
Toward the end of the nineteenth century there was hope that science, then
gaining ascendance, might furnish the comfort of moral clarification. Yet,
as scientists became increasingly aware, there is no deriving "ought" from
"is," that is, no means of declaring what people ought to do on the basis
of observing and studying what they actually do. Or, as commonly put,
we must distinguish between facts and values. Science deals with facts,
and has its roots in systematic observation and rigorous logic. The realm
of values is separate, and scientists make no claims to expertise in such
matters. At worst, if scientific knowledge is driven by values, it is likely to
be biased. It may be politically desirable to say that "all persons are born
equal," but from the scientific perspective, when all the evidence argues
for the inheritance of differences in basic intelligence, it would corrupt the
science to report otherwise.

As this view of science developed there was diminishing interest in
deliberation on values. Science, it is said, is beyond ideology: its focus is on
"what is" and not "what should be." In the early decades of the century,
such a view provided a refreshing and much-needed counter to emerging
forms of fascism; with the rise of Nazism science stood for many as the very
champion of a world uncontaminated by ideology. The expansion of the
scientific world-view was especially noticeable in the university. Whereas
nineteenth century education typically required intense immersion in
issues of ethics, value, and spirit, such topics were gradually abandoned in
the twentieth century and replaced by strong scientific curricula. The social
sciences – such as psychology, anthropology, economics, and political
science – which were either minor or non-existent in nineteenth century

curricula, became dominant forces in twentieth century education. The humanities and religious studies receded in significance. The scientific conception of truth beyond the hubbub of competing value biases was regnant. And then came the 60s!

In the extended anguish over the domination of the weak by the powerful – whites over blacks, the haves over the have-nots, the US over North Vietnam, government over the people, men over women, educational institutions over the students – the science establishment was almost invariably found on the side of domination. Scientists seemed unflinchingly to supply the technologies of domination, control, and exploitation; claims to neutrality seemed naive if not ludicrous. Constructionist ideas, then in infancy, grew in significance precisely because they furnished intellectual ammunition for piercing the armor of scientific neutrality – objectivity beyond ideology. As outlined in previous chapters, the languages used by scientists to describe and explain are not required by whatever is the case. We have enormous latitude in our accounts of the world. Further, because scientific languages enter social life as means of sorting people into categories, giving credit, and laying blame, this language is never value-free. If certain data are called "indicators of inherited intelligence," and used to privilege certain groups ("the intelligent") and penalize others (those of low IQ), then scientific descriptions are scarcely neutral. They enter society with all the impact of a police force. On this account, all scientific propositions should be open to question on moral and political grounds. Thus we find that the constructionist critique of the distinction between fact and value invites scientists – indeed, all of us – to speak out on issues of the good. This is not because we are trained experts, but because we participate in the cultural generation of meaning, and thus the creation of our ways of life – today and in the future.

Yet, while constructionist arguments do invite moral and political deliberation, they do not champion one ideal over another. Constructionism furnishes a mandate for feminists, ethnic minorities, Marxists, gays and lesbians, the elderly, the poor, and indeed all of us to challenge the "truth" and "the facts" of the dominant order. There is respect here for all traditions of value – religious and spiritual, political, social. However, constructionism does not select a victor among the competing voices. In this sense it is relativistic; all positions may possess legitimacy in their own terms. However, one should not make the error here of saying that constructionism espouses relativism. There is no *position of relativism*, that is, a transcendent standpoint from which we can rule on the relative merits of various contenders without espousing any values. All evaluations, deliberations, or comparisons of competing positions will necessarily carry with them presumptions of the real and the good. To be intelligible at all is to render support to some view of the world and what constitutes proper action within it. Constructionism may invite a posture of continuing reflection, but each moment of reflection will inevitably be value-saturated.

With this said, let us consider a contrasting condition: what would it be for constructionism to heed the voice of the critics, and offer a slate of values? For example, we might find in constructionism a commitment to justice, equality, and universal peace. Here is an inviting *raison d'être*, and we might willingly condemn all those who stand in the way of these goals. At the outset, you quickly realize that there are no foundations for such an agenda, no warrants, no authority. These are simply our pronouncements. But consider, would you truly wish constructionists to establish the nature of the good, a universal political and economic system, or the way of life to be followed by all people? Chances are you do not. Further, those who criticize the moral shallowness of constructionism are seldom interested in establishing just any value commitment. It is not simply a moral posture of some kind that is being demanded of constructionists, but typically a commitment duplicating that of a specific group – whether it be Marxist, liberal, feminist, humanist, Christian, or otherwise.

It is at just this point that the difficult questions arise. How are we to establish the "universal good," to make a decision of the best way of life in a broad sea of committed competitors? Who is to make a decision for all, and on what grounds? Further, most all of us are mixed even in our own values, unable to make easy decisions in a sea of competing goods. There is no single value, moral ideal, or political good that, when fully pursued, will not work toward the obliteration of some alternative value – even those we might especially wish to sustain. Pursue individual freedom to its limits and we lose community; favor honesty above all and personal security is threatened; champion community well-being and individual initiative may be destroyed. Again, do we truly wish foundational commitments, ethical codes against which all people at all times can be judged?

It is at just this point that the constructionist "failure" begins to open new vistas on problems of ethical and political value. First, consider the account of ethical value emerging from the preceding pages. As proposed, in coordinating ourselves with each other, we develop patterns of action that are "ours," "what we do," a viable mode of going on. This is so for the mother and the infant, friends out camping, strangers on a train, and even man and dog. Moral discourse is not essential to establishing these patterns of preference; when there is perfect harmony there is little need to declare good and evil. However, moral discourse may come into being when corrections are required ("This is wrong; don't do it again!"). Or when there is a threat to a way of life it is useful to credit or praise adherence to the tradition and to punish deviation. Realize that on this account we do not "do good" because there is a language of the good – rules, laws, principles, a bill of rights and the like. Moral discourse may go into making up a way of life; however, it neither generates the tradition nor does it alone sustain the tradition.

If this seems reasonable, then we find that neither constructionism nor any other credo can dictate a way of life. Rather, there will be tendencies toward creating the good wherever there is successful coordination among people (Chapter 3). Or, in effect, some form of local morality will "grow naturally into being." We can scarcely anticipate a single good, but rather a virtual infinity of local goods – coming into being at all times people are challenged with coordination. The challenge, then, is not that of creating ethical or political dispositions; ethics and politics are always already under creation.

If each community of the good lived in total separation from all others, we would have little problem about political or moral stands. Each community could live by its own standards without interference, which is to say, no challenge to its local credos and commitments. But of course, this is seldom the case, and as the world rapidly shrinks and its peoples increasingly collide, so are value conflicts increasingly in evidence. This is not only evidenced in movements of identity politics (see Chapter 2) and myriad techno-cultures (Chapter 8), but more globally, for example, with a range of explosive ethnic and religious conflicts. The major challenge, then, is not the existence of values, but how we are to manage in a world of pandemic value conflict. It is at just this point that we find constructionist resources particularly useful. The constructionist may recognize the legitimacy of the competing value investments, each within its own tradition. The constructionist may even share in one or more traditions. There is nothing about constructionism that argues against having values. However, there is also the recognition that strong commitments lend themselves to eradicating the other, to eliminating any voice antithetical to one's own. The end of this process of elimination is the single voice – the one and only word. The existence of the single voice is simultaneously the end of conversation, dialogue, negotiation – or in effect, the death of meaning itself. Thus, in hostile conflict we lurch toward the end of any values, ethics or politics.

It is precisely here that constructionism offers a positive alternative. As previous chapters demonstrate, there is keen interest among constructionists in the problem of multiple and competing realities. Springing from this concern are a range of practices designed to facilitate productive interchange. Recall, for example, the work of the Public Conversations Project, and the relevant discussion of transformative dialogue (Chapter 6). This discussion was precisely concerned with sustaining processes of making meaning in otherwise hostile conditions. Also prominent is the practice of appreciative inquiry (Chapter 7), used broadly in organizations to enable antagonistic groups to build a mutually viable future.

Do these offerings imply that constructionists are, then, committed to a foundational value – namely that of sustaining meaning and thus value itself? No, it simply means that constructionists too are participants in cultural history, and act within traditions. Thus, to offer such practices is an expression of a tradition. However, it does not follow that such values are presumed to be universal. They are "goods within a tradition," but not ultimate – not the final word. But as an invitation to a particular way of being they seem to hold great promise.

What is Worth Doing: the Question of Engagement

> If I took all your arguments to heart, I wouldn't have
> anything to do on Monday morning.
>
> Personal communication from a colleague

Many critics feel constructionist arguments are disillusioning because they reveal the artificial basis of truth, rationality, morality, and political principle. Once this bitter message is understood, the argument goes, how can we justify anything we do? If helping others or fighting injustice has no intrinsic merit, if it is only a form of cultural bias, then why bother? If we learn that the mind is a social construction, then how can we take seriously the study of psychology, or the education of minds? If love is something we make up, then doesn't this undermine our most committed relations? If intentions are culturally constructed, then why should we hold anyone responsible for what they do? What is worth doing at all?

In reply to this line of questioning, we must first ask what is assumed in this expression of disillusionment? One obvious presumption is that the worth of an action or a way of life depends on its having some sort of foundation, something that deeply justifies it above all. If we didn't embrace the view that people should live according to what is true, fundamentally moral, or intrinsically worthy, then it would not be disillusioning to find such assumptions problematic. The constructionist arguments wouldn't be painful because nothing would be lost. Of course, these assumptions have deep roots in Western religion, science and politics; we cannot simply shake them off by virtue of an insight. However, it is important to recognize that the lament of "what is worth doing" is situated historically and culturally.

Having said this, we may further ask whether such assumptions are necessary for committed, fully engaging, joyous, or even rapturous action. Or again, are beliefs in fundamental truth or value necessary prerequisites for a nourishing sense of life? The answer would appear to be "no." Has the infant grasped the discourse of fundamental truth or value before it laughs at a funny face or plays peek-a-boo? Does the child who grasps a toy and cries "mine" do so out of a foundational belief in justice? Or does the child learning arithmetic, answer "four" to "what is two plus two" because he or she knows that the answer is transcendentally true? It seems highly doubtful. In effect, the discourse of fundamental truth or value seems quite tangential to the level of one's engagement in cultural life. Moreover, the constructionist asks, what is it that does generate commitment, the sense of worth, or nourishment of action? What does give champagne a kick? As the preceding chapters have attempted to demonstrate, one generative answer to this question lies within the sphere of relationship. It is within relationship that we acquire the sense of the real and the good, the sense of value, justice and joy. Or to use the metaphor of the game, we may thrill at the goal, or feel anguish in loss not because the game is based on fundamental truth or morality. When in the thrall of the game, it *is* the real and the good – for that moment. Or in Hans Georg Gadamer's words, "... all playing is being played ... The real subject of the game ... is not the player, but instead the game itself. The game is what holds the player in its spell, draws him [*sic*] into play, and keeps him there."[5]

To this the constructionist also adds, perhaps we are better off as human beings with this view of the "serious game" than with notions of foundational realities or moralities. For it is when we can understand out commitments as situated within culture and history, as expressions of traditions, that we may be less inclined to eradicate the other. It is in the reflexive moment that we may be able to appreciate the limitations of our commitments, and the potentials inhering in alternatives. In this sense the constructionist invitation is not to "give up and do nothing," but rather, to open oneself to the enormous potentials of human relationship.

Constructionism and the Dangers of Elitism

One central focus of constructionism is on meaning as solidified within a group, and the dangers involved in fixing a particular version of the real and the good. As proposed, once a group of people enter into a "way of understanding," it is difficult to comprehend or appreciate those who don't agree (cf. Chapter 6). Yet, as you may have realized, this same argument can be turned on constructionism itself. What is there to prevent constructionism from becoming just another isolated enclave, a self-satisfied group that aims to undermine all other orientations in the service of its own expansion? Certainly the present work has functioned so as to generate suspicion of all those claiming truth, objectivity, or superiority in understanding. Such a deconstructive effort typically alienates the targets of analysis. Why aren't social constructionists, then, simply functioning as a closed and self-congratulatory society?

This criticism is not insignificant. Constructionists are indeed prone to seeking others of "like mind," and with a sense of intellectual if not moral righteousness. Such tendencies are certainly possible. However, there are three saving moments in constructionist dialogues, each of which can place constraints on such tendencies and invite broad connection. First, constructionism makes no claims to foundations; it offers no means to justify itself. As a result, there are no ultimate grounds for claiming superiority of any kind. To be sure there is criticism of other positions, but from this standpoint such criticism has no claim to the only or final word. The attempt is not to eradicate traditions of meaning that are disagreeable to its own assumptions. Second, because alternative orientations are also embedded in traditions or ways of life, constructionism invites interest in their positive potentials. In what ways might human communities benefit

from particular ways of conceptualizing the world or self, the constructionist would ask, and how might these meanings be shared?

To illustrate these points, Zen Buddhists speak of a state of *no mind*, a
rarefied state reached primarily through meditative sitting. Such a state of
mind, it is claimed, enables the individual to transcend local cultural
meanings and to gain access to a transcendent level of being. Intellectually, constructionists might question the possibility of anyone transcending cultural meaning. However, because constructionism makes no claims
to truth, the criticism is more an attempt to reflect on limitations of the Zen
tradition than to replace Zen with constructionism. Rather, we are encouraged to ask about the positive implications of the concept of no mind and
its associated practices. In what ways are forms of meditative sitting,
within particular cultures of meaning, deeply nurturing? And are there
interesting connections to be made with other points of view? For example, in its suspicion of commonly accepted realities – and our tendency
to equate language with the real – Zen Buddhism is very similar to social
construction. Let us then approach the possibility of no mind with an open
curiosity, and attend to the consequences for our lives together.

There is a third argument emerging from constructionist dialogues
which also helps to avoid the tendency toward objectification and isolation of the venture. It is essentially the recognition of meaning's fragility.
That is, constructionists take meaning to be continuously negotiable; no
arrangement of words is self-sustaining in the sense of possessing a single
meaning. The meanings of "I love you", for example, border on the infinite. Such reasoning suggests that all bodies of thought are fundamentally
porous or spongy. Whatever is said can mean many different things;
meaning can be changed as conversations develop. It is largely for this
reason that you may find scores of books attempting to interpret the words
of any major philosopher, from Plato to the present. This feature of language also applies to constructionist assumptions. The vocabulary is also
porous, and every concept is subject to multiple renderings depending on
the context. Each different meaning also generates a bridge to another
community, to other conversations, and to still other meanings. In effect,
the profound malleability of words works to destroy firm boundaries, and
lends itself toward broadening the range of participants in the conversation.

Recognizing this point has positive implications. To illustrate, there is
a strong intellectual and therapeutic tradition often called "constructivism." It is a tradition with deep roots in rationalist philosophy, but is
represented in recent psychology by such figures as Jean Piaget,[6] George
Kelly,[7] and Ernst von Glasersfeld.[8] Constructivists propose that each individual mentally constructs the world of experience. In this sense, the mind
is not a mirror of the world as it is, but functions to create the world as we
know it. From this perspective there could be as many realities as there are
minds to conceptualize or construe. As you can see, the constructivist perspective is similar to the constructionist in the emphasis it places on

human construction of what we take to be "the real." It is largely for this reason that many scholars will use the words "constructivism" and "constructionism" interchangeably. However, you can also appreciate a fundamental difference: for constructivists the process of world construction is psychological; it takes place "in the head." In contrast, for social constructionists what we take to be real is an outcome of social relationships. This is no small matter, either intellectually or politically. Constructivism is allied with the individualist tradition in the West, the individual mind is the center of interest. Yet, many constructionists are deeply critical of the individualist tradition and search for relational alternatives to understanding and action (Chapter 5).

These differences have also generated substantial cross-criticism between the two camps. Yet, for social constructionists there are limits to the critique; the attempt is not to "defeat the opposition," but to reflect on limitations and potentials. Most important in terms of the present argument, there is no reason for resisting forms of amalgamation. Because the meaning of terms is indefinite, we can locate openings to new forms of intelligibility and action that draw from both domains. Inquiry into such hybrid forms has already commenced, as scholars now explore the affinities between the positions and the practices of therapy they invite.[9] One result has been the emergence of a position called *social constructivism*. In this case, it is proposed that individuals mentally construct the world, but they do so largely with categories supplied by social relationships. For the social constructivist therapist, for example, there may be an intense interest in the narratives an individual brings into therapy, but these narratives are treated as psychological. The therapist might thus explore what they mean to the person, and how central they are to his or her ways of thinking. In effect, we have a new position that borrows from both traditions, and thereby opens a new range of possibilities.

Constructionism and Scientific Progress

Constructionist arguments seem most powerful when you aren't certain that there are actual states of affairs to which words can be associated. For example, few are shocked to learn that terms such as "social structure," "the unconscious," and "neurosis" are socially constructed, because most of us were never quite convinced that these words reflected real entities in the first place. However, suspicion mounts when we turn to the work of sciences such as biology, chemistry, and physics. Scientific terms for the physical world are virtually taken for granted. It is partly for this reason that previous pages have gone to great lengths to elaborate the sense in which our presumptions about "atoms," "chemical elements," and the "earth as round" are socially constructed. Yet, even with these arguments in place you may sense a residual resistance. One of the most important dimensions of this resistance is the commonly shared belief that somehow natural science research over the years has yielded increments in knowledge. Regardless of constructionist contentions, who can deny that natural science research has not generated a harvest of resources for human benefit – the electric light, cures for smallpox and typhoid fever, jet propulsion, atomic power, and more? If science does create socially constructed worlds, how can we account for these estimable advances? That science generates useful increases in knowledge seems a major fly in the constructionist ointment.

There are several points of reply. First we must be careful about what constructionism is arguing here. There is no attempt to deny that "something is happening" when the scientific community is at work; constructionism doesn't challenge the possibility that science is oriented to "what exists;" however, the significant question is whether the scientist's terms for naming or describing this "something" reflect what is actually the case. To be sure, we have a language of atomic properties, chemical elements, and neuro-transmission. The danger is in concluding that these words are somehow privileged in "reflecting" or "mapping" what exists, that these terms tell or inform us about the nature of the real. From a constructionist perspective, for example, all that we call "chemical elements" could be given the names of Greek gods. Or, with no loss in accuracy, in physics we could substitute the term Neptune for the neutron and Zeus for the proton.

Yet, you might rejoin, it is not simply words we are talking about here. Scientific formulations make predictions; our scientific theorizing leads us to conclude that a rocket can be sent to Mars, and lo, we witness the success of the prediction. How can constructionism account for the fact that theories can make successful predictions? To reply, it is a mistake to hold that theories make predictions. How, the constructionist asks, can a theory – a body of discourse, an arrangement of syllables, a set of markings on paper – predict anything? Let us say you discovered a bottle floating in the sea, and in the bottle was a paper that said "I predict that when thronesis occurs we shall witness the collapse of quintabia." Here we have a possibly profound prediction. However, when these words are cut away from a community of users it doesn't tell us anything. There are no consequences. For the constructionist, then, it is the community of users that is crucial in this matter. "Predictions" are effectively moves in meaning, born in relationships. The particular words themselves are simply partial constituents of a social practice we call "prediction." And similarly, whether a prediction is verified or falsified depends on the local agreements of a community. Thus, by common standards we did succeed in landing a rocket on Mars. However, this is not because of some magical predictive power contained in the words of the NASA community. The creation of a prediction and its success are community achievements.

Finally, in considering the progress of science, we must carefully consider what we mean by "progress." As the preceding arguments demonstrate, there is little sense to be made of the view that scientific research moves us ever closer to "the truth." There is no convincing account of how an array of syllables (scientific theory) can increasingly "capture the contours" of what exists. Further, there are important advantages in abandoning the view of science as a march to the truth. First, we remove the competitive posture of the sciences; the attempt to narrow the range of ideas to the "single best" approximation of reality. Rather, we are invited by constructionist arguments to sustain a multiplicity, to keep myriad images and metaphors alive. In this respect it is not an embarrassment to physics to sustain both the wave and particle theories of light; nor is it a problem of psychology that there are multiple theories of mental disorder. With multiplicity comes flexibility. Further, by removing the ideal of "the single truth," we open the door to wide-ranging participation in the dialogues of science. Progress for one is peril for another; the social and ethical significance of scientific inquiry should be subject to broadest scrutiny (see Chapter 3).

Finally, we are drawn by constructionism to an appreciation of those disciplines or practices often discredited for their lack of progress. For example, therapy and visual art often take a secondary role to the "natural" sciences, because the former are said to be non-cumulative. In therapy and art we simply move from one style, fashion, or fad to another, as it is put; the movement is horizontal rather than vertical. However, as we have seen, the claim to vertical movement – progress in scientific understanding – has no grounds. As we move from Aristotelian physics, to Newtonian mechanics, and then to atomic physics, we come no closer to the truth. We simply move from one domain of meaning to another. However, in each case the theories function within communities of action; certain accomplishments and certain values are favored. In this sense, we now see that the continuous shift in schools of therapy and styles of art is not a defect. Each form of therapy and artistic fashion leaves the culture with an option, a form of life, a possible move in relationship. And for many people, these options provide enormous nourishment.

Reflection

This book now draws to a close, and with its completion comes a certain sense of sadness. As I have carried the outcomes of a thousand conversations into this writing, I have also carried out an imaginary conversation with you my reader. And as I imagine you, you have been so caring in your attention, so curious in your questions, so willing to follow strange twists of logic into exotic lands, and so indulgent of my passions and prejudices. So, as I complete the writing, this preciously projected relationship comes to an end. Every disconnection is a small death, and this one is not trivial. So what can I, as the extension of my human embeddedness, now hope? Perhaps it is that these pages might have offered you a relationship of some value, an internal conversation that will have its own power of provocation and leave you wishing to speak further, act anew, carry the dialogue forward. Perhaps this book will enable our relationship as writer and reader to live again in our relationships with others. As the dialogues go on, vestiges of our present communion may be projected into the future. We shall in this case meet again.

Notes

1 Eliade, M. (1971) *The Quest: History and Meaning in Religion.* Chicago: University of Chicago Press. p. 67.
2 Quoted in Crimp, D. (1992) Portraits of people with AIDS. In L. Grossberg, C. Nelson and P. Treichler (Eds.) *Cultural Studies.* New York: Routledge.
3 Ibid., p. 118.
4 Nagel, T. (1997) *The Last Word.* New York: Oxford University Press. pp. 10–11.
5 Gadamar, H.G. (1976) *Truth and Method.* New York: Seabury. pp. 95–6.
6 See for example Piaget, J. (1954) *The Construction of Reality in the Child.* New York: Basic Books.
7 Kelly, G.A. (1955) *The Psychology of Personal Constructs.* New York: Norton.
8 von Glasersfeld, E. (1988) The reluctance to change a way of thinking. *Irish Journal of Psychology,* 9, 83–90.
9 See for example issues of the *Journal of Constructivist Psychology.*

Further Resources

Critical Deliberations

Eagleton, T. (1996) *The Illusions of Postmodernism.* Oxford: Blackwell.
Gross, B. and Levitt, N. (1994) *Higher Superstition: The Academic Left and its Quarrels with Science.* Baltimore, MD: Johns Hopkins University Press.
Held, B. (1996) *Back to Reality, A Critique of Postmodern Psychotherapy.* New York: Norton.
Nagel, T. (1997) *The Last Word.* New York: Oxford University Press.
Michael, M. (1996) *Constructing Identities: The Social, the Nonhuman and Change.* London: Sage.
Parker, I. (Ed.) (1998) *Social Constructionism, Discourse and Realism.* London: Sage.
Phillips, D. (1997) Coming to grips with radical social constructivisms. *Science and Education,* 6, 85–104.

Constructionist Reflections

Edwards, D., Ashmore, M. and Potter, J. (1995) Death and furniture: the rhetoric and politics and theology of bottom line arguments against relativism. *History of the Human Sciences,* 8, 25–49.
Gergen, K.J. (1994) *Realities and Relationships.* Cambridge, MA: Harvard University Press.
Gergen, K.J. (1997) The place of the psyche in a constructed world. *Theory and Psychology,* 7, 724–45.
Hacking, I. (1999) *The Social Construction of What?* Cambridge, MA: Harvard University Press.

Ruse, M. (1999) *Mystery of Mysteries: Is Evolution a Social Construction?* Cambridge, MA: Harvard University Press.

Simons, H.W. and Billig, M. (Eds.) (1994) *After Postmodernism.* London: Sage.

Smith, B.H. (1997) *Belief and Resistance.* Cambridge, MA: Harvard University Press.

Squires, J. (Ed.) (1993) *Principled Positions: Postmodernism and the Rediscovery of Value.* London: Lawrence & Wishart.

INDEX